To John

in memory of your
Ordination

from Catherine and Harold

THE WISDOM OF FAITH

The Wisdom of Faith

An Introduction to Theology

By Msgr. Charles Journet

Translated by R. F. Smith, S.J.

THE NEWMAN PRESS

Westminster, Maryland

1952

Nihil obstat Edward A. Cerny, S.S., D.D.
Censor Librorum

Imprimatur Most Reverend Francis P. Keough, D.D.
Archbishop of Baltimore

May 17, 1952

The nihil obstat and imprimatur are official declarations
that a book or pamphlet is free of doctrinal and moral
error. No implication is contained therein that those who
have granted the nihil obstat and imprimatur agree with
the opinions expressed.

This Translation Is Dedicated

to

M Y   P A R E N T S

with Gratitude, Respect, and Love

Author's Preface

From the beginning of his *Summa Theologica* Saint Thomas affirms the existence of three distinct and mutually irreducible wisdoms: the wisdom of the Holy Spirit, which attains knowledge, not by way of rigorous demonstration, but by the instinctive impulse of love; the wisdom of sacred doctrine, which is based on the infallible testimony of Absolute Truth and which is contained in the canon of Scripture; and the wisdom of metaphysics, which is founded on reason. The first and the second of these are supernatural, though each wisdom is so in its own fashion; while the second and the third—this last is natural—both use concepts, though again in different ways. The doctrine of these three wisdoms is the consummation of a traditional teaching which was implicitly maintained by both Eastern and Western Christianity; it pertains, in fact, to the treasury of Christian truth.

At the beginning of this essay I shall point out briefly the role of the wisdom of love [Chapter One], and at the end of the volume I shall recall the work of the wisdom of reason [Chapter Eight]. But the principal purpose of this book is concerned with the wisdom of faith: Christian doctrine or theology. For some years this subject matter has

been a preoccupation of professional theologians. Many of
these have studied the subject and have presented interpretations which differ in some cases in only accidental respects,
and in other cases in a more profound and more serious
way. Certain of these theologians, because they did not take
a sufficiently lofty view of the matter, seem to me never to
have reached the point where old and new aspects are recon-
ciled instead of being mutually opposed. Nor is the discussion yet closed.

Since it was my duty at one time to teach the first question of the *Summa Theologica*, I was obliged to take account of the new and to me authentic aspects of theology
which have recently been brought to light and, as it were,
to determine their position in the total question. I was
assisted in this by the conversations I had at the Angelicum
last October with Father M.-R. Gagnebet, who has devoted
himself to these studies and who in his charity disclosed to
me the orientation and the results of his work in this field.
The usefulness of the present work will consist in no small
part in calling attention to his writings. They have, besides,
given me the courage to examine certain other aspects of the
theological problem.

At the same time, my teaching of the first question of the
Summa has given me the occasion to propose a solution to
a problem which has occupied my mind for some time: the
problem of the nature of positive or historical theology.
Here too private conversations have assisted my thinking. If
I mention no names, it is only because I fear that by so
doing I might attribute to others contestable points for
which I alone am responsible.

Had this slight work achieved a more definitive shape, I would have dedicated it to Saint Augustine and Saint Thomas Aquinas, who have never led me astray and whom I love ever more spontaneously. I date the book at the place where it was first conceived and six months later completed, at that Rome to which the Catholic heart grows ever more devoted. The flamboyant splendors of the Renaissance can not succeed in drawing our attention from the overwhelming testimony to the Gospels given by the silent tombs of those saints who for the last two thousand years have died near the See of Peter, as though thereby to justify that See's divine authenticity, true purpose, and everlasting fecundity.

Rome, May 3, 1946
Feast of the Finding of the True Cross

Delays in printing have permitted me to perfect my text. I would add that this little book has been written *for* the truth and not *against* any individual.

Fribourg, August 28, 1947
Feast of Saint Augustine

Acknowledgments

Except where the context denotes otherwise, all citations from the Bible are taken from the translation by Msgr. Ronald A. Knox, copyright Sheed and Ward, Inc., New York: Old Testament, Vol. I, 1948; Old Testament, Vol. II, 1950; New Testament, 1944.

Numerous quotations from other books have been used throughout the text and the footnotes. For the use of such citations I wish to acknowledge the kindness of the following publishers: Benziger Brothers, publishers and copyright owners of the English translation of the *Summa Theologica* by Saint Thomas Aquinas; The Dial Press for quotations from *The Angelic Doctor* by Jacques Maritain; B. Herder Book Co. for quotations from *Christ the Savior* by Father Garrigou-Lagrange, O.P.; The Macmillan Company for quotations from *Dionysius the Areopagite* translated by C. E. Rolt, 1920, and *A Literary History of Religious Thought in France* by Henri Bremond, Vol. II; Random House, Inc., for quotations from *The Basic Works of St. Augustine*; Charles Scribner's Sons for quotations from *The Spirit of Medieval Philosophy* by Etienne Gilson, and from *The Degrees of Knowledge* and *Science and Wisdom* by Jacques Maritain; Sheed and Ward, Inc., for quotations from *The Mystery of the Church* by Humbert Clerissac, O.P.

xi

Contents

Contents

8. BENEATH THEOLOGY: THE WISDOM OF REASON . 157

9. THE VITAL STRUCTURE OF CHRISTIAN KNOWLEDGE 186

THE WISDOM OF FAITH

1. Beyond Theology: The Wisdom of Love

1. The Teaching of Dionysius the Areopagite

The highest knowledge of God which is accessible to man in this life is described by Dionysius the pseudo-Areopagite in the five brief chapters of his *Mystical Theology*. It consists in abandoning the sensible and the intelligible to unite oneself, through an ignorance that is higher than any knowledge and through an ecstasy that is completely free and yet irresistible, to Him who is beyond all essence and who hides Himself in darkness.[1] This experience presupposes, of course, the knowledge that comes by faith and the acceptance of the revealed truths which are contained, for example, in Scripture and clarified in the teaching of the Fathers. But it is not reducible to the simple knowledge that comes from faith. It is rather a wisdom in which Dionysius recognizes three distinguishing marks: 1) its proper mode is to use no concepts, whether these be positive or negative, but, by avoiding them, to enter into silence, to rest speechless in a union with the Ineffable;[2] 2) it is not communicated by teaching nor discovered by study, but it is attained when a person who is

3

united to God experiences and "suffers" divine realities; [3]
3) finally, it is the fruit of an ecstasy.

2. *Saint Thomas' Commentary on Dionysius*

It is our opinion that no one has commented on this
teaching of Dionysius with greater penetration than Saint
Thomas Aquinas nor has anyone excelled him in the exact-
ness with which he describes the distinctiveness of this
mystical knowledge. Let us watch him for a few moments
discuss—though in reverse order—the three characteristics
of mystical knowledge which Dionysius has pointed out.

Mystical knowledge is the fruit of an ecstasy. What, then,
is the nature of this ecstasy? Is it some miraculous and
fleeting grace? Is it the ravishing of which Saint Paul was
the prey, the secret of which the Apostle confided to the
Corinthians: "There is a man I know who was carried out
of himself in Christ fourteen years since; was his spirit in
his body? I cannot tell. . . ." (2 Cor. 12, 2)? It is not in
this passage of the Apostle—or at least, to be more exact,
not in the measure in which he there describes an exceptional and extraordinary favor—that we are able to recognize
the ecstasy of mystical theology.[4] The Areopagite himself
when speaking of this ecstasy refers rather to another text
of the Apostle: "And the Divine Yearning brings ecstasy,
not allowing them that are touched thereby to belong
unto themselves but only to the objects of their affection.
. . . And hence the great Paul, Gal. 2, 20, constrained by
the Divine Yearning, says, with inspired utterance, 'I live,
and yet not I but Christ liveth in me.'"[5]

But let us return to the admirably clear and penetrating
commentary which this text of Dionysius has inspired Saint
Thomas to write.[6] Love, says the Saint, as distinct from
knowledge, draws us to things. Nevertheless, not every kind
of love can be termed ecstatic. There is one kind of love

that makes us love things, not because of what they are (as happens when a thing is loved for itself, *secundum se*), but because of an advantage it brings to the lover (as when a thing is loved for a reason other than itself, *per accidens*). For example, I love (that is, I want, I desire) wine or justice, but only for my own sake; such a love may be legitimate, but it is not ecstatic. But the love which tends towards objects because of what they are, which desires the very goodness of the thing loved, such a love causes ecstasy and carries the lover outside himself. Now if the beloved is God, the lover has nothing to keep back; he can and should abandon everything; and it is in this very abandonment of self for God that the creature recovers himself, that he returns to himself, to his condition as a creature. If, however, the beloved is a creature, the lover exists alongside the beloved, and his good alongside that of the beloved: the abandonment will not be entire.[7]

Charity, by which we love God for Himself and all other things for God, is in all its degrees and of its very nature an ecstatic love. Here then—but how can we realize the profundity of this gift of God?—is the ecstasy and the mystical knowledge offered to all Christians: "So many athirst; who will not come to the water? So many destitute; who will come and get him food, get wine and milk free, no price to be paid?" (Isaias 55, 1). "Come, you who are thirsty; take, you who will, the water of life; it is my free gift" (Apoc. 22, 17).

Since mystical knowledge derives from the ecstasy of love, it is a knowledge by way of sympathy. Love brings with it the mutual clinging together of the lover and the Beloved. Secretly, intimately, imperceptibly the Beloved begins to enter into the lover because of the intrinsic pleasingness of the Beloved; as a consequence, the lover, while yet remaining himself, loses himself in the Beloved. This is the mystery of love, similar in its way to the mystery of knowledge: the lover dwells in the Beloved, lives in Him, abandons himself for Him; in some mysterious fashion he experiences all the vicissitudes and all the riches of the Beloved, as though they affected his own being; as Dionysius dares to say, the lover "suffers" divine realities; by means of sympathy he experiences them in the way God Himself does.[8] He knows these realities, not as one separated from them, but as one enveloped by them, plunged into them. And all this, according to Saint Thomas,[9] is told us in the words of Saint John: "He who dwells in love dwells in God, and God in him" (1 John 4, 16).

Finally, mystical knowledge does not use concepts as a formal means of cognition. It is, however, a true knowledge —though as such it is only one part or one aspect of mystical experience; but it is a knowledge without concepts or, more exactly, a knowledge beyond concepts. Mystical knowledge presupposes the conceptual data of revelation, believes them through supernatural faith, and lives by them; and yet it surpasses them in the silence of its mystic night. For, as Saint Thomas explains, there are two ways of knowing God, two wisdoms. One of them proceeds by using human concepts; it is the wisdom of sacred doctrine, the principles of which come to us through revelation. The other proceeds by way of the impulsion of love; it is the experimental wisdom that is a gift of the Holy Spirit.[10] ". . . Dionysius says that Hierotheus is perfect in Divine things, for he not only learns, but is patient of, Divine things. Now this sympathy or connaturality for Divine things is the result of charity, which unites us to God, according to 1 Cor. 6, 17: 'He who is joined to God is one spirit.' Consequently wisdom, which is a gift, has its cause in the will, which cause is charity, but it has its essence in the intellect. . . ."[11]

The mystical wisdom of love, then, supposes the doctrinal wisdom of faith, however implicit and latent this latter may be. On the path which faith opens to view by means of concepts, divine love urges along our intelligence and even faith itself to points beyond the limits of conceptual knowledge.[12] In other words, mystical wisdom is distinct from the wisdom of faith but is not separable from it.

This, then, is the teaching on love and the gift of wisdom as it was understood and expressed by Dionysius the Areopagite and Thomas Aquinas. It is a doctrine that pertains to our Christian inheritance and is common to both the East and the West. Only ignorance of either Dionysius or of Saint Thomas, or a misunderstanding of their teaching, could lead one to contrast their positions and thereby to create an abyss between an Orient that is naturally "mystical" and an Occident that is naturally "rationalistic." [13]

3. Bremond and the Nature of Mystical Knowledge

When Henri Bremond attempted to summarize what he found to be the basis of the experience of the mystical authors whose writings he had studied, he rediscovered—rather than merely repeated—the same teaching. As he remarks: "Mystical knowledge is unlike the common stock of doctrinal knowledge which is formed by the acquisition and successive elaboration of a certain number of concepts and judgments—both sharply defined—and therefore presents 'teachable' matter. It is a veritable knowledge, since by it human intelligence assimilates a spiritual object, the God present; but it is not either science or speculative theology. . . . With ordinary knowledge, as for instance in the recital of the Nicene Creed, we collect and detail a series of affirmations and negations. . . . Mystical knowledge is not like this, built up gropingly, precise, fragmentary, and progressive. . . . The mystic's capture is truly magnificent above all captures, but it is Truth rather than truths, Light rather than lights, a Presence rather than a doctrine. The Truth is the source of all truths, the Light is the central heart of all lights, the Presence radiates out doctrine, but the mystic contemplates directly the Source and not the streams, the Fire and not the flames, the Sun and not its rays." [14]

4. The Growth of Mystical Experience

Eternal life, which is the knowledge of the one true God and of Him whom He has sent, the life of love in which are fulfilled the promises made by the Saviour to His disciples and related in the discourse after the Last Supper (John 14–17), has never been extinguished in the heart of the Church; so mysterious and so rich is it, that it has never ceased to manifest new powers in and through the souls which it possesses. If an attempt be made to trace the progress of this manifestation, it will be seen that up to the twelfth or thirteenth century, the progress is patently the same for both the Eastern and the Western Churches. Whether Benedictine, or even Cistercian, spirituality is considered, all is nourished by the memory of the Fathers of the desert and fitted into the framework that stems from the monasticism of the Orient. But from the twelfth and thirteenth centuries on, the mystical life—inexpressible though it may be in its essence—begins in the West to be colored by new hues [15] and to venture forth into hitherto unexplored profundities which correspond to the growth in the life of dogma.

When we speak of such a deepening of mystical experience, it need hardly be pointed out that the point of comparison is not with the mystical experience of the Apostles and their immediate disciples,[16] but rather with the mystical experience of the general faithful of the early periods of our religion. And even here it is necessary to be more exact. As compared with the mystical experience of previous centuries, this deepening does not always require a greater intensity of love; but there is required in every case a new and more explicit consciousness of the mysterious riches implied, for example, in the fundamental revelation that there can be no Christian life except that which is had through configuration with Christ. But let us indicate more clearly how the growing comprehension of the truth just mentioned was accompanied by a deepening of mystical experience.[17]

The first revelation of the Gospels which it was necessary to explain to men was that their salvation was begun by the mere fact of the Incarnation of the Word who put on our humanity that we might put on His divinity. This above everything else was the task of the Greek Fathers (as also of Saint Augustine). The second revelation which it was necessary to explain and which presupposed the former was that this salvation was accomplished only by the sufferings and blood of the cross. This deepening consciousness of the mystery of the Redemption—occurring especially but not exclusively in the West—could not begin until the awareness of the mystery of the Incarnation had sufficiently increased, especially but again not exclusively in the East.

At the time when this increasing consciousness of the Redemption began, was mystical love to be excluded from the progress? Was it not rather this very love that secretly aroused the theological development, somewhat as the love of Saint Francis caused the appearance of the art of Giotto? Can it be denied that this love was an active force in the heart of Saint Anselm even before he wrote his *Why God Became Man?* [18]

What is it, then, that this love produced? In a manner hitherto unknown it caused the realization of a truth that had always been present in Christianity, since it fills the writings of Saint John and the epistles of Saint Paul. And the truth was this: if we are destined to be one day configured to Christ ("He will form this humbled body of ours anew, moulding it into the image of his glorified body," Philip. 3, 21), yet this will take place only after we have gone down to the depths of His suffering and death, after we have "shared his sufferings" and have even been "moulded into the pattern of his death" (Philip. 3, 10), after having been crucified with Him (Gal. 2, 19).

Moreover, in a way that was new and that gradually but relentlessly destroyed the all too human illusions of medieval imperialism, Christian love reached the social consciousness that just as Christ had been in His lifetime a crucified King, so His kingdom, before being glorified in heaven, would be here below a crucified one; it became conscious that the Church, which is the Body of Christ (Ephes. 1, 23), ought to follow the same path as her Head and that just as Docetism had not spoken truly of the suffering Christ, so it was no truer when applied to the Church.

But can this new realization of the cross of Christ and of the depths of the mystery of evil be compatible with the transfiguration and the glory of Christ? In our opinion, it serves to deepen our realization of that glory. An example of what is meant can be found in that contagious enthusiasm which each year seizes the whole of Russia at Easter time. This is no unconscious survival of Docetism nor an illusory conviction of the impassibility of the Mystical Body of Christ, but a true, deep, and authentic impulse of the Catholic faith; it is the unconquerable certitude in the inevitable, imminent, and awesome resurrection of this Mystical Body, which is now truly crucified; it is an example of the purest hope of the Gospels that the resurrection of the entire Body will be all the more glorious as its compassion and configuration to its suffering and blood-stained

Head are here below more complete, more pure, more loving.[19]

The discovery, then, of the mystical depths of this co-suffering of the Church for Christ, with Christ, and in Christ [20] does not suppress but rather emphasizes the final sharing of the Church in the glory of Christ. This is the reason why the exterior manifestations of the Church's suffering with Christ have not eliminated the exterior signs of our future transfiguration: stigmatic phenomena, for example, have not eliminated the phenomena of levitation, of aureole, or of incorruption.

While it is true that the Church is even now divinized and even now has begun her eternal life, still the essential law of her existence until the end of time is to lead the divine life of Christ on the cross and not the divine life of His glory; her transfiguration, as His during His mortal lifetime, appears now only as a sign of things yet to come.

5. *The Relation of Mystical Wisdom to Discursive Forms of Expression*

This mystical wisdom can sometimes be "ineffably concentrated on the passion of divine things, as is the case in mystical contemplation." [21] In this case its only desire is to be silent, for it knows even to the point of suffering the radical helplessness of words and concepts to express the divine fullness. Nevertheless the wisdom of love—she is as free as the wind—can also make a contrary choice, "royally overflowing in communicable knowledge . . . in the endeavour to express lyrically, as does a Saint John of the Cross, or if I may say (with no play upon words) oratorically, as does a Bérulle, mystical experience itself." [22] Such expressions, however, are never more than approximations; they cannot be fully understood except by those who have already experienced what these signs try to evoke.

But there is a larger way in which mystical wisdom flows over into a knowledge that by nature is communicable. In order to feed the apostolic zeal with which it burns, the wisdom of love can make use of all the conceptual and discursive knowledge which it encounters in order to preach to souls and to persuade them to approach the feast to which the King of heaven invites them. Such is the way in which mystical wisdom throughout the centuries has built up under the impulse of the Holy Ghost that sovereignly free and eminently varied rationale of the faith which we call Christian doctrine. In the Fathers of the Church it can be seen in a state exceptional for its condensation and richness. Their teaching is shaped by the wisdom of the gifts and whatever may accompany them. "Such is the wisdom of an Augustine (and, more generally, of all the Fathers). The wisdom which is common to all Christians . . . reaches its supreme proportions, rightly fatherly and episcopal, in the wisdom of these great spiritual shepherds. . . . The supreme wisdom conquered all things, appropriated all, drew them all into its universal current: all the spoils of Egypt, all the treasures of philosophy. Let it be said, in order to draw a clear boundary about these things, that these treasures are here the instrument, not precisely of theology in so far as it is distinguished from philosophical science (which were neither of them as yet explicit in their essential natures), but of infused wisdom, of the wisdom of the Holy Ghost, which dominates and absorbs them, and which is bound up with faith and charity." [23]

Mystical knowledge, moreover, can influence the workings of our reason in a way which, while not necessarily less profound, is certainly less immediate and more distant. Saint Thomas Aquinas, who began the golden age of theology, attempted to organize the extensive material of Christian doctrine, not in terms of an immediate preoccupation with souls linked as this always is with the changing needs of human beings, but in terms of the real but mysterious internal connections which unite and order them. In his heart, as in that of the Fathers and the mystics, there blazed the flame of the inexpressible gift of wisdom; it was this gift that brought forth his tears each time he celebrated the holy sacrifice of the Mass. Nevertheless his life work unfolded itself on the plane and according to the laws of a wisdom that of its nature is communicable, conceptual, and discursive—the wisdom of theology. His labors extended even to the yet lower level of knowledge that is philosophy. Like some brother gardener of a contemplative monastery who, although his soul abounds in mystical graces, is yet glad to descend for the common good to the humblest of work, Saint Thomas observed with the greatest respect and the sweetest patience the rules which were imposed on him by the nature of the matter entrusted to his care.

It is mystical and superconceptual wisdom, then, which in the Fathers uses the treasures of philosophy as its instrument to further an apostolic evangelization; with Saint Thomas, however, it is faith and its conceptualized dogmas which use the data of reason as an instrument of exploration and explication [24] in order to achieve a scientific organization of theological knowledge. But even here the roots of this faith must be deeply embedded in mystical wisdom. We shall see later that henceforth both apostolic evangelization and the scientific organization of theological knowledge are indispensable if the brilliant splendor of the Church is to shine forth.

2. The Wisdom of Faith and the Use of Concepts

In the first question of the *Summa Theologica* Saint Thomas uses the phrase "sacred doctrine," *doctrina sacra*, to designate a wisdom based on faith in the teachings of divine revelation. The interpretations which the commentators give to this phrase vary somewhat, but the differences are nothing more than shades of the same basic meaning. We can say, then, that according to Saint Thomas sacred doctrine signifies the teaching of revelation together with all the truths related to it [1] insofar as the whole of this is presented in an ordered and organized way, *secundum ordinem disciplinae*. [2] With this in mind we can explain how it is that Saint Thomas in one and the same question can discuss not only revealed truths, their necessity for the salvation of the human race (article one), and the manner in which Sacred Scripture communicates to us these truths (articles nine and ten), but also can explain the work of theological speculation, which, by a process of deduction from certain revealed truths used as principles, thereby

14

attempts to illuminate other truths which are therefore considered as conclusions, whether these latter truths are already formally revealed or only virtually so.[3]

In our study of the nature of this Christian doctrine which is the wisdom of faith we shall first consider the use which it makes of human concepts. Then in the following chapter we shall discuss the two states in which that wisdom can exist, the spontaneous and the scientific.

1. *The Divine Use of Concepts by Faith*

The mode proper to that knowledge by faith which is necessary for all men (Heb. 11, 6), but which nevertheless is better appreciated and cherished by the mystic than by the ordinary Christian, is to use concepts. For faith uses expressions such as these: "In the name of the Father and of the Son and of the Holy Spirit"; "I believe in God, the Father Almighty, Creator of heaven and earth"; "Our Father, who art in heaven, Thy kingdom come, Thy will be done." Such concepts are its distinguishing instrument and formal means of reaching God. They are, to be sure, but weak human concepts, but faith never forgets that they have been chosen and confirmed by divine revelation and it seeks to use them in a divine fashion.

It is not an infrequent experience that a word hitherto regarded as commonplace can suddenly reveal to our minds a hidden meaning which gives the word unthought-of connotations. There can come a time in the life of a human being when in the passing of a moment he discovers the reality that lay hid under the word *calumny* or *love* or *death* or *despair* or *freedom* or *forgiveness*; such an experience is a frightening one: up to then he has been living on the surface of things, he has heard only the physical sound of words—and now he has stumbled into hidden depths and glimpsed unsuspected abysses.

So it is when divine faith is born in a heart, when the Light which enlightens every man (John 1, 9) penetrates to the innermost being of a person: the man is changed. He may be unconscious of the transformation, like some pauper who has become wealthy but is not yet aware of it, or like a sick person who does not yet know that he has already been cured; but for all that he is no longer what he once was. If now he says: "God is," "God is good," he does not make such assertions on natural grounds, as a philosopher might if left to the unaided resources of his reason; but—presupposing that he speaks from the depths of his heart and not with his lips only—he makes such assertions in a supernatural way, urged on as it were by the power of affirmation of the Spirit. Such an affirmation, such an activity of the soul does not pertain to the sphere of purely human achievement, but is concerned with the kingdom of God.

We can not know whether or not a human being who by his unaided reason has discovered and taught natural truths concerning God has also been able to elicit with the help of divine inspiration an act of supernatural faith; this must remain the secret of God. Plotinus, for example, was able to write and to teach that we have in heaven our true fatherland and a Father who there awaits us; he was even able to teach that the evil that exists in this inferior world is held in check, as it were, by the bonds of His beauty. Nevertheless we shall not know until the Last Judgment whether he also made an act of supernatural faith in these realities; until then we shall remain ignorant whether or not the heart of Plotinus received some stray spark of the supernatural faith which shone so brilliantly in that Origen who so troubled the spirit of the pagan philosopher.

2. Ambivalent Propositions

It is altogether necessary to insist on the mystery of the double use of the same concepts by reason and by faith. When we say that God is one, that He is good, that He is wise, as well as when we say that God exists and rewards those who seek Him, the propositions we affirm can veil two different profundities. They can signify a philosophical mystery, the mystery of perfect Unity, of absolute Goodness, of the fullness of Being and its Providence, as these can be glimpsed by the human reason through the mirror of creatures. In this case God is known only by the fringe of His garments.

But they can also signify a revealed mystery, a mystery of faith, incomparably more profound—the mystery of the Unity, Goodness, Being, and Providence of the God who is a Trinity and of Him who became flesh for the salvation of the world. And in this case God is known as He is in Himself, in His personal life, but in the darkness of faith. When our Saviour said: "God is good and he only" (Matt. 19, 17); "God is a spirit, and those who worship him must worship him in spirit and in truth" (John 4, 24); when the Apostle writes: "God is light, and no darkness can find any place in him" (1 John 1, 5); or "God is love; he who dwells in love dwells in God, and God in him" (1 John 4, 16); when the Epistle to the Hebrews teaches that "God exists . . . and rewards those who try to find him," and when it tells us that it is necessary to believe these truths as the patriarchs of old did, since "it is impossible to please God without faith" (Heb. 11, 6); these truths show us the uttermost profundities of God. They reveal to us God as He is in Himself, the God that is inaccessible to reason and whom we shall see in heaven, the God, however, who is attained here below only in the darkness of faith.

3. *The Ambivalence of the Proposition "God is Pure Act"*

Even the affirmation that God is pure Act does not have a single meaning, but covers two depths of significance. On the metaphysical level, it signifies that God is attained by our intelligence, not as a composite and evolving being such as Jacob Böhme imagined (the amazement which is experienced at the idea of a real and dramatic conflict in the interior of the Divinity is one caused by the folly and incoherence of the concept), but rather as a Plenitude of Being (and the amazement which is thereby experienced is the wonder aroused by a mystery of infinite peace, the existence of which can be established by reason without, however, reason's having the power to understand its nature).

But on the level of sacred doctrine, the proposition that God is pure Act signifies, among other things, that the personal processions of the Divine Persons in the bosom of the Trinity are not successive and that they existed from eternity. "The Father," says Saint John Damascene, "has never existed without the Son; as long as the Father has existed, so long has the Son generated by Him existed." [4] And Bossuet in his turn writes: "At the beginning, before the origin of things, He was; He did not begin, He was; He was not created or made, He was. And what was He? . . . Was He a chaotic matter of some sort that God began to shape, to move, to form? Far from that; what existed from the beginning was thought, reason, intelligence, wisdom: in short, the Word, the interior Utterance of God. . . . What overwhelming and unutterable mystery have I stumbled onto? Be silent, my reason; and without reasoning, without anxiety, without human effort, let me say from the interior

of my heart under the influence of faith and with an understanding held captive and subdued by it: At the beginning,
without beginning, before all beginning, beyond all beginning, He was Who is and always will be, the Word, the
substantial and eternal Utterance and Thought of God." [5]
Here is a staggering knowledge of a completely supernatural
mystery, which would have been forever unknown to us
had not God sovereignly and freely revealed it to us.

4. *Analogy and Transanalogy*

There exist, then, two orders of knowledge which differ
in their principles and in their objects and which present us
with mutually irreducible meanings, even though these are
communicated to us by the same words. Thus, for example,
the expressions "God is" and "God is good" mean different
things when they are said by reason and when they are said
by faith. All this is Catholic doctrine [6] based on Holy Scripture, which tells us, on the one hand, what pagans can learn
of God by contemplating Him with their natural reasons
through the help of creatures (Rom. 1, 20) and, on the
other hand, informs us of a mysterious and hidden wisdom,
unknown to the wise of this world, which does not spring
from the heart of man, but which the Spirit of God has
revealed to His Apostles (1 Cor. 2, 6–11).

We are forced, then, to admit even in the case of the
same words and the same concepts a double transposition
and a double analogy. One of these analogies is the means
by which human reason, having seen certain perfections
existing in creatures, transfers them to God, where they
exist as in their source. An example of this is found in the
assertion: "God exists and is the Remunerator." Here, then,
we have what is known as metaphysical analogy. The second
of the two analogies we have mentioned is that by which
faith uses certain perfections which are mentioned in Scrip-

ture and which at times may be the same as those used by
metaphysics. By scrutinizing these perfections to their uttermost extent, faith elevates itself to approach and give full
and complete consent to the mystery of the Divine Being
insofar as it contains, formally but implicitly, the entire
revelation of the Trinity. In a similar manner it assents to
the mystery of Divine Providence insofar as it too contains formally but implicitly the redemptive Incarnation.[7]
This second kind of analogy we can call the superanalogy
or transanalogy of faith. These two analogies—that of
metaphysics and that of faith—do not belong to the same
order. As the theologians say, the notion of analogy is itself
analogous and proportional.

5. Analogy and the Gospels

It is in this transanalogical light of faith that the Christian reads Scripture and in particular the Gospels. Under its
illumination the texts which tell us of the beneficence and
the forgivingness of God or the obstinacy of men appear
greater and more overwhelming; they open to us perspectives hitherto unknown. Each word and each action of the
Word made flesh is loaded with mystery, the depths of
which can not be plumbed. An ancient sage, a prophet
could have said: "Blessed are those who weep. . . . Blessed
are the clean of heart," and his words would have been able
to move us. But if the second Person of the Blessed Trinity
descends from heaven to pronounce them, what mortal can
ever hope to fathom their complete meaning? Similarly
each of the actions of our Saviour conceals unlimited meanings; for it is God Himself who enters a boat intent on
reaching the other side of the lake in order to heal a raving
madman; it is God Himself who prays in the solitude of the
night; and it is God who weeps at the tomb of Lazarus.

6. *The Christian Use of Concepts*

Since faith and, more generally, Christian doctrine and theology [8] can not speak of God and the things that pertain to the kingdom of God without straining and amplifying the meaning of words even more than the unaided reason does, we can understand how faith uses the same dialectical procedures as reason does and for the same purpose. We can understand how it is that Dionysius can borrow from the neo-Platonic philosophers the ways of affirmation, of negation, and of eminence by which these philosophers reached God. The Areopagite, however, transposes these procedures to a theological level. He says, for example, "God is one and triune"; thereafter he asserts, "God is neither one nor triune," that is, in the imperfect manner in which these perfections can be found in creatures; finally he remarks, "God is one and triune in an eminent way," since He completely transcends every other being to which these names can be applied.[9]

We must remember, however, that the purpose of such negations is not to destroy [10] the previous affirmations, but to surpass them. In this respect they are even superior to the affirmations. They force the soul which can no longer return to its previous affirmations to pass beyond them into the inexpressible vision of faith as it transcends the weakness of all concepts, both positive and negative.[11]

7. *Negative Theology and the Way of Negation*

This use of negations to surpass previous affirmations is technically known as the use of the way of negation. On the other hand the term "negative theology" is used to signify mystical knowledge which abandons both affirmation and negation; and, while it presupposes the concepts of faith, it does so, not because these are its necessary means of knowledge, but only because they constitute a necessary condition for that knowledge.

Negative theology, then, discards discursive reasoning and its negations. On the contrary, sacred doctrine or theology retains the use of reason and employs its affirmations and its negations, the positive and negative ways.

8. *Christian Paradoxes*

The dialectical procedure of juxtaposing two opposite concepts in order to startle the intellect into surpassing mere words and to enter into silent adoration is a permanent technique of Christian preaching and piety. Such, for example, is the procedure of the Fathers, who proclaim a God made man to make men God; it is found also in the *Confessions* of Saint Augustine, who invokes a God who is at once hidden and yet present, unchangeable and yet changing all things. It is the method of the Paschal Sequence with its amazement at the respective triumphs of life and death; it can be seen in the Litany of the Holy Name of Jesus, who is All-powerful and yet All-suffering; it is present in the *Dies Irae*, which contrasts the justice and the mercy of God. Pascal was likewise aware of this procedure, as when he wrote: "Faith embraces many truths which appear to be contradictory. . . . There are a great number of truths pertaining to faith and morals which seem to be opposed to each other; yet all of them exist in an admirable order. The source of all heresies is the exclusion of some of these truths. One example of such truths is that Jesus Christ is both God and man. . . . Another example can be found in the Blessed Sacrament. We believe that Jesus Christ is really present there. This is one truth, but another is that this sacrament is also a figure of His cross and of His glory." [12] Elsewhere he remarks: "A person does not show his greatness by being at one extremity, but by touching both extremities at the same time and by occupying the space in between them." [13]

Every authentic theology, in the East as well as in the West, realizes that it must grasp simultaneously the complementary aspects of each divine truth, of each ineffable mystery for the precise purpose of "occupying the space in between them." [14] Properly speaking, this procedure does not belong to mystical theology but is a characteristic of every true theology, of all Christian doctrine. [15] It is of the nature of theology to use such conceptual oppositions, rising thereby to an understanding of the truth of the mysteries of the kingdom of God. By such complexities does theology arrive at a knowledge of what in itself is entirely simple. [16]

9. A Citation from Father Gardeil

"If we wish to understand correctly any dogma of the Church, we must always view it in the light of the analogy of proportionality. If it is a matter of the divine realities themselves, this necessity is only too apparent. However purified, clear, and understandable may be the terminology we use in speaking of them, however justified may be the relations we find among them, however sound may be our synthesis of them, let us never pretend to have there a knowledge that is on the uniform level of univocity.

"Take, for example, the phenomena of the most important facts of the life of Christ as these were known by the first witnesses, His birth, His suffering, His passion, His death; or take the least action of Christ: there you will find a mystery, the source of which is found in the interior of God; you will find there a divine nature which you can never fully comprehend. Each one of these actions is the act of the God-Man; each of them belongs to the eminence of the Divinity in Its fullest reality. Popular piety uses the term with due precision when it calls scenes from the life of Christ mysteries, as, for example, when it speaks of the mysteries of the Rosary.

"In a similar way, the Church is a society, the sacraments are signs, sanctifying grace is a reality that exists in man, charity is a virtue. . . . All this is true, but it is not at all true if the words are taken in their usual and ordinary meaning as might happen in a first consideration. Rather, to take one example, it is necessary to say that what signs are in our natural life, the sacraments are in our supernatural lives. Have you, in fact, ever seen signs that by their own power efficaciously effect what they signify? And what is it that these sacramental signs effect? They produce something divine, a participation in our souls of the divine life itself. What a sacrament is in its innermost nature is inaccessible to our minds, just as is the Holy Trinity. And in the final analysis the mystery in both cases is the same." [17]

A true theologian and a true follower of Saint Thomas can be known by a double characteristic. First of all, he knows that the concepts of revelation actually and really signify the realities of the kingdom of God. He knows that we are speaking, not in poetic images, but in the proper sense of the words when we say that God exists, that He is just, that there exists in Him the procession of the Word and the procession of Hypostatic Love, that the sacraments of the New Law are the signs and the causes of grace, that created grace is an accident, that the Blessed Virgin is our Mother, that the Church is a society, that Scripture is inspired, that Christian marriage causatively is a contract, but formally a society. In the second place, however, he realizes that these same concepts must undergo a transposition of meaning, the profundity of which is unique and has nothing in common with the transpositions of meaning found in poetry, but which stems from the nature of divine faith and

which we have called transanalogical. How insignificant is
the natural mystery of the caterpillar become a butterfly,
when compared to the mystery of these words which, although contrived in this world of moth and rust, have
finished by signifying in a true and proper sense the hidden
profundities of the kingdom of its Ruler!

These are the teachings of classical theology, of the only
theology that is of importance. And they are understood,
sensed, even rediscovered, as well as lived daily by souls
who are very humble and very loving. For the highest
theology and the most ardent love are such that they always
agree.

10. *The Use of Metaphors*

It is apparent that there are many metaphors and parables
in Scripture.[18] The truest reason for this, perhaps, is that an
image has the power to diffract in some way the truth and
to present it to each soul according to the soul's need, since
it offers little to him who seeks little, much to him who
seeks much. "And he used many parables of this kind, such
as they could easily listen to, in preaching the word to them;
to them he spoke only in parables" (Mark 4, 33–34). But
immediately after, the Evangelist adds that He "made all
plain to his disciples when they were alone." These images,
then, had to be explained. "Hence," says Saint Thomas,
"those things that are taught metaphorically in one part of
Scripture, in other parts are taught more openly." [19]

In the organization of his theology Dionysius consecrated
an entire treatise called *Symbolic Theology* (it is no longer
extant) to a discussion of the meaning which words expressing sense realities can have when they are applied to God.
What, for instance, does Scripture mean when it speaks of
the shape of God, His members, His throne, His anger, His
sorrow, His vengeance, His jealousy, His oaths, His sleep,

His awakening? [20] A chapter in the *Exposition of the Ortho-dox Faith* by Saint John Damascene [21] gives us the key to most of these figures: the oath of God signifies the un-changingness of His decisions; the anger of God, His hos-tility to and His action against evil; the forgetfulness and the sleep of God, the delays which He uses in His dealings with His enemies and His friends, and so forth.

Moreover, Saint John Damascene does not forget to recall in the same passage that ever since the Word was made flesh many of these sensible qualities can be attributed to God in a proper and literal sense. There can be no doubt that it is in this way that one is to understand the text where the Saint says that in the life to come "the Lord will be seen by those who have served Him perfectly as He was seen by the Apostles on Tabor." [22] In the same way the Areopagite teaches that when we become incorruptible and immortal, we shall experience "the visible theophany of the Lord." [23] What could the text mean, if there be excluded a corporeal vision which we shall have of Christ in His glory? The interpretation we have given is certainly that which was adopted in the scholia attributed to Saint Maximus [24] and in Saint Thomas' commentary on the work of Dionysius. [25] As the Angelic Doctor says, "We shall be enraptured by the visible appearance, that is to say, by the sensible and corporeal vision, of God Himself, as He is manifested in the radiant humanity of Christ."

By way of parenthesis, let us remark that the teaching of Saint John Damascene should certainly throw light on the Palamite controversy [26] concerning the nature of the glory of Tabor. What in reality was the light of the Transfigura-tion?

First of all, its source and its cause were the uncreated light and glory of the divinity of the Word. For, as Saint John explains, the glory which the Word possessed from eternity in the bosom of the Father remained His even when He became flesh.[27] The glory of Tabor, then, was the illumination of the holy humanity of Christ by this glory; it was the created effect of this glory as it was received in the weak and passible Body of Christ. "The divinity," as Saint John Damascene says, "was so invincibly impassible in spite of the passible humanity, that it could make the Body participate in its brilliance and glory." [28] And before him Saint Andrew of Crete had already written: "Since the Apostles could not endure the miraculous presence in Christ's immaculate Body of the brilliance which shone forth from the divinity of the Word to which that Body was hypostatically united, they fell prostrate on the ground." [29] It is by reason of this hypostatic union that the humanity of Christ is always and everywhere adorable, whether plunged in the suffering of the Crucifixion or in the glory of the Transfiguration. Finally, the light of the Transfiguration consisted in an impression of the divine glory on the external world, on the garments of Christ and on the luminous cloud which enveloped the Apostles.

Gregory of Palamas, then, had good reasons for wishing to adore the light of Tabor, but no less valid were the reasons that led Barlaam to consider it as a corporeal and transitory phenomenon. If these two had only expressed their convictions more exactly, truth would have triumphed instead of confusion and dispute.[30] But we must return to our main consideration.

Very often the theologian can not remain content with merely establishing the proper sense which underlies the metaphorical meaning. He must also recall that this proper sense must itself be transposed and understood in the light of the transanalogy of faith. It is in this way, for instance, that we must understand how the Church can be called the Mystical Body of Christ. Since the words *head, body, member,* directly signify a biological reality, they do not on this level of meaning surpass the animal order. It is only by metaphor that they can be transferred to the sociological level, that is, to the level of human society.[31] In this case, *body* means an ordered multitude, while *head* signifies the organizing principle of this multitude.

By using an analogy of proportionality, the notion of an ordered multitude can be applied in its proper sense to different societies of the natural order, to the family, for example, and to the State. And if we make use of the transanalogy of faith, the proper meaning of this notion can be extended still further to apply also to the supernatural society that is the Church. In the same way, the notion of organizing principle can be applied in a proper but analogous sense to the father of a family and the ruler of a State, while by virtue of the transanalogy of faith, it can be applied in its proper sense to Christ in the Church.

So it is that when the Apostle asserts that God has made Christ "the head to which the whole Church is joined, so that the Church is his body" (Eph. 1, 23–24), the words *head* and *body* metaphorically stand for organizing principle and ordered multitude respectively. It is not sufficient, however, to convert this metaphorical meaning into its proper significance; there still remains the necessity of transposing to the supernatural order the notions of ordered multitude and organizing principle. For their validity depends on the transanalogy of faith.

Another example of this is found in the notion of *person,* which can be subjected to the same procedure as we have just used with *head* and *body.* The word *person* was first used to signify a mask, an actor, a role; therefore it was used as a metaphor to designate something capable of playing a role in the world, an independent being, undivided and incommunicable, intelligent and free. Even today the legal use of *person* to designate inanimate beings such as a house, an annuity, a trust fund, and so forth is nothing more than a metaphor and a fiction.

On the other hand the notion of an undivided and subsistent totality that is intelligent and free can be predicated in a proper though analogous manner both of substantial totalities such as a man or an angel and of accidental totalities such as perfect human societies.[32] And the same notion can be predicated in a proper but transanalogous manner of such substantial totalities as the three divine Persons of the Holy Trinity[33] as well as of the collective totality which is the Church united with her Head, Christ. It is this mystical and collective totality which Saint Paul (Eph. 12, 12) calls "the Christ." Saint Thomas in turn writes: "The Head and members are as one mystic person."[34] Elsewhere he adds: "Grace was in Christ . . . as in the Head of the whole Church, to Whom all are united, as members to a head, who constitute one mystical person."[35] It is clear that this mystical person, though collective,[36] is a real person, whose ontological unity is of the accidental order.[37]

The constant effort of the theologian, then, will be to attain to the reality underlying the figures used by Scripture, the Fathers, and mystical writers. What other task does the theologian Saint John of the Cross have, except to explain the metaphors of the poet Saint John of the Cross? Recall, for example, how in his commentary on the second verse of the fourth strophe of *The Living Flame of Love*, the holy Doctor shows us in terms of the highest theology the effects of the marvelous awakening of God from the sleep into which He apparently falls for a given period in the center of a soul transformed by the union of love. Under the tutelage of such a master, we cannot help perceiving that the images he uses—whether they be his own or borrowed from Scripture—conceal a profundity that is

truly divine. Nor can we escape understanding what an ir-
reparable error it would be to judge them only by the
canons of poetry, and not with those of faith and the wisdom of love.

11. *An Unpublished Text of Maritain on the Tears of the*
    Blessed Virgin

It is impossible to refrain from quoting here a brilliant
text of Jacques Maritain, which, though written some years
ago, still remains unpublished. In the text, which was occa-
sioned by a consideration of the tears of the Virgin of La
Salette, Maritain points out to us the serious attention that
those statements deserve which depict for us the sorrow
our sins cause in God, in Christ, in the Blessed Virgin, and
in the saints.

"She [the Blessed Virgin] wept on the mountain of La
Salette. She said that her strength was gone and that she
was forced to let go the hand of her Son: 'That hand is so
strong and mighty that I can no longer keep it from strik-
ing. Since that time, how I have suffered because of you
sinners. . . . Though you pray much and live well, you will
never be able to recompense the suffering which I have
endured for your sakes.' Is it possible, we may ask, that tears,
sufferings, and sorrow exist in paradise?

"It is easy to reply that we have here only a manner of
speaking which is not infrequent in Holy Scripture, where
God is said to be repentant, to be angry, and so forth. Confronted with the sins which merited the flood, God was
touched with sorrow at the very core of His heart. We must
be on our guard not to diminish the truth of such passages
by our commentaries nor to change the language of God
into mere rhetoric or hyperbole. If our Lady has wept, if
she has spoken as she has, it is because in the system of
signs which men can understand, no other image could

better express the ineffable reality that actually exists in heaven. Our manner of expression, implying though it does some imperfection or some real sorrow incompatible with the happiness of heaven, does not sin by excess but by default in describing to us this reality. Everything [38] which exists in creation, insofar as it possesses being and goodness—whether it be the force of torrents or the swiftness of birds or the grandeur of the ocean—exists in God in a virtual and eminent way. If, then, there is in tears any beauty or any goodness, any being or any life, this, too, though separated from all sorrow and all imperfections, exists virtually and eminently in God by reason of His essence and, by participation in His essence, also exists in those who see God. Even so the tears of the Queen of Heaven are far from giving us an adequate knowledge of the sovereign horror which God and His Mother experience because of our sins; nor do they allow us to realize fully the surpassing mercy which they feel for the misery of the sinner.

"In the light of this explanation, the apparitions—increasingly more numerous since the time of Saint Gertrude—where our Lord shows Himself to saintly souls filled with sorrow and with the wound of His Heart bathed in blood, can show us, together with the tears of the Blessed Virgin at La Salette, that we can speak of a virtual sorrow in Jesus and in Mary. Though the sorrow be virtual in them, yet throughout the length of time it is a real sorrow in the Church of which Christ is the Head and the Virgin Mary is the neck. During Christ's life on earth, His soul already enjoyed the Beatific Vision; nevertheless by a miraculous hindering of the effects of this vision, Christ was subject to suffering. Now, however, He can not suffer in the real sense of that word. Nevertheless do not realities exist that of their nature would tend to cause sorrow in Him? Is not each soul that is lost a piece of flesh torn from the Body of Jesus? And are not we sinners—lepers rather—the very children of the Immaculate Mother? If, as we know, the vision of God and the state of happiness prevent the blessed from suffering, still from the side of man the reasons that exist for them to suffer constitute a veritable ocean of sorrow. The Sacred Heart overflows with blood, the eyes of our Lady are filled with tears; and this is done only to show us that they would suffer, if they still had power to feel pain.

"Finally we must never forget that when our Lady could actually suffer, Mary in her role of co-sufferer really wept for each one of us and for each of our sins, just as Jesus in His passion was sacrificed for each of us and for each one of our sins."

Throughout this chapter, then, we have discussed the use of concepts in the teaching of Christian doctrine. It remains for us to say a word now about the two states in which this doctrine is found. The first of these is the unpolished and spontaneous state that is found in preaching; the second is the elaborated and scientific state of theology.

3. Supernatural Rhetoric and Science

If we take an over-all view of the truths of the Christian message, we can distinguish two different forms or states in which this message presents itself. In the first place it can be found in an unpolished state in which the Divine Wisdom seems to use the weaknesses as well as the strength of men in order to cry out and make Itself heard in public places. The result is a mysterious rhetoric, the key to which is possessed by the Holy Spirit. Secondly, Christian doctrine appears in an elaborated state where its message is ordered and organized according to the internal exigencies of its constituent elements; this is the scientific state of sacred doctrine and is generally called theology.

1. The Preaching of the Holy Spirit

It will be profitable to begin these considerations by seeing in Christian doctrine an announcement, a message, a teaching, a vast and ardent sermon which the hidden God preaches to men to free them from their unhappiness and to invite them to eternal happiness, to a participation in the divine life. If we forget for the time being the secret illuminations which are placed in the heart of each man, we can say that it is the Trinity Itself which speaks openly and publicly by the Prophets and the Apostles, who, under Its inspiration, were able to reveal new truths. Even now it is the Holy Spirit who speaks openly and publicly through His Church, whose task it is, with His assistance, not to announce new revelations destined to be the foundation of a new faith,[1] but to preserve during the course of centuries a revealed deposit of faith which never ceases to live and which is rich in practical applications and dogmatic developments.

For the man of faith there can be no question that there exists an ordering principle which commands the appearance, manifestation, and actual presentation of this immense body of teaching, intercrossed as it is with divine invitations and human responses, speculative as well as practical truths, definitions and anathemas, commandments and counsels, magisterial pronouncements and religious facts like the lives of the saints which give us a reflection of the example of Christ; nor can it be doubted that there is a Wisdom and a Love that orders this teaching for the purpose of building up in the womb of time the Body of Christ (Eph. 4, 12) and of establishing the kingdom which Christ at the end of the world will present as a homage to His Father (1 Cor. 15, 28).

Nevertheless, the principle of this order escapes us, since it is hidden in the heart of a God who is both Light and Love and whose knowledge far surpasses our divisions of speculative and practical knowledges.[2] We can not know the nature of that order because it is hidden in a God who reveals to men not only what He does for them, but also what He is to them and, in addition, what He is in the light of His own eternal gaze ("In the beginning was the Word. . . ."). And He does this because He wishes to be known and loved by men as He is in Himself and to give Himself to them in all His reality. Precisely because the infinite liberty of the divine decree which is the ordering principle of this vast and universal preaching remains incomprehensible to us, the preaching itself can appear to us as though it were without order, like the fragments of a vase shattered under the pressure of its own contents.[3]

2. Divine Rhetoric

When ancient thinkers tried to classify the different ways of communicating knowledge, they distinguished the scientific mode with its exclusive attention to the objective requirements of truth from the oratorical manner with its emphasis on the disposition of the hearers.[4] When, then, we look on Christian doctrine as a supernatural preaching whose purpose is to awaken men to the knowledge of divine realities, we can see that its procedure will not be scientific, but oratorical. It will be a sort of supernatural rhetoric in which can be discerned to a certain extent the procedures and methods of human rhetoric, but used with complete purity and freedom.[5]

But it must be added at once that such a rhetoric exceeds in a thousand ways the limits of a purely human one and even disregards it. Though the imagery of poetry can rise above the weaknesses of earthly things, still by its very nature it remains infinitely removed from the divine obscurities of revelation.[6] Nor must we forget that if Saint Paul was at pains to take into consideration the sensibilities of the Athenians (Acts 17, 22), he nevertheless did not hesitate to shock those of the Corinthians (1 Cor. 1, 17).

The Holy Spirit who preached prophetically and lovingly [7] in Holy Scripture continues the same preaching in the Church. He enlightens the teaching Church, no longer, it is true, by the oral or scriptural inspiration (these accompanied the Apostles into heaven), but by the assistance of an illumination that varies in its degrees. At the same time the Spirit illuminates the heart of the Church, as He did those of the Apostles, by the gifts of counsel, of knowledge, of understanding, and of wisdom. In this way the spreading of the gospel continues to be conducted in the world with a liberty similar to that which it had when it was first born.

Christian preaching continually rediscovers the means by which it can appeal to pagans or to dissidents and call them to eventual union with the one true flock. Similarly it rediscovers the ways by which it can lead sinners to penance and by which it can instruct and exhort the faithful while stirring up the love of the generous followers of Christ. Mystical experience itself constantly rediscovers from age to age the ways by which it can proclaim openly the marvels with which it overflows. The supernatural rhetoric of the Holy Spirit, then, which speaks to men and through men, continues to be enriched until the end of the world.

3. Theology: The Scientific Presentation of the Christian Message

We may well ask the question whether there can be found a unifying principle [8] in this vast ensemble of teaching the greatness of which overpowers our minds and at times throws them into confusion and discouragement. Is there an interior unity which would permit us to order and to organize this multitude of truths? Is it possible to understand these truths not as isolated realities, but as related among themselves? Is it possible to induce our minds to see one mystery in another?

There can be no doubt that we can, and the task of performing this is precisely that of reason, which, because it is discursive, can attain knowledge by deducing one truth from another. The reason, however, which attempts this task can not be "rationalistic" nor even "rational" as Aristotle would have understood that word. It is rather a reason that is unknown to philosophers, a reason that is purified, directed, and elevated by faith and thereby enabled to discover the relationships which exist between the supernatural mysteries of revelation.

Once this effort of reason has begun, theology springs into existence. The sacred teaching is seen to be capable of becoming the object of a true science.[9] But in this connection the word "science" must be transposed to a new level; to avoid all possible misunderstanding, it would be better to speak here of a "superscience." Within its vast stretches, then, sacred doctrine conceals a profound and sanctifying unity which, when it is discovered, brings a supernatural peace to our souls.

4. *Patristic and Scholastic Presentations of the Sin of Schism*

When the Fathers read in Scripture (Num. 16, 28) that the earth opened to swallow up those who had cut themselves off from the people of Israel, they were led to conclude that schism is a greater sin than infidelity.[10] But the speculative method obliged Saint Thomas to compare the sins of schism and of infidelity according to their natures, independently of circumstances which might make a particular sin of schism more grave than a given sin of infidelity. From the scholastic point of view infidelity, since it is a sin directly against God Himself, is a graver sin than schism, which is directed against the created unity of the Church.[11]

"In this example," says Father Congar, "we can see the consequences of the Patristic method of theology and how it differs from the scholastic method. The Fathers consider a Scripture text exactly as it stands, with its historical and its doctrinal implications as well; they explain such a text without subjecting it to critical scrutiny with the result that a text of Scripture the nature of which is not in all respects homogeneous and the intention of which is neither speculative nor systematic leads them to make affirmations which would not be made by a theology that was scientifically constructed. In other words, there exists in the Bible not only a revelation of speculative truths that show us the inner nature of the realities they express, but also a supernatural politic and a supernatural pedagogy which at times give precedence to the conditions of the hearers and to the opportunities and occasions of teaching rather than to a rigorous precision in the statement of the truths to be expressed. Scholastic theologians, therefore, although they were well acquainted with the Bible and were profoundly docile to its teachings, generally attempted, especially in moral considerations, to construct their theology according to the essential nature of things; consequently they felt themselves free to comment on, explain, and adjust any Scriptural texts where a different perspective was apparently to be found." [12]

It was pointed out in the preceding paragraphs that the sacred teaching conceals under its profusion of lessons a supernatural and peace-bringing principle of unity. The question now remains how this principle can be discovered and made evident.

5. *The Division of Theology into Speculative and Positive*

This principle of unity has a double aspect. Just as we can understand a living being in two ways, either by attempting to make clear the internal relations of the different parts of the being (this may be called the constitutive method) or by trying to show the process of its development (the genetic method), so human reason when illuminated by faith, can attempt to show in Christian teaching either the internal, ontological ordering of its truths according to their profoundest exigencies and their mutual relations of dependence; or it can attempt to point out the unity in their historical succession, in the way in which they have been known and stressed during the course of time.

In both cases it is human reason under the illumination of faith that makes this attempt to find the principle of order in Christian teaching; in both cases there is the same luminous light of intelligibility which is due neither to faith alone nor to reason alone; in both cases, therefore, we have one and the same theology. But this theology has two spheres, the purpose of both being to make Christian teaching understandable; but one attempts it by examining its constitutive, internal order, the other by considering its order of appearance in time.

Though the first sphere of theology is termed scholastic theology, and the second, positive theology, these names are not in every respect appropriate. The first of them gives only a non-essential description, for it makes allusion to the educational procedure of the Middle Ages, to the *disputatio magistralis in scholis*, which attempted to render revealed doctrine intelligible.[13] And the second term is even less exact.[14] However, since this terminology has at least the advantage that it is classic, we will be forced to preserve these terms, at least as secondary nomenclatures.

What we have called scholastic theology is nothing else than a divine-human science of the internal order of what has been revealed.[15] It can be called systematic or even speculative theology. In connection with this last term, however, it must be remembered that it is termed speculative only in opposition to historical research, and not in opposition to practical science, for, as will be seen, scholastic theology is both a speculative and a practical science; and it is both in an eminent degree. The word which we prefer to use is to call this sphere of theology doctrinal theology.

On the other hand, what we have called positive theology is the divine-human science of the historical development of revelation, and in a wider sense, of the Church, the kingdom of God here on earth. It is a theological explanation of the history of salvation, and in this sense can be termed historical theology.

In the rest of this book we shall examine successively these two major functions of one and the same theology.

4. The Need For a Doctrinal Theology

This present chapter will treat of matters that have reference to the necessity for speculative or doctrinal theology; the next chapter will then consider in detail the nature of this theology and indicate briefly its divisions.

1. Divine Authorization of the Argumentative Procedure

Doctrinal theology is the divine-human science of the internal and ontological order to be found in what has been revealed by God. The technical procedure which gives birth to this science is an argumentative one flowing from a reason which studies the faith to discover therein the mutual relationships that exist between the revealed truths. Such a method is both legitimate and holy, for it is to be found even in the pages of Scripture. If Christ is our Head and if we are His members, if He is our Leader who has come to carry us with Him to His destiny (this is the major of the argument), then from the fact that He has arisen from the dead (and this is the minor proposition) we must necessarily conclude with Saint Paul (1 Cor. 15, 20) that we too shall arise with Him. This is the classical example of theological procedure and is utilized by Saint Thomas.[1]

Moreover, one can find numberless passages of Scripture where in one way or another faith makes use of reason. In the same epistle which we have already utilized, Saint Paul at first is satisfied to disabuse those catechumens who were seduced by the teachers of this world; for this purpose he sets up an irreducible opposition between the folly of God and the wisdom of men (1, 25). Thereafter, however, he makes use of rational considerations to strengthen and increase their faith. This he does by leading them to consider the multiplicity of forms which matter can take on here below; thereby he shows them that the glorified body is not an impossibility (15, 39–44).

Holy Scripture, then, not only gives us revealed truths to which we must adhere by faith alone and by reliance on the Cause of all truth, but also teaches us to use our reasoning powers under the illumination of faith by proceeding from one revealed truth to another truth which itself (as we shall see later) may also be revealed. In this procedure the first type of truth is a principle of knowledge; the second is a conclusion.[2] Throughout the entire process none of the truths involved are considered directly in themselves (for this would be a matter of faith alone), but in their mutual relationships; we consider the first insofar as it is the cause of the second, and we view the second insofar as it is implied in and explained by the first. Such is the scientific procedure of theology.[3]

2. Intuitive Faith, Discursive Theology

The knowledge of faith is, as it were, intuitive, while the knowledge of our reason under the illumination of faith is discursive. Between faith and theology there exists a proportion that is similar to that which is found in the natural order between the understanding of first principles and the science of conclusions. The understanding of first principles is acquired by the light of simple insight; knowledge of conclusions, however, is obtained by the light of the complex process which we call reasoning. As Saint Thomas remarks, just as in the natural order the habit of first principles is given to us with our natures, while the habit of conclusions is acquired, "so, in the case of sacred doctrine, the habit of faith which plays the role of a habit of first principles is not acquired, but the habit which deduces conclusions from these principles and defends them, is acquired." [4]

Nevertheless, it must be emphasized that the procedure of theology is neither rationalistic nor even purely rational. It is the procedure of an intellect that is immersed in the light of faith and which seeks to understand the truths of that faith. "It is for this reason," says Saint Thomas, "that this science is higher than the science of divine things which philosophers have taught, for it proceeds from higher principles." [5]

3. Two Functions of Theology: The Organization and Extension of the Revealable

That which specifies theology and makes it distinct from faith and from natural disciplines is, then, the discursive procedure of reason under the illumination of faith and from the data of faith. This discursive procedure can begin with one truth of faith—for example, one of the articles of the creed—and conclude to another truth of faith. In such a case, the procedure of theology permits us to organize the truths of faith. In a true sense we can say that we know a truth of faith only when we know its place in the hierarchy of all revealed truths and when we understand its importance for and its relationships with the other truths that have been revealed.

However, the discursive procedure of theology can also begin with a truth that has been revealed and deduce there-

from another truth which is not known as a revealed truth
of the faith; in other words our reason can proceed from
the formally revealed to the virtually revealed.[6] In this case
it permits us to extend the sphere of the "revealable," [7] and
in some cases may allow us to discover intermediate links
between two truths, both of which are formally revealed.[8]

"The principal thing in theology . . . [is] to know in a
more detailed and organic form the truths of faith themselves, and to penetrate ever deeper into their principles.
The science of theology is not confined to theological conclusions which expand the area of its field of knowledge.
It includes also, and chiefly, the very truths of faith which
are penetrated and connected one to another with the aid
of human inference—*ut connexae*, said John of Saint
Thomas, *et penetratae modo naturali et studio acquisito*.
For a theological inference which starts from a truth of faith
can join up with another truth of faith. This augments
theological knowledge in depth and is of primary importance to it. Moreover, when it examines questions which
concern the supernatural last end and the states of human
nature theology discovers many truths which are not all of
them matters of faith." [9]

4. *The Light of Theology*

It is the same characteristic light of theology which permits us both to organize and to extend the riches of the
deposit of faith. This light of theology is neither that of
pure faith nor that of reason, but is a combination of both.
While faith commands us to adhere after the fashion of
simple insight and intuition to the mysteries of faith insofar
as these are formally revealed and proposed as such in the
ordinary or solemn teaching of the Church, theology uses
the discursive powers of our reason under the guidance of

faith to attempt a consideration of these formally revealed mysteries insofar as they contain virtually other mysteries. It is because of this light that theology can both organize as well as extend the riches of the Christian deposit of truths.

Faith proceeds by an infused light and sees the truths of faith insofar as they are formally or immediately revealed; theology, on the other hand, proceeds from discursive reason illumined by faith and looks on revealed doctrine insofar as it is virtual or mediate. The former is concerned with the formally revealed; the latter with the virtually revealed.

5. Theology in Service to Faith

Though faith is always necessary for theology, the proposition can not be reversed. Nevertheless, theology can be useful for the diffusion of faith. Frequently it opens the way by which faith is made welcome in the hearts of men and "is there engendered or nourished or defended or strengthened." [10] It is of infinite service to the Church when she teaches, since theology prepares her doctrinal decisions. It is of untold value to preachers, if they wish to give forth not a letter-dead doctrine but a pure and living teaching, to present the mysteries in their true sense and in a true perspective, and to build upon the foundation which has been revealed with materials which the flame of Divine Truth will not destroy (1 Cor. 3, 10–15). Actually there can be no question whether or not theology is necessary. For all men theologize. The only question worth asking is whether the theology that exists is good or bad, true or false, complete or incomplete. [11]

6. Reason and the Understanding of Scripture

The manifestation of how some truths are contained in other revealed truths is not the only function of reason which Scripture points out to us. It constantly urges us to use the light of our reason when it is penetrated by faith to scrutinize the notions of the natural order of which Scripture itself is composed and made up; it is only in this way that we shall be able to understand in what way they are capable of being purified and transposed in order to bear a supernatural meaning. We have just seen, for example, that Saint Paul draws our attention to the multiple states of matter in order to permit us to envisage the possibility of a glorified body. But we must not be content with that example alone. The passage from the sphere of the natural to that of the supernatural fills all of Scripture. It is to be found wherever a word of human origin is used to designate realities of the kingdom of God: at times this is done through the use of a metaphor, the true meaning of which we must discover (for example, the anger, repentance, sorrow, sleep of God); at times words will be used in their proper and rigorous meanings, but according to a transanalogy (for example, the being, goodness, wisdom, love, mercy, justice of God; the Trinity, Father, Son, Word, Spirit, processions; the Church, baptism, grace, and so forth). But such passages in Scripture necessarily presuppose a preceding exercise of our reasons, however momentary and spontaneous this may be; our reasons must grasp the immediate sense of the words, judge whether they are used in the passage in a proper or metaphorical sense, and decide under which of these meanings the sense is applicable to supernatural realities.

From all this it follows that faith needs reason in order to read Sacred Scripture. This is not to say that faith depends on reason; it means rather that like a queen it makes use of reason.

The Wisdom of Faith 47

7. Antischolasticism

The violent antischolasticism of Luther as well as that of
Erasmus must be attributed to abuses, the reality and extent
of which it would be useless to deny.[12] Nevertheless, it must
be admitted that besides these abuses the reason for such
attacks, especially in the case of Luther, is to be found in
an out-and-out refusal to make use of reason, and this in
spite of the fact that Scripture nowhere forbids the use of
reason, but rather employs it in its own pages or at least
constantly presupposes it. Though Luther spoke in the
name of Scripture, he himself was lacking in fidelity to the
holy books. This tragic mistake of Luther was made at
Heidelberg, when he gave his exegesis of the words of Saint
Paul on the knowledge of God possessed by the Gentiles.
Today his exegesis is generally recognized as a misinterpreta-
tion of the text he was explaining.

8. The Value and the Danger of Theology

Theological abuses have always existed; they are always
ready to spring up again. When Saint Thomas asks the
question "Whether it is permitted to investigate divine
realities," [13] he answers that it is not only permitted but is
highly desirable, since man should employ all his resources
in order to approach God. Hence he must use not only his
intelligence to contemplate divine realities but also his
reason to search for them, as the words of the Psalmist suggest: "It is good for me to cling to God." Nevertheless the
Angelic Doctor does not hesitate to add that by so doing
man exposes himself to a real danger: "Nevertheless, man
can sin in this manner." [14] The case is an exemplification
of the principle that the more beautiful a thing is, the more
dangerous it is also. Our question, then, is whether a Chris-

tian man, whose choice must be made between heaven and hell, should flee the peril involved in theology or whether he should accept the risk.

The danger of which Saint Thomas speaks can be succumbed to in three principal ways, which both Scripture and the Fathers point out to us. The first of these is to forget that an infinite distance separates him who seeks from Him who is sought; Job is infinitely removed from the Omnipotent God. The second way is to forget that this search for God is a unique human activity and must be directed by faith, not by natural reason. Finally, the third way is to forget that the resources of different men are unequal, that the hunger of one man is satisfied when that of another has scarcely begun to be awakened.[15]

Nevertheless, says Saint Thomas, none of these dangers can cancel the obligation that the human spirit has to seek an ever-growing knowledge of God according to the abilities of each man.[16] And even the silence of the human heart before its God—let us recall that Saint Jerome terms such silence a true act of praise—is not so much a mere abstention from words and thoughts as a tension of the spirit because it comprehends that God is incomprehensible.[17]

9. *Saint Thomas Aquinas, Patron of Theologians*

Whatever may be said concerning the above matters, the theologian must pray ardently and humbly that while he applies himself to a task that is imperatively needed for the salvation of the entire human race, he may not forget that he himself is a man created and redeemed by a God who, before everything else, demands from him the gift of his life and his love. He must plead that the substance of his soul may not be devoured by the insatiable exigencies of his theology; he must beg that his fundamental and directive intuitions [18]—for in a certain manner they are transconceptual—may not be falsified or mutilated; and he must ask that his theology itself may not be subtly vitiated.

Saint Thomas himself read the *Conferences of the Fathers* for fear that his spirit would be withered by his studies.[19] And Reginald of Piperno assures us: "He [Saint Thomas] never undertook to write any work whatsoever without first praying and weeping over it; and when he had doubts about anything, he had recourse to prayer and would return bathed in tears but with his doubts banished and removed." [20]

Since theology is not a work of pure reason nor of Aristotelian philosophizing, but in a special sense is the endeavor of Christian reason; and since it is concerned (we shall return to this point later on) not with merely cultural activities but with activities that pertain to the kingdom of God, it demands to be placed in its entirety both in its speculative and practical endeavors under the light of the gifts of the Holy Spirit. It is necessary that the secret influence of these gifts should be exercised in a powerful and decisive manner on the master intuitions which, though preconceptual, control the conceptualized organization of revealed truths. This is the reason why the Church never confers the title of Doctor on any of her children except on those bishops or simple theologians whom she can canonize.[21]

Nevertheless, the individual theologian—not theology itself—will always be troubled by the question whether, when he is in the presence of a revealed truth, he has any other right than that of permitting himself to be inflamed with love for that truth. Yet there can be no doubt that another right does exist. When Saint Ignatius Loyola was immersed in the light of divine consolations, he was still able to comprehend that if he wished to give efficacious assistance to souls, he would have to study. Accordingly he applied him-

self to the pursuit of learning, but found that he was forced
to defend himself against his God, who lay siege to him,
never ceasing to speak to his heart and to ravish his soul.
And this strange battle lasted for some twelve years.[22]

10. *Theology in the Fathers*

With the Fathers theology already began to be constituted as a science, though it remained with them in an
inchoative and imperfect state. Under the illumination of
faith the Greek and Latin Fathers made constant appeal to
the resources of discursive reason in order to establish the
precise meaning of revealed mysteries by considering the
meaning of human words; they used reason to show the intimate connections that exist between these mysteries and
to display the folly of heretics who attempted to disjoint
these mysteries; finally they employed their reasons in an
attempt to develop the implicit content of the revealed
truths. In this appeal to theological reasoning, there is apparent an exigency that is peculiar to Christianity and which
transcends the geographical divisions of East and West.

It was in this way that through their consideration of
Divinity and Sonship, the Fathers were led to conclude to
the dogma of the numerical consubstantiality of the Father
and the Word. Similarly from a consideration of the maternity of Mary and the divinity of Christ, they were led
to conclude to the dogma of the Divine Maternity.[23] It is
true that today the consubstantiality of the Father and the
Word, and the Divine Maternity are defined truths of our
faith; but they continue to find even now their explanation
in those primordial truths which originally gave birth to
them.

11. *An Example: The Dogma of Subsistent Relations*

In order to be able to affirm the identity of essence in
God as well as the real distinction of Persons in Him, the

Fathers were forced to elevate their minds to the infinitely mysterious but in no way contradictory notion of a subsistent relation.[24] The Divine Persons are subsistent relations. They are opposed to each other insofar as They are relations, but They are identical with the Divine Essence insofar as They are subsistent.

"O wisest of men," exclaimed Saint Gregory Nazianzen to the Arians, "the name Father is not, as you think, the name of an essence"; for in such a case you could say that as the Father is distinct from the Son, so His essence is distinct from that of the Son. "But the name of Father signifies a relation, the relation of the Father to the Son and of the Son to the Father." [25] Hence the Father and the Son are truly distinct. But They have, They are, identically the same Essence. The Father is God, He is the very Essence of God; the Son likewise is God, He is the very Essence of God. Nevertheless the Father is not the Son.[26]

It is this same Gregory (whom the Greeks called the Theologian) who tells us in a celebrated text: "Though He [the Son] is not the Father, there is nothing lacking in the Son to be the Father. . . . The Son is not the Father, since there is only one Father, but the Son is that which the Father is." [27] And again the holy Doctor says: "In order to save the distinction of Persons in the Trinity, we must say that the Father is one Person, the Son another Person, and the Spirit another Person; but we can not say that the Father is one thing, and the Son another thing, and the Spirit still another thing; for the three Persons are one and the same Thing as far as Their divinity is concerned." [28]

Because of its superiority to differences of place and time, this same doctrine is found in its purity in Saint Augustine [29] and in the Councils of the West: "The Father is not the same Person as the Son . . . but He is the same Thing as the Son. . . ." [30] "The Father is one Person, the Son another, and the Holy Spirit another; nevertheless they are not different things or realities. But what the Father is, so also identically are the Son and the Holy Spirit." [31]

When the Arians and the Sabellians charged that the Church by preaching her doctrine of the Trinity and the divinity of Christ was replacing the message of the Gospels with one of incoherence, the Church replied that the Trinity and the divinity of Christ were ineffable mysteries, disconcerting to reason, and above reason, but that they were in no way unreasonable, or contradictory, or incoherent. Between a mystery of faith which is beyond reason and a contradiction which is a denial of reason, there yawns an infinite abyss.

It is not philosophical reason, but the light of faith which both in the West and the East has dared by means of a transanalogy to elevate the notions of essence and of relation to signify the intimate life of God; the relations precisely as relations are opposed each to the other, and each of them, precisely because it is subsistent, is really identical with the Divine Essence. Certainly it was not philosophical reason but the light of Christian faith which maintained through the words of these Doctors that if the Persons were realities distinct from the Divine Essence, as Gregory of Palamas and his followers upheld at the beginning of the fourteenth century, then it would follow that the Father would possess a reality which did not belong to the Divine Essence; similarly the Son would possess another reality which did not belong to the Divine Essence; accordingly the Divine Essence would not Itself be infinite but limited, while there would be in the Father a reality which the Son did not possess and vice versa. In other words, there would be something lacking to the Son for Him to be the Father. But as we have seen, Saint Gregory said: "There is nothing lacking to the Son for Him to be the Father."

The dogma of the real distinction of the Persons and the

unicity of the divine nature obliges us today as it obliged Gregory Nazianzen and Augustine in days gone by to elevate ourselves to the notion of a subsistent relation and to the principle formulated by the Council of Florence according to which in God "everything is one, except where there exists an opposition of relation." [32] We have here an eminent example—though it be but one of innumerable cases—of the manner in which theology relates the mysteries of our faith to each other.

12. Believe, in Order to Understand

We have seen, then, that by taking as our point of departure something which we believe on divine faith, we seek by means of discursive reasoning an explanation of other things which we already believe with the same divine faith or which we will believe when they are defined as revealed by the teaching power of the Church.[33] Therein is contained the entire function of theology.

This is not to say that faith is ordered to theology as something inferior is ordered to its superior, or as a means to an end. Faith is a theological virtue and completely supernatural. Theology, on the other hand, is the work of reason under the illumination of faith; theology it is which is the inferior and its highest dignity is to engender, nourish, defend, and strengthen the faith in the souls of men.[34]

Nevertheless, it is true that there is an ordering of faith to theology, but it is the order that exists between a superior and an inferior, as a tree is ordered to its foliage, a mother to her son, a teacher to a student. Faith in its superabundance gives birth to theology, and theology in turn has as its task to prepare the way for faith. It is necessary "to believe in order to understand." But this is only the first stage; the second will always be "to understand in order to believe still more."

In a book which he at first wished to entitle *Faith Seeking Understanding*, Saint Anselm wrote: "I do not seek to understand in order that I may believe"—that is to say, I do not attempt to comprehend first by my reason what later I shall believe by divine faith; I do not attempt to base my faith on my reason—"but I believe in order to understand"—that is, I believe first of all in order that the superabundance of my faith may enable me to understand. "For I am sure of one thing, namely, that if I do not begin by believing, I shall never reach understanding." [35] Such, in effect, is the first stage in passing from faith to theology; it is the characteristic of theology which many ancient writers loved to discover in the Septuagint version of Isaias, 7, 9: "Unless you believe, you will not understand." [36] The second stage in passing from faith to theology is to put theology in the service of faith in the world and in our own hearts.

13. *Mysteries Explained by Mysteries*

The principal function of theology is to manifest the order that exists in the truths of revelation and to show how they mutually explain each other. It shows, for example, the mutual relations between the mystery of the divine relations *ad intra* and the mystery of the divine relations *ad extra*; it does the same for the mystery of the eternal processions and the mystery of the temporal processions, especially of the visible missions of the Incarnation and of Pentecost, which conferred on the Church her essentially missionary characteristic. It explains the profundities of sin by those of the Incarnation and the profundities of the Incarnation by those of sin. By extending the privileges of Christ, who is the Head, theology explains the privileges of the Church, which is the Body. Through the mystery of the being of Christ, it explains the mystery of the activity and the causality of Christ; similarly through the mystery of the in-

strumental causality of Christ it explains the mystery of the
instrumental causality of the sacraments of the New Law.
The mystery of the Incarnation is used to explain that of
the Divine Maternity of the Blessed Virgin. And through
the revelation of the "Word made flesh" it understands
better the revelation of "this is my Body."

What is surprising in all this is that in this confrontation
of mysteries, the resulting illumination is mutual. For if the
higher mysteries by their own power and, as it were, from
on high clarify the lower mysteries, still these latter frequently have a marvelous power to reveal to us—and, as it
were, from below—the profundities concealed in the higher
mysteries. Something similar to this happens in everyday
life when the tone of a voice reveals to us the state of a
soul. In a similar way the Incarnation gives us an understanding of the Eucharist, but the Eucharist itself can throw
further light on that very Incarnation.

Those who study theology and who love it know that in
this world there is no explanation more simple, more unifying, or more quieting to the soul than that in which the
greatest things are explained by the greatest things and
the greatest mysteries by the greatest mysteries. "And if to
explain these things for us, other mysteries are used, these
mysteries are similar to those that exist between husband
and wife or between mother and child; they are real, and
though they escape our understanding, are yet a source of
overwhelming interest and of piercing joy and of life. Our
faith gives a perpetual dignity to these things since they
will exist eternally as they do now." [37]

After affirming with Saint Thomas the coexistence in the
soul of Christ our Saviour of the highest happiness and the
deepest sorrow, of a desire for glory and a desire for the
cross, Father Garrigou-Lagrange adds: "All these statements
pertain more to the teaching of faith than to theology. They

transcend it. Yet theology is most useful in showing the subordination of these statements in the body of doctrine; in fact, the principal part of sacred theology is not the deduction of theological conclusions through the medium of a natural premise, but it is the explanation of truths of the faith and their logical subordination. In the manifestation of this subordination, theology in some manner hides itself; somehow as Saint John the Baptist says of Christ: 'He must increase, but I must decrease.' This means that sacred theology no longer uses strictly technical terms, but speaks in the words of Sacred Scripture, which are like precious stones logically arranged by it, so that in their subordinate and doctrinal setting they may interact as searchlights. This most exalted part of theology proposes the object of faith in a doctrinal manner, that is, in logical order, and thus it is of great service to contemplation, because thus it prepares for us a general synthesis of the truths wherein we have a view of the whole doctrine of faith, as also a complete and intelligent grasp of it." [38]

14. *The Importance of the Argument from Fittingness*

When the theologian advances reasons in support of divine decisions which he knows were entirely gratuitous and which could be entirely different or might never have existed at all; when, for example, in order to explain the reason for creation [39] or for the Incarnation,[40] he appeals to the principle of the natural superabundance and diffusibility of the good; or when he explains the relationship between the sin of Adam and the Redemption of the second Adam [41] by appealing to an infinitely good and powerful God who would never permit evil unless He could derive some great good from it; or when the Assumption of the Blessed Virgin is explained by the principle that the Saviour should associate His Mother with His perfect vic-

tory over sin, death, and the devil; or when he explains the
order that exists in the seven sacraments by reference to
the parallelism between our supernatural lives and our
physical lives; [42] he does all this under the impulsion of a
secret yet forceful instinct that these arguments from suitability are very precious, since, as far as this is possible here
below, they justify to us the actual choices that God has
made, and since in the light of eternity they will appear to
contain more truth than can be proved in our actual state.

The same remarks are applicable to the arguments given
by the theologian in support of a mystery the intrinsic necessity of which is known to him only by revelation, even
though these arguments can never completely manifest the
mystery in this life. If every created intellection of the
natural order requires the production of a "word," we
can understand that the Divine Intellection engenders a
Word; [43] if there exists within us a second procession by
way of love, we can understand what our faith means when
it teaches that there is a second procession in God and we
can divine that it takes place by way of Love; [44] moreover,
if the Father generates a perfect and completely adequate
Word, we can understand how it is that the Son and the
Holy Spirit can communicate in the Divine Intellection
without producing another Word.[45] Nevertheless, however
valid these arguments may be—and they are not mere
images or metaphors—they are, as it were, blinded by the
glory of the divine splendor; they would lead us nowhere,
had we not the signposts of our supernatural faith.

When Saint Thomas establishes the existence of the second divine procession by arguing from the existence of the
first procession, he does not intend to give a rigorous demonstration, even though he uses the term "evidence." [46] Father
Garrigou-Lagrange remarks in this connection: "He [Saint

Thomas] simply wishes—and this is customary with him—to show that there is nothing in this mystery that contradicts reason; for this reason he adduces an argument of suitability which is unquestionably profound and which appears more and more so, the more one contemplates it, but which never becomes strictly demonstrative. For the contemplation of which we are speaking, as it sees ever more profoundly into the argument, tends to resolve itself not in the evidence of a strict demonstration but in the higher evidence of the beatific vision. Such an argument from suitability belongs to a higher sphere than that of demonstration. Should someone attempt to propose it as a true demonstration, the attempt would diminish rather than increase its value. Accordingly the argument of Saint Thomas does not give a rigorous proof that there is in God a second procession; and without revelation it would not suffice to establish the existence of a third Person." [47] Saint Thomas himself tells us that there are two kinds of proof; there are those which are sufficient to establish a truth, as, for example, the proofs of the existence of God; but the second kind of proof is based on a reality already known and simply clarifies the suitability of the consequences that flow from that reality. It is this latter kind of proof by which the theologian manifests the Trinity.[48]

If our arguments from fittingness are deficient, even if our entire theology is similarly deficient, the reason is not that its discursive efforts necessarily tend to lessen or to bend or to alter truth; rather the reason is that what is certain in the terms of its arguments will some day appear to be more profoundly true than theology itself can now realize. To think otherwise would be to offend against the sanctity of our intellect and of that image of Himself which God has placed in the soul of each man.

15. *An Important Text of Saint Augustine on Reason and Faith*

An important and explicit text of Saint Augustine on the use of faith and reason in theology is to be found in the Saint's *Letter CXX*, in which he was forced to answer Consentius, who, while begging for enlightenment on the mystery of the Trinity, still was confident that men should seek to know the truth more through their faith than by their reason. "For if the faith of Holy Church were a matter of a reason which disputes and not of a piety which believes, only philosophers and orators would enter into happiness. But since it has pleased God to choose here below the weak to confound the strong and to save those who believe through the folly of human preaching, we ought rather to follow the authority of the saints than to invoke our reasons."

"But," exclaims Saint Augustine, "how could I, even with the help of God, give you even the least understanding of so profound a mystery as that of the Trinity, if I did not try my utmost to show you the reasons for the Trinity?" Consentius indeed should learn to express himself more exactly. He should learn not, of course, to reject faith, but to consider under the light of his reason what he already holds with complete certainty by means of his faith.[49]

This use of our reason which, as Saint Augustine here says, takes its point of departure from faith, is precisely what we mean by theology. Moreover, the Saint goes on to show that theology uses in its own proper way a faculty the exercise of which is required even in supernatural faith and in the beatific vision; consequently it would be a grave danger to contemn this faculty even in the case of theology. How, continues Augustine, could God hate that part of man by which He Himself had made man superior to all the other

animals? How could God want us to believe for the purpose
of thereby renouncing or giving up our reasons? For how
could we even believe, had we not a rational soul? Moreover, our reason, far from being hostile to our faith, realizes
full well that in certain matters of salvation which it can
not yet understand but which it will one day see, it must be
preceded by faith, whose task it is to purify our heart and
make it capable of receiving and holding in due time the
light of the supreme reason,[50] that is, the light of intuitive
vision.

It was not without reason, then, continues Saint Augustine, that the Prophet Isaias exclaimed: "If you do not believe, you shall not understand," [51] thereby asking us to
believe first that later we might comprehend. It is advisable
and reasonable that in the matter of these incomprehensible
mysteries faith should precede our future vision. And however weak our reason may be when we use it to persuade
ourselves of the correctness of this position, still under this
aspect it may be said that it precedes faith. With these last
words Saint Augustine touches on a new use of reason, that,
namely, by which it establishes the rational credibility of
revelation, thereby demonstrating that it is reasonable to
believe, and unreasonable not to believe, the suprarational
mysteries of Christianity.[52]

As Saint Peter remarks (1 Pet. 3, 15), we ought to be
ready to give anyone who asks us our reasons for our faith
and our hope. If an unbeliever puts the question to me, I
must realize that in this case faith must precede understanding, and therefore I must try to show him how unreasonable
it is for him to hope to understand until he first believes.
In such a case to give our reasons for our faith is merely to
establish its credibility. On the other hand, if a believer puts
the question in the hope of understanding what he already
believes, then to give a reason for one's faith would be to

establish its intelligibility. I should try to lead him to an understanding of the faith that is proportioned to his abilities, more or less profound depending on his capabilities. It follows that we shall always remain on the road of faith as long as we have not yet attained to the fullness and the perfection of knowledge.[53] Nevertheless, if it is true to say that one gives a stronger assent to things which he understands and at which he is no longer startled, and if it is true that this startling of the intellect tends to disappear in the measure in which the truth becomes familiar,[54] then it is necessary—and this is the hope of Saint Augustine—that the faith of Consentius should be one that loves to understand: *Haec dixerim ut fidem tuam ad amorem intelligentiae cohortor.* When Consentius opposes the wisdom of men to the folly of God, he must be on his guard not to misinterpret the Apostle. For (and this gives the justification for a philosophical use of reason) if some philosophers have rejected Christ, others have received the grace to profess belief in Him.[55] Moreover (and this is the justification of a theological use of our reason), why can not faith make common cause with our reason when it dispels from our hearts those material and idolatrous representations which our imaginations form of the Trinity? [56] For true it is that faith has eyes to see in some fashion objects which it does not see as yet. But the man who by a legitimate use of his reason now sees what formerly he only believed is certainly in a more enviable position than the person who still seeks to understand what he believes. And if this latter does not even seek to understand but thinks it sufficient to believe things that demand to be understood, he does not understand the purpose of faith, that it is orientated towards the hope for and the love of complete vision.[57]

In the case of the Trinity, says Saint Augustine to Consentius, first of all believe with an unshakeable faith that the Father, the Son, and the Spirit are only one God; that the divinity which is common to them is not a fourth reality but is the Trinity Itself; that the Father generates, that the Son alone is generated, and that the Spirit proceeds from the Father and the Son.

"And while meditating these truths, avoid, reject, disdain, repulse, and flee all corporeal images which present themselves to you. For in the case of the knowledge of God it is of no small importance to realize that before we can know what He is, we must first know what He is not. Above all love to comprehend; have a great love for understanding: *Intellectum vero valde ama.* For Holy Scripture itself, even though it advises us to believe these great realities before we understand them, will be of no use to you if you misunderstand it. Every heretic has acknowledged the authority of Scripture; each of them persuaded himself that he was following Scripture, though in reality he was following his own errors. Such men are heretics, not because they reject Scripture, but because they have not understood it: *non quod eas contemnant, sed quod eas non intelligant.*" [58]

The entire soul of that doctrinal theology which burst out in the schools of the Middle Ages, the entire spirit of the faith which gave birth to such theology, all the dynamism which that theology entails—are not all of these found in this beautiful letter of Saint Augustine? As for the Saint's command to love understanding, who has carried it out better than Saint Thomas Aquinas?

We may close this section by a citation from the concluding pages of Saint Augustine's *The Trinity*: "Directing my purpose by this rule of faith, so far as I have been able, so far as Thou hast made me to be able, I have sought Thee, and have desired to see with my understanding what I believed; and I have argued and labored much. O Lord my God, my one hope, hearken to me, lest through weariness

I be unwilling to seek Thee, 'but that I may always ardently seek Thy face.' " [59]

16. *The Understanding of Faith*

If we ask the questions "What is this understanding of faith which was the soul and the moving power of all Augustinianism? What is this understanding which appears to us to be neither pure reason nor pure mysticism, but which apparently combines both?" [60] the answer would seem to be that this understanding of faith is an impulse of an intellect that comes from God and which is eager to rejoin the divine mystery by employing all the resources at its disposal (even before it has had an opportunity to make a definitive inventory of them); it makes use of theological faith in order to adhere to God; of the gifts of understanding and wisdom in order to touch and taste Him; and of the discursive reasoning of theology to seek Him, to preach Him, and to defend Him. Even today the expression "intelligence of faith" should retain the plenitude of its powerful dynamism. For if, in seeking out the distinctive differences of this intelligence of faith, we fail to return constantly to its nourishing roots and its original implications, in short, to its parent idea, we shall end only by unbalancing, withering, and abusing the notion.

Beyond this intelligence of faith, there is the understanding of the Beatific Vision; beneath it there is the understanding of pure reason. Those who possessed this latter were called by Saint Augustine, following Consentius (though the Saint did not always use the terms in a disparaging sense), "the wise men," "the philosophers," "the orators."

5. The Nature of Doctrinal Theology

In the time of Saint Thomas Aquinas theology had become completely aware of its nature as the science of the order to be found in revelation; consequently it took stock of its purpose, of its means to this purpose, and of its limits. In our present consideration of doctrinal theology as a science, we intend to point out various aspects of its nature and to give a summary indication how it can be divided into its parts. The first point to be considered is the question of "theological places" or of topological exposition.

1. Theological Places

Since the purpose of scholastic or doctrinal theology is to manifest the mutual connections and interdependence of the Christian mysteries, it is necessary that before it attempts any of the problems which it proposes to itself, it should make a preliminary and careful investigation of the authentic documents which contain the problem and which are able to furnish information that is either certain or at least prudent. Accordingly an inventory of theological places, a topological exposition, will precede the properly speculative or doctrinal exposition.

This topological treatment will naturally refer to documents and in this sense it deserves to be called "positive," [1] and in fact it is currently referred to as "positive theology." But it may be questioned whether it is in a complete sense a theology at all. Since theology is essentially an explanation, it would be better to say that this topological exposition prepares the way for theology rather than that it is a constituent of theology. It is a precursor of theology, since it furnishes it its principles; and this is its chief glory.[2] Moreover, it can be doubted that this process can be called "positive" in a strict sense. For its interest does not lie chiefly in the historical vicissitudes of what has been revealed, but in the degree of explicitation which revelation has received; it studies and investigates the documents from the point of view of a scholastic theologian who believes in order to understand and whose efforts are directed towards a doctrinal synthesis. This certainly is a perspective that is quite different from that of the mere historian; it is just as different, too, from the task which belongs to the true positive theologian, who studies the history of salvation.

By reason of the purpose which it hopes to attain, scholastic theology is first of all concerned with making contact with the mature and precise magisterial teaching of the Church in its most evolved and recent forms; for this reason it takes account of the degree of certitude, of the theological notes, of these statements. The antiquity of a given text is of no direct interest to scholastic theology; its concern is with its weight of authority, the richness of its content, the virtualities of a text, whatever be its age or modernity. Accordingly the method of inquiry which, although not obligatory, is certainly normal, natural, and basic for scholastic theology, consists in beginning with the present and working back to the past in an attempt to arrange the testimonies on a given point insofar as these have expressed throughout the ages the mind of the Church and insofar as they now constitute the declarative or manifestative places (*loci declarantes vel manifestantes*).[3] In other words the method of inquiry proper to a scholastic theologian will be a regressive one.[4] And since he realizes that the Church, because of the assistance of the Holy Spirit, can manifest throughout the course of time only what is truly contained—whether expressly or virtually and implicitly—in the revealed deposit which she received from Christ and the Apostles, the speculative theologian will consummate his inquiry when he rejoins one of the two great theological places, Scripture or Tradition, which, between them, contain all of revelation (*loci continentes*).

For these reasons, the "positive" or documentary part of scholastic theology, the inventory of theological places in which historical succession is merely accessory and in which the normal method of procedure is regressive, does not seem to us to deserve the title of "positive theology" in its full sense. Rather it appears to us to be but an initial moment, a fundamental phase of doctrinal theology—the phase of topological exposition. The second phase of this theology will be that of doctrinal exposition in the proper sense.

From this it must be evident that at the beginning of any given treatise the scholastic theologian will be free to devote a more or less considerable part of his time and effort to an elaboration of an inventory of these theological places. In his preface to his commentary on the *De Trinitate* of Boethius, Saint Thomas remarks: "According to Saint Augustine, we can speak of the Trinity in two ways, either by citing authorities or by giving reasons for it. Saint Augustine, as he himself tells us,[5] has recourse to both methods. Some of the holy Fathers, such as Ambrose and Hilary, used only the argument from authority. Boethius, on the other hand, chooses the other method of procedure and presupposes that the arguments from authority have already been established by his predecessors." [6]

When theology is anxious to right error and to enlighten the Jews or the Manichaeans or the Eastern dissidents, it tries to show that a given point of doctrine is actually taught either in the Old or New Testaments or in the Greek Fathers; in this case it is dealing with the question whether a thing is true or not (*an ita sit*). But when it is desirous to lead the faithful to an understanding of what has been revealed, its efforts are directed towards manifesting the radical relations that exist between one truth and a higher truth; in such a case it is seeking to explain and to give reasons and is concerned with the question *why* or *how* a certain thing is true (*quomodo sit verum*). "And if the teacher settles a question by recourse to authority alone, his students will doubtless be convinced that the thing is true, but they will acquire no science or understanding and will go away without satisfying their intellects (*vacuus abscedet*)." [7]

The above may serve as an indication of the connection between the use of authority and reason. "What we believe," says Saint Thomas,[8] "we owe to authority; but what we understand, that we owe to reason"; [9] for it is our reason that shows us with certitude the inclusion of one mystery in another. Moreover, the more one believes, the more one desires to understand. All of this, it may be noted, was already contained in the phrase of Saint Anselm: "Faith seeking understanding."

2. The Light of Theology

"The proximate efficient cause of theological inquiry," says Saint Thomas, "is the intellect of the theologian which is, as it were, a small flame. . . . The human soul is weak, its purity is disturbed by its union with the body, its light

is hidden, its powers are weak, its flight towards the heights
is retarded. This is the reason that its ability can be compared to that of a small flame. This is the reason too that
it does not suffice to discover the truth in such questions
as those of the Trinity, unless it has been enlightened by
the Divine Light. Hence in theology the Divine Light is
the principal cause, and the soul is the secondary cause." [10]

We can not resist translating here a relevant text from
the Council of the Vatican, italicizing the most important
parts: "Reason, indeed, *enlightened by faith*, when it seeks
earnestly, piously, and calmly, attains *by a gift from God
some, and that a very fruitful, understanding of mysteries;*
partly from the analogy of those things which it naturally
knows, partly from the relations which the mysteries bear
to one another and to the last end of man: *but reason never
becomes capable of apprehending as it does those truths
which constitute its proper object.* For the divine mysteries
by their own nature so far transcend the created intelligence
that, even when delivered by revelation and received by
faith, *they remain covered with the veil of faith itself, and
shrouded in a certain degree of darkness,* so long as we are
pilgrims in this mortal life, not yet with God; 'for we walk
by faith and not by sight' (2 Cor. 5, 7)." [11]

We may add that the third annotation of the first *Schema*
of the Constitution of the Vatican Council on Catholic
Doctrine against the errors of the rationalists [12] also treats
of the nature of theology, though certainly with a profundity and an authority that is less than that of the Council
itself. Theology, it remarks, is a science of the mysteries
whose existence and whose truth (*an sint, quid sint*) are
inaccessible to philosophical reasoning, since it proceeds
from revealed principles believed by faith. "There is no
question here of excluding all understanding, for a large
part of sacred theology is constituted precisely by a certain

kind of understanding. Once faith is supposed, the human mind inquires first of all into the manner in which truths are proposed in revelation; this is called positive theology. Afterwards, by using even natural truths and rational principles, our minds are led to an analogous [13] knowledge of the things contained in revelation, a knowledge of what they are in themselves; it is a case of faith seeking understanding; it is speculative theology. The meaning of the dogmas which are contained in revelation and defined by the Church are regarded here as the norm in accordance with which philosophical notions should be elaborated for the purpose of giving us a certain analogous understanding of the mysteries, as in fact the holy Fathers and Catholic theologians have always done. It is not, however, legitimate to reverse the order, to begin with purely rational notions of philosophy for the purpose of thereby rediscovering the dogmas, since in this way one would give to them a meaning other than that which is contained in revelation and which the Church teaches and professes. As the current expression puts it: in matters of religion, human reason and philosophy should not be queens but handmaids."

All the texts which we have quoted give a clear indication of the nature of the unique and characteristic sovereignty of faith over reason in theology. Reason does not operate in the same way in theology, where it is but a handmaid—but of what a queen!—as it does in Christian philosophy, where it is a true mistress.

3. Theology and the Kingdom of God

Theology belongs to the activities of the kingdom of God; reason is torn from its own proper domain to be given wings with which to soar aloft. On the other hand, Christian philosophy—and let it be noted we are not here speaking of the influence of Christian doctrine, which is the

guiding star of Christian philosophy and which enlightens
it from above in both a positive and negative manner—pertains to cultural activities, where reason remains in its own
proper sphere in which it walks or, better, runs along. The
truth of this last statement is forcibly imposed on us by
the spectacle of so many non-Christian philosophies which
misunderstand the nature of the dependence of the world
on God.

We may say, then, that under a supernatural and divine
illumination, the human mind can function for the sake of
the kingdom of God after the fashion of an instrumental
cause, provided we make this instrumentality wide enough
to include all activities characteristic of this kingdom even
though they be on different levels and elevated in different
ways; this instrumentality, therefore, will include activities
which flow from the infused and non-discursive habit of
faith as well as those which flow from the acquired and
discursive habit of theology. Nevertheless, under the influence of a divine and supernatural revelation the human
mind can also function for the sake of cultural purposes as
a secondary but autonomous cause, as, for example, in the
case of Christian philosophy. But the watchfulness with
which the Church attends to the progress of theology belongs to her by a special title, since her care for it is on the
level of the activity of the kingdom of God, not on that of
mere culture.[14]

4. Who Should Study Theology?

From what has been said it must not be inferred that the
study of theology is reserved to clerics alone. On the contrary, it is our belief that at the present moment of the
disintegration of the old "sacral" Christianity and of the
preparation for a new "lay" Christianity, it is more than
ever necessary that the Church should see to it that a good

number of her laymen should not only possess a solid initiation in theology but should have a theological sense that is at once sure, vivifying, lucid, and penetrating. It may well be that the Church has need of such laymen today as she did in the time of Saint Justin or of Saint Thomas More; it may be that the hierarchy of the Church, which by beginning the work of Catholic Action has manifested in our day a great confidence in the modern layman and has called for his services in many pressing circumstances, will bless the efforts of laymen to break their long-drawn-out silence and to renew their testimony to the faith on the same level as that on which a Justin or a Thomas More gave his.

It remains true, however, that clerics are the specialists in the spiritual tasks of the Church. It is to them that the *Code of Canon Law* entrusts the mission of teaching theology in seminaries (Canon 1360) and of preaching in churches (Canon 1342). Laymen in their turn are the specialists in the temporal tasks of Christianity. To achieve these, the love of theology must illuminate their minds and their hearts. This testimony of the layman specialist will have its immediate impact on a cultural level, in matters of philosophy, politics, economics, law, ethics, pedagogy, history, art, and so forth. It is by being refracted in the prism of the temporal vocation of these laymen that the light of theology will be able—and at times very powerfully—to affect the world and, as a consequence, produce conditions favorable for the growth of the kingdom of God. Moreover, this task of refraction does not at all prevent them from anticipating and forestalling the theologians. In fact, such an anticipation will often occur when it is a case of applying spiritual values to the level of an always changing culture. Such laymen, therefore, will at times anticipate the theologians, but only in their own proper sphere of activity.[15]

5. *The Authority of Theology*

In each of its stages of progress, the authority of theology doubtless comes from an interior grace of the mind by the help of which theology progresses from one supernatural mystery to another through a reasoning process expressed in transanalogous formulas; its authority likewise comes from the profundity of its explanations, from their intrinsic correctness as well as from the rigor of their interconnections. The principle of identity, for example, is not extinguished in the interior life of God, but on the contrary is there realized in an unsuspected way; consequently the principle of identity controls the entire order of faith and of theology in a way the human mind of itself could not grasp.

Nevertheless, an individual theologian can not know with certitude whether he has been entirely faithful to the theology in which he believes, to which he has consecrated the labors of his life, which he loves, and for which he would suffer anything rather than betray it. Likewise the theologian can not know whether or not he has failed to respect perfectly the royal—more, the divine—exigencies of this science; he can not know whether he has penetrated its principles and understood the interior logic, the profundity and correctness of its explanations, and the rigors of its reasoning. Such is the disproportion between the misery of his being and the nobility of his vocation that he is always obliged to doubt whether he has done his part. But this is a question not on the level of essence but on that of existence; it is a question, therefore, not about theology, but about a theologian.[16]

The answer to such doubts can come only from the teaching authority of the Church, which can draw on its experience throughout the centuries. It is the Church's position to settle such doubts either by condemning or by giving tacit or express approbation, not indeed to the theologians (save in those exceptional cases when she canonizes one or declares him a Doctor), but to the views which they have proposed and which the Church allows gradually to enter into the common patrimony of Christianity.[17] The theologians, it is true, are useful in the Councils of the Church; theology itself is necessary for the Councils; but it is the teaching Church alone that gives the final decision.

6. Theology: An Individual and a Collective Task

It can be seen that theology (and we include in the term the preparatory elaboration of the great dogmatic formulas) is an activity that is highly personal; what indeed could be more individual than the encounter of the mind of a baptized person with the profundities of the Christian mysteries? From another aspect, however, it is a highly collective task; for what could be more de-individualized, more purified, more eponymous (though not more anonymous) than an approbation or a definition of the Church? How could personality not be erased in the face of the supra-spatial and supra-temporal personality of the Holy Spirit? [18]

This constant yet mysterious interlinking of the personal and the collective in the elaboration of the synthesis of Christian doctrine has not been perceived by some Pravoslav thinkers who have at times heatedly maintained that there exists an individualistic form of religious thought which is characteristic of the West and a collectivistic form of religious thought proper to the East.[19]

7. The Subalternation of Theology.

This constant dependence of the theologian on the teaching power of the Church emphasizes what Saint Thomas taught on the subalternation of theology.[20] The Saint points out that just as in the natural order the science of optics or of acoustics depends on principles, the certitude of which can be demonstrated by the mathematician, but which the science of optics or of acoustics accepts on faith without being able to prove them, so in the supernatural order the theology of Christian believers who are still on this earth depends on principles which are seen in the knowledge possessed by God and the blessed but which theology must accept in the night of faith, not in the clarity of vision.[21] If, then, a theologian possesses a true science, this science does not extend to the principles (these, on the contrary, are presupposed) but only to the conclusions which are deduced in a necessary way from those principles. In brief, the theologian believes the principles; he knows the conclusions.[22] It is impossible for him to demonstrate the principles of theology; but once they are given, his reason is able to establish the results that flow from these principles.[23]

It is necessary, then, that the theologian grasp fully the principles of his science, if he does not wish his deductions, however rigorous they may be, to go astray. But he can grasp these principles only through faith. How, then, will the theologian be able to tell whether or not his faith is profound enough (however greatly he may desire to believe) to coincide perfectly with the faith of the Church so long as in a given case the Church has not given a definite pronouncement? For the faith of the Church is a hidden one by which she has believed from the beginning—at least implicitly—the dogmas which she has defined later on in the course of time.[24] It may well happen that the deductions which a theologian draws from a principle of faith may tend to externalize against his will the fact that this principle was not grasped by him in its true perspectives and its authentic connotations; thereby his deductions oblige the Church to react against such a contracting (involuntary though it be) of what has been revealed.

With what fullness, then, must a theologian receive the

revelation of the Word made flesh in order to be able to deduce from it in all rigor the two natures of the Saviour, His two wills, His inerrancy, His beatific vision, His infused knowledge! With what fullness must he understand the angelic phrase "full of grace" and the revealed privilege of the Divine Maternity of Mary to be able to make a logical deduction from it of her exemption from mortal, venial, and original sin, as well as of her Assumption and her co-redemptive mediation! How complete must be his interpretation of "You are to be perfect, as your heavenly Father is perfect" and of "The man who unites himself to the Lord, becomes one spirit with Him" in order to discover therein all the depths of the doctrine of the *The Dark Night of the Soul* and the *Spiritual Canticle!*

In all truth, theology is a testing ground for faith. By its explorations, its advances, its bold undertakings, it forms the test, not merely of a verbal or even well-intended orthodoxy, but of the genuine orthodoxy of the theologian's faith.

8. Theology: A Speculative and a Practical Science

It is by a unique, infinitely simple knowledge that God knows what He is and what He does. In the first case, the purpose of His knowledge is simply to know; it is, consequently, speculative in its nature; in the second, the function of His knowledge is to produce and hence is practical. Nevertheless, it is one and the same identical knowledge; notwithstanding its perfect simplicity, it is eminently and truly speculative as well as practical—speculative, first of all, and then practical. Hence, if it be true that theology, since it depends on faith and is immersed in the light of faith, is an impression or an imprinting in us of the divine knowledge,[25] we must conclude that theology itself, though in an inferior way,[26] is eminently and truly speculative as well as practical—speculative in the first place and then practical or affective. In other words, theology does not break down into two sciences, one of which is speculative and the other practical.

What, then, does theology embrace in its considerations? It embraces the same thing that God considers, in other words, God Himself. And in considering Him, theology is speculative. Secondly, theology considers the order which God independently of us has put into the universe of nature and the universe of grace and by which all things are referred to Him as to their First Principle and their Last End. On the part of God such an order is the object of a practical knowledge, but for us it is the object of a speculative knowledge which comes to us from God to tell us what He has made that we might be able to know and contemplate His creation. Finally theology considers the order which man himself ought to introduce into his own activity to orient it "towards the perfect knowledge of God in which eternal happiness consists." [27] It is in this last case that theology is a practical science.

Theology, let it be repeated, is both speculative and practical. To wish to make it only practical or even primarily practical would be to misunderstand it and to mutilate it.

9. *The Subject of Theology*

The "formal subject" of theology, that is to say, "the real being existing outside the thinking subject, the knowledge of which theology seeks" [28] and which is the center of intelligibility to which theology relates everything else, is God, the Deity, the Trinity, considered primarily as He exists in Himself, and then insofar as He is the Principle and End of the universe of nature and of the universe of liberty.[29] Everything in this science is ordered to this center; everything in it is illumined by it. For example, the mystery of the "whole

Christ," Head and Body, is viewed by theology in the way in which God views it: centered on the mystery of the Trinity. Since the mystery of the Trinity is not centered on the mystery of the whole Christ, it follows that the theology of the whole Christ does not constitute the whole of theology, but it is only a part of it.[30]

Similarly the practical aspect of theology, which is concerned with the direction of human activity and the progress of the rational creature towards its God,[31] is not the whole of theology; if it attempts to be the principal element in this science; if it attempts to organize all the notions that have been revealed under the idea of the Good considered as the keystone of all theology and not of moral theology alone, this would mean in the first place that it hopes to enclose the whole in one of its parts and secondly that theology would cease to be an impression in us of the divine knowledge, which, though it is both eminently speculative and eminently practical, is first of all speculative and then practical.

10. Progress in Theology

There are two types of knowledge and two types of progress in knowledge.[32] The first type of knowledge (it is the type that includes all empirical sciences) fails to grasp the mystery of reality which admittedly lies outside its domain and which is regarded as an irrational core; such a science reaches reality only obliquely and, as it were, blindly and enigmatically through the observable facts and appearances which manifest reality and which constitute its phenomenological wrappings. The definitions of this first type of knowledge are descriptive; it characterizes, for example, a vegetable, not by attempting to define vegetative life (for this is considered as an irrational and prescientific element), but by distinguishing one vegetable from and relating it to other vegetables.

The purpose of such knowledge is to give us "substitutes for the reality that is unknown, myths and symbols which are well-founded indeed, but which are constructions of our reason built up by our minds from observed and measurable data and by which it hopes to advance to the knowledge of real things." [33] In other words, the purpose of such knowledge is to obtain some universal viewpoint which is capable of grouping together all observable facts and of "saving the appearances." It never fails to happen that a moment comes when new discoveries oblige us to sacrifice an old myth which has become too restrictive and to replace it by a new and more comprehensive one. As a result, the progress of truth is affected in such sciences by a process of substitution. The physics of Newton is replaced by that of Einstein or of Heisenberg, the cosmogony of Laplace by the "hypothesis of the primitive atom." Only facts and their measurements remain.

The second type of knowledge (it includes all ontological sciences) is directly concerned with reality which, however, is admitted to be mysterious. Faced, for example, with a vegetable, such a science seeks to grasp the mystery of vegetative life. The definitions, then, of such a science are constructed not in function of the observable or the measurable, but in function of the mystery of being and of its necessities. The nature of life, for instance, is rendered intelligible by reason of the distinction of activity into transient and immanent activity; the mystery of vegetative life is made clear by its opposition to the mysteries of sensitive and spiritual life. Such definitions are not descriptive, but philosophical. Once they have been achieved, they are never abandoned, never lost. In these sciences, then, progress in truth takes place by a deepening, a developing, and an explicitation of indefinitely fecund data; likewise this progress is achieved by an assimilation of the true insights which are contained in erroneous doctrines. But this assimilation will not be possible for us unless we ourselves already are in possession of a body of doctrine. Otherwise it is we who will ourselves be the ones to be assimilated.

Should a person imagine that theology is a science of the first type, he must admit that theology, whatever may be its protestations, leaves the revealed mysteries outside its grasp; moreover he would have to admit that the definitions of theology are descriptive rather than representative; that the task of theology is to translate the Christian mysteries into the master symbols appropriate to each culture; and finally that its law of progress is that of substitution and that after being Platonic and then Aristotelian, it will successively become Cartesian, Hegelian, existentialist. "There has been much hasty talk," said Pope Pius XII, "of a new theology which should evolve as everything else evolves, always advancing without ever coming to a term. If we adopted such a point of view, what would happen to the immutability of Catholic dogmas, what would happen to the unity and the stability of our faith?" [34]

But if theology belongs to the second type of knowledge, then by reason of its transanalogous method what it grasps by its concepts is the innermost mystery of what has been revealed. The definitions which it proposes are truly representative of a reality which nevertheless surpasses those definitions. Its task is to propose an organic body of revealed doctrine and the truths connected with this, not, of course, by becoming dependent on the successive cultures in which it finds itself, but on the contrary by utilizing as instruments of its activity the resources, the difficulties, and the problems of each culture.[35] And its law of progress will be to proceed by teaching an ever more precise awareness of its own riches; it will manifest the inexhaustible virtualities of its principles and of its preceding acquisitions; in short, it will progress by constantly bringing to act its power to assimilate the truths which are deformed or mutilated in the great but mistaken systems which rise up throughout the course of time.

11. *The Divisions of Doctrinal Theology*

It may well be questioned whether it is advisable to sketch a provisory division of that theology which we call scholastic, systematic, speculative, or doctrinal in opposition to that theology which we term positive or historical. The answer to this is to be found by considering that since theology is formally and essentially one, the divisions which can be made are only material and accidental, arising from different points of view, from the envisaging of different ends, even from mere pedagogical convenience. In the table of divisions which immediately follows, the numbers in brackets after a given section refer to the remarks which constitute the rest of the present passage.

We can assign to doctrinal theology:

A *defensive* function. Apologetics, or the science of the rational credibility of the ensemble of the Christian faith, is an extensive part of theology. It can also be termed in all strictness fundamental theology, not in the sense that reason is the foundation for faith but in the sense that it establishes the credibility of faith [1].

An *expositive* function. This is divided into:

> *General* or fundamental theology (though fundamental here is taken in another sense than in the preceding division). This treats in general of the principles or the foundations of theology. It is nothing else than the treatise on theological places [2].

Special theology, which embraces a topological exposition as well as a doctrinal one. This special theology is again subdivided into:

Speculative or *dogmatic* theology. This branch of theology is immediately concerned with knowledge for the sake of knowledge. Nevertheless it is evident that such a knowledge creates a favorable atmosphere for love [3].

Practical or *moral* theology. This seeks to know in order to direct and embraces two moments or phases [4]:

In its *first* phase this theology is only remotely ordered to action; it is speculative in its mode of knowledge, though practical in its object. As a result it is more concerned with knowing than with directing, and can be termed a speculatively practical knowledge. Examples of this knowledge can be found in the moral doctrine of the *Summa* or in the ordering of the *Code of Canon Law* [5].

In its *second* phase, this theology is immediately ordered to directing action. It is practical both in its mode and in its object; consequently, it is more concerned with directing than with knowing. It is a practically practical knowledge. Examples of this can be found in the spiritual writings of Ruysbroeck, Tauler, Suso, and Saint John of the Cross, as well as in pastoral theology [6].

As was mentioned before, the numbered notes which follow refer to the numbers in brackets in the preceding outline.

[1] As Saint Thomas points out in his *Summa Theologica*, I, 1, 8, since theology is a wisdom which of its nature makes use of concepts and of reasoning processes, it should have a defensive function. The identification of this defensive function of theology with apologetics has been definitely shown by the works of Father Gardeil and of Father Garrigou-Lagrange. The most notable work of the first author in this matter is his *Crédibilité et apologétique*; the contribution of the second is chiefly to be found in his *De Revelatione*. Rational credibility is required in order that the decision to make an act of suprarational faith may be seen to be, not unreasonable, but completely reasonable, and that faith in a certain sense may come from reason.[36] It is in this sense that "right reason shows the foundations of faith," [37] that is to say, insofar as it treats of the extrinsic credibility of the faith, for its intrinsic credibility is of a higher and a supernatural order.[38]

[2] Theology has for its principles and foundations the truths of faith contained in Scripture and in Tradition and defined by the organs of the Church's teaching power. In the strict sense of the term, fundamental theology is constituted by the treatise on theological places. Here, however, these places are not considered principally from the point of view of whether they are true or not, nor even with the intention of defending them from external attacks, but rather chiefly from the point of view of what they are (*quid sint*) and insofar as they have the power to give the theologian the plenitude of revelation. It may well have happened that these two points of view—both of which are legitimate—have been neither sufficiently distinguished nor sufficiently united, since the first viewpoint has receded into

the background of theological activity and the second is cavalierly treated in apologetics.

[3] It is customary to include in dogmatic theology the different treatises from the first to the third part of the *Summa Theologica*. Each of these treatises requires the establishment or at least a review of those theological places which refer to its subject matter. The topological exposition is with full right the basis for the doctrinal exposition.

Missiology constitutes one of the aspects of the theology of the Church, since it studies the penetration and the expansion of the Church into regions where it is practically unknown or into those in which it has practically ceased to exist. This doctrine, however, of the expansion of the Church, if it be seen in its completeness (and the same holds true for the formation of the Church), is related to the Trinitarian doctrine of the missions of the Divine Persons.[39] Moreover, speculative missiology seeks its complement in a pastoral missiology.[40]

Let us note that the *Summa Theologica* of Saint Thomas Aquinas is only one link in the uninterrupted chain of works of dogmatic theology which includes, for example, Saint Athanasius' *Discourses against the Arians*, Saint Basil's *Treatise on the Holy Spirit*, Saint Augustine's *The Trinity*, Saint John Damascene's *Exposition of the Orthodox Faith*, Saint Anselm's *Why God Became Man*, and Peter Lombard's *Sentences*. In all of these it is but a mere accident of circumstance or of personal temperament that leads a theologian to manifest or conceal his own wonder at and love for the dogmas which he teaches. Whether he does so or not has no bearing at all on the intrinsically speculative nature of his theology.

[4] The two phases of moral theology which are here distinguished permit us, for example, to clarify the relations between the spiritual theology of Saint Thomas Aquinas

and that of Saint John of the Cross, and this without falling into any kind of eclecticism or without sacrificing the originality that belongs to each of these theologians. On this point it would be well to consult Jacques Maritain in his *Degrees of Knowledge*, pp. 382 ff. Also see Yves Simon, *Critique de la connaissance morale* (Paris, 1934), p. 81. These two phases likewise allow us to compare the teaching of Tauler and that of Saint Thomas.

[5] On speculatively practical knowledge Jacques Maritain has this to say: "When Saint Thomas treats of morality and of human activity, when he treats of that supreme activity which is mystical contemplation, it is from the point of view of this science. His teaching is enshrined in doctrinal theology, in knowledge in the speculative and explicative mode. And if we are seeking for a sure speculative elucidation of mystical theology, as of other supernatural mysteries, it is to him first and before all that we must address ourselves" (*The Degrees of Knowledge*, pp. 386–387). The Code of Canon Law is also on this level; consequently the study of it must also be on the same level.

[6] On practically practical knowledge, Jacques Maritain remarks: "The very method of knowledge is here reversed: for the entire mode of knowledge is practical. What does this mean? It implies that what is significant here is no longer to explain, to resolve a truth, even a practical one, into its reasons and principles. What is significant is to prepare an action and assign its immediate rules. . . . It is important to comprehend that in regard to that action *par excellence* which is the passion of divine things and the contemplative union with God, there is also not only a speculatively practical science which is that of theology: there is also a practically practical science, which is not so much occupied with telling us what perfection is but with directing us thither, the science of the practician of souls, of the

masters of spirituality, of the artisans of sanctity, the science which broods over our miserable hearts and would bring them at any cost to the possession of their supreme joy. It is in this practical science of contemplation that Saint John of the Cross is a master" (*The Degrees of Knowledge*, pp. 388 and 390). The remarks apply equally well to Saint Teresa, Tauler, Saint Francis de Sales, and so forth.

It is on this level of practically practical knowledge that pastoral theology should descend if it is to be constituted as a complete discipline and respond perfectly to its object. This holds true whether it treats of pastoral care in Christian countries or in missionary territory. Let us be sure, however, that we are certain of what we are talking about. Pastoral theology is not merely a question of transmitting a conceptualized doctrine, even though it be remotely ordered to regulate action; doubtless such a doctrine will constantly be appealed to and presupposed, but of itself it remains on the threshold of pastoral theology. Nor is it a question of transmitting experimental knowledge; such knowledge can not be taught, it can only be experienced. Of what, then, are we speaking? In order to understand what pastoral theology is we must presuppose that we have a master who possesses a large outlook and an exceptionally rich nature which has been gifted with profound supernatural graces, and who has, through the power, penetration, and amplitude of his qualities as well as because of his exceptional ability and true sanctity, experienced a fruitful pastorate in a Christian country or in a missionary land. In any case his experience should have been among sufficiently diversified human backgrounds. To such a man let us give our students with the purpose of preparing them to become missionaries in the world. What will be the purpose of such a man's knowledge and efforts? He would attempt to place his students in the best conditions possible for him

to lead them in accordance with their abilities to experience in some fashion what it means to be an apostle. The
discipline which such a man would teach and which should
be sufficiently general to be addressed to all the students
will have for its purpose to open to them more promptly
and more surely the way which will lead them to know and
to experience in their turn what makes a good pastor who
gives his life for his sheep; he will, therefore, lead them to a
type of knowledge that of itself is incommunicable. If now
such a man wrote out his teaching in an orderly and organic
manner, he would be termed the founder of pastoral theology and it would be in the light of his teaching that future
professors, or rather masters, of pastoral theology would
advance.[41]

12. *Scientific and Kerygmatic Forms of Christian Doctrine*

We have given the name of systematic, speculative, or
scholastic theology to the entire ensemble of the truths of
the Christian treasury, to all of Christian doctrine, but only
insofar as these truths are presented and taught according
to their internal hierarchy and their organic interdependence; moreover, a necessary condition for such a theology
is a technique of doctrinal precision and purity. Such a
theology includes all Christian doctrine but only insofar as
it is assembled and organized by means of its own proper
intelligibility.

There exists, however, an infinite number of other ways
of presenting and teaching the truths of the Christian
treasury, according to the interior impulses and free inspirations of the Spirit and the innumerable needs of the apostolate. The "doctor of Catholic truth" of which Saint
Thomas speaks in the beginning of the *Summa* is not only
the teacher of theology in universities and seminaries, he is
also a priest in the midst of his people, among whom are

both the learned and the ignorant. The priest, then, has need of great liberty in his choice of means for instructing adults, catechizing children, exhorting the sick. Besides there are lay catechists, among whom parents hold the first place. All this teaching, in the measure in which it is pure and authentic, constitutes Christian doctrine, even though it is not assembled and organized in the light of its own intelligibility, but dispersed and, as it were, broken up into parts in the night of souls and the world.

These two forms of presentation of Christian doctrine, the one scientific or scholastic, the other oratorical, adapted for preaching, kerygmatic [42]—this latter form corresponds to what the ancients called rhetoric and which of its nature is ever changing—are both in their own way necessary for the Church. Neither can one supplant the other. Consequently it is foolish to distinguish as some have done three successive periods in the presentation of Christian doctrine according to the following outline:

1. First, a kerygmatic period, that is, a period of free presentation of Christian doctrine by the Fathers.

2. Second, a scholastic period, that is, a period of logical, coordinated, and scientific presentation which substituted itself for the first period.

3. Finally, a new kerygmatic period to supplant the period of doctrinal or scholastic presentation which will reach its limits in our own day.

Such a division is too facile. There is a great deal of technical, systematic, and doctrinal theology in the teaching of the Fathers, for they were forced to defend the transcendence of the deposit of faith against the subtlest errors of heretics. Likewise there is a great deal of "supernatural rhetoric" in the preaching of Saint Francis, Saint Dominic, and of Saint Vincent Ferrer; and in general the Middle Ages invented a "religious eloquence" which was characteristic of that age. Moreover, the Middle Ages were careful to distinguish "teaching," which looked to the transmission of scientific erudition to its hearers, from "preaching," which tended to the moral and religious instruction of its listeners.[43]

The truth of the matter is that doctrinal and kerygmatic presentations ought always to be contemporaneous and mutually helpful. Preaching—and we understand the word in its widest sense as a synonym, not for vulgarization, but for divulgation—continually profits from the illuminations of scholastic theology, provided these illuminations have shaped the life, the convictions, and the interior liberty of the preacher. On the other hand, scholastic theology receives an equal profit from preaching, for it is this area in which Christian doctrine is constantly confronted with problems and difficulties which necessarily arise from the encounter of the inexhaustible riches of Christian revelation with the exigencies of a world that is always in flux.

But it is time for us now to say a word about that kind of theology which we have termed historical or positive.

6. The Nature of Historical Theology

In this chapter we shall attempt to give the precise nature of historical theology and to distinguish it from merely scientific historical disciplines as well as from doctrinal theology and from faith; we shall also discuss the need for an historical theology and illustrate by examples how historical theology operates. In the following chapter, we shall suggest some of the themes which historical theology must resume if it would prepare the way for the realization of its great ambition to rewrite *The City of God*.

1. The Characteristics of Historical Theology

In our opinion positive theology is the divine-human science of the historical development of revelation and more generally of the kingdom of God. Reason enlightened by faith can apply itself to discover not only the internal ordering of what has been revealed (scholastic, systematic, speculative, doctrinal theology) but also the successive order to be found in its dispensation and unfolding in time (positive, genetic, historical theology). Strictly speaking these are not two theologies, but two functions, two spheres, two points of application of the single light of one theology.

Hence the division into doctrinal theology and historical theology is only a material one.

Doctrinal theology insofar as it is a technically organized science is already well founded. In its dogmatic and speculatively practical aspects its founder was Saint Thomas Aquinas. In its practically practical aspects, we may say that it was founded by Saint John of the Cross insofar as it is a technical science for leading the soul towards mystical union with God; under this same aspect, however, it still awaits its founder insofar as it is pastoral theology; this is so at least in the eyes of those who think we still have far to go on the path opened up by such treatises as Saint Augustine's *First Catechetical Instruction* or Saint Gregory the Great's *Pastoral Care.* Similarly the practically practical aspect of theology still awaits its founder insofar as it is the science of missiology. Nevertheless, if we take an over-all view, it is fairly easy to obtain a precise idea of the nature of doctrinal theology.

Historical theology, however, if it is to be thought that its purpose is to put into operation an intention that was roughly sketched in *The City of God,* has not yet been founded; nor is it so easy to conceive its nature with great preciseness. Nevertheless, it is worth our while to attempt to see what it is.

2. *The Directive Principle of This Investigation*

The question we are trying to answer is this: Is it possible for the light of human reason, when directed by faith, to furnish an explanation of what has been revealed, of the truths connected with this, and in general of all salvific realities (the "revealable" and all that this denotes) by considering, not the internal and reciprocal order of its parts (the constitutive order), but the successive order of its growth in time (the genetic or historical order)? If we answer the question in the affirmative, then there exists a part of theology which may be called positive or historical and which is distinct from that part which we have termed scholastic or doctrinal. We can, then, assign to it its proper sphere of activity, discern its originality, notice how it comes into existence, and indicate by way of illustration some of its advances.

In order that there should exist a true historical theology, it is necessary that it should be 1) an ultimate explanation 2) of the historical order to be found in the revealable 3) by theological reason, that is, by reason operating in the light of faith and concerning the data of faith. The first condition permits us to exclude historical theology from all ordinary historical disciplines, while the second distinguishes it from doctrinal theology. The third condition serves to mark the separation between historical facts to which we give assent by means of supernatural faith and the light which arises from a consideration of the relationships between such facts, which relationships are given a theological assent.

But let us examine more closely the first of these three conditions.

3. Historical Theology and Historical Disciplines

The notion of historical theology implies an ultimate explanation; it is not an explanation that is induced from documents and facts, but one that depends on divine revelation and in this sense may be called deductive. This is what constitutes it and distinguishes it from all purely historical and informative disciplines, even though these latter may be absolutely indispensable for historical theology. Historical theology even seeks to promote the historical disciplines and at times secretly raises them up to its own domain. Nor can it be denied that many historians tarry in the confines of that historical theology of which perhaps they may one day be devoted servants.

There can be no doubt that when historical disciplines treat of religious facts and above all of the facts of the Christian religion, they must be exercised under the light of faith, which serves as their guiding star.[1] Nevertheless, the role of these disciplines is not that of theology. Their duty is to establish documents and facts, to adhere to them as closely as possible, to describe them in their concrete material conditions, and to clarify them by reference to their immediate and cultural milieux. We can say if we will—and it is true in the best examples of historical disciplines—that they also attempt explanations, though these will always be strictly limited by the fear of unconsciously substituting poetic creation in place of a restoration of historical verity. In any case, historical disciplines will never attempt to explain their facts in function of the mystery of the City of God nor in function of the supernatural organism of salvation which has been present in the interior of time from the fall of man and which, like grain among weeds, will not cease to grow until the day of the harvest.

4. Scientific and Theological Types of Historical Explanation

From what we have remarked, we can distinguish two kinds of historical explanation, one scientific (in the modern sense of this word), the other, theological.[2] The aim of the first is to understand even the most mysterious events in terms of their temporal appearances and by reason of the painfully inadequate circumstances with which they are clothed because of their insertion into a given period of time; through these there is offered to the diligent observer an undeniable minimum of understanding. This type of historical explanation seeks to coordinate and explain events in function of the concrete, immediate, and visible tissue of history.

The second type, however, of its very nature, attempts to understand its documents and its facts by reason of their mysterious content, insofar as it has been instructed about these by the clarities of revelation. It seeks to restore to them the full meaning which God intended them to have and with which they entered history to perform therein their secret but efficacious work. Historical theology seeks such a meaning, even though this was imperceptible to persons contemporaneous with the events in question. It seeks to coordinate and explain its facts in function of the designs of Providence in regard to the growth of the kingdom of God.[3]

Accordingly historical theology operates on the level of ultimate explanations, that is, in dependence on revelation. So-called scientific history, even when it treats of Christian facts, operates on the level of phenomenological explanation. Such disciplines may constantly treat of realities that have been directly or indirectly revealed, but they see these realities only from below as data which surpasses them and sits in judgment on them. Historical disciplines are never able to view them on their own level, as data which would furnish them a principle of explanation.

5. *Scientific History and Religious Facts*

To these historical disciplines is reserved an important part of the teaching in Catholic colleges, seminaries, and universities. Their study, their practice, their growth appear each day to be more indispensable. Though they themselves are not theology, they demand to be kept in touch with theology, to be sciences auxiliary to theology, to serve it more or less closely. They receive their greatest glory when they can be used and employed by either doctrinal or historical theology.

We can divide these disciplines into two groups, historical sciences and exegetical sciences, each of which will be considered in turn.

6. Historical Sciences

In this first group of disciplines is included first of all the study of non-Christian religions. The purpose of such a study is to give a faithful presentation of the facts, institutions, and doctrines of these religions, without, however, judging their value. Such studies achieve their task only by way of induction within the limits of their documentation. At this moment, it is true, such studies border on positive theology, but it is at this precise moment that their task is finished.

A scholar reaches such heights and lays the keystone of his work when, for instance, he aids us to discern in Vedantic thought two ways of deliverance, a laborious one directed towards the self of the soul, the other one a way of love directed towards the Self of God.[4] Another example of such achievement is the case of the scholar who is able to conclude that Islam must be classified, not among non-Christian religions, but among the dissident religious groups.[5] These are data which, when plunged in the light of revelation from which they receive their full significance, serve historical theology as points of departure from which to descend once again to actual events in order to explain the vicissitudes of the kingdom of God.

In this same group of disciplines must also be classified all studies of the Jewish people and their destiny before and after the coming of Christ. A Christian historian could not treat of these matters without taking into account the revelation of the New Testament concerning both the choice and the rejection of the people of God. But his proper task will be only to describe the succession of contingent events in their history and to explain these by inserting them into their immediate historical context. Historical theology, on the other hand, seeks to explain them by placing them in the perspective of revelation, which shows theology the stages in the divine plan for the salvation of the world.

Finally we must include in this section researches on the history of the Church, on schisms and heresies, and on the dissident Churches. Here, too, the Catholic historian, if he is not to go astray even in regard to historical matters, must have constant recourse to the light of faith. It is faith, for instance, that teaches him that this Church, the progress of which in the course of time he studies step by step, is actually the Body of the Divine Christ; it is faith which leads him to accord an attention to the canonical books that is different from that he gives to the apocryphal ones; it is faith, too, that prevents him from considering the "robber council of Ephesus" as a Second Council of Ephesus; and it is faith that permits him to say with perfect assurance where there is continuity and where there is dissidence in the history of Christianity. From such a point of view the Catholic historian can legitimately discuss the history of the Councils, the history of dogmas, or the history of patristic and scholastic theology; [6] in doing so, however, it is clear that the life of the Church is not directly reached by him, but only its phenomenological wrappings. Though he measures the traces which these events have left in the sands of time, he does not attempt to measure their spiritual dimensions nor to estimate their significance in relation to the destiny of the kingdom of God.

7. Exegetical Sciences

The second group of pre-theological disciplines includes the exegetical sciences of the Old and New Testaments.

There is no need to remark how constant is the need of the exegete for the clarities of faith and the certainty of a sure theology. He needs their help to establish the list of canonical books; to determine the notion, extent, and importance of inspiration; to affirm the existence of a typical sense in Scripture; to decide at times the value of variant textual readings [7] and, more frequently, to determine the exact sense of a passage. He needs their help, for example, in interpreting such passages from the Old Testament as the following: the text on creation in time (Gen. 1, 1), on the fall (Gen. 1), on the eternal priesthood of the Messias (Ps. 110, 4), on the expiatory sacrifice of the Servant of Jahweh (Is. 53, 3–12), on the perpetuity of the house of David (Jer. 33, 17–18), or such texts in the New Testament as the Word made flesh (John 1, 14), on the Last Supper (1 Cor. 11, 23–32), on the descent into hell (1 Pet. 3, 18–20).

All of Scripture should be read under the direction of the teaching power of the Church; it is for this reason that exegesis is so close to positive or historical theology. Nevertheless, the distinction between the two is extremely precise. What the exegete attempts to do is not to give the highest sense of a revealed text, with its different depths and resonances as well as the authentic interpretations given to it throughout the course of time (in brief, its theological sense), but he is concerned with the sense that is immediately accessible; the sense that would have been taken by readers contemporary with the writing of the text; a sense that is doubtless exact, but superficial and perhaps incomplete; in brief, he is concerned with the historical sense. As Father Lagrange puts it: The exegete "makes it a point of honor not to mingle any of his own concepts, however true they may be or even if they are of faith, with the text he is interpreting. His sole purpose is to extract from the words

the pure sense of the text." [8] For example, in the texts of
the Book of Kings and of Isaias, in which God at the time
of the general defections of His people reserved for Himself
a remnant of the people, the exegete of the Old Testament
endeavors to search out only the direct sense and not the
transpositions which Saint Paul made of these texts to the
Israel of his own time, no matter how illuminating in ret-
rospect the words of Saint Paul may be. In the same way
in the passage of Saint John's Gospel where Christ pro-
claims His dependence on the Father, the exegete's attention is riveted on the immediate sense, which is limited to
Christ's birth in time; he is not concerned with the more
hidden sense, which refers to the eternal generation—a sense
which the Fathers were led to bring to light in the time of
the Arian controversy.

There are, however, moments when exegesis borders on
positive or historical theology. These occur when the exegete has finished his work of clearing the ground and
makes an attempt to assemble his results and to give a view
of the whole by sketching what he himself calls a theology
of Saint John or of Saint Paul. Thereby he hopes to turn
our minds towards the divine preparations and plans contained in the revelations recounted by a Saint John or a
Saint Paul. But at this point his true work as an exegete is
behind him and he begins his task of organization under
the illumination of a higher light. This is what the encyclical *Divino Afflante Spiritu* seems to point out when it
speaks of the means of making progress in Biblical studies:
"With special zeal should they [commentators on Scrip-
ture] apply themselves, not only to expounding exclusively
these matters which belong to the historical, archeological,
philological and other auxiliary sciences—as, to Our regret,
is done in certain commentaries—but, having duly referred
to these in so far as they may aid the exegesis, they should

set forth in particular the theological doctrine in faith and morals of the individual books or texts so that their exposition may not only aid the professors of theology in their explanations and proofs of the dogmas of faith, but may also be of assistance to priests in their presentation of Christian doctrine to the people, and in fine may help all the faithful to lead a life that is holy and worthy of a Christian." [9]

8. *Historical Theology, Doctrinal Theology, and Faith*

As we have seen, the first condition required for the existence of an historical theology is that it be an ultimate explanation, that is, it must proceed from revelation. Two other conditions, however, are equally necessary; namely, that it be a search for an historical order under the light of theological reason, that is, under the light of reason functioning as a servant of faith. It is by these last two conditions that historical theology is distinguished both from doctrinal theology, with which it shares the title "theology," as well as from faith, on which both it and doctrinal theology depend. We have already noted that historical theology presupposes the activity of what we have termed scientific historical disciplines, which are ecclesiastical sciences that prepare the way for theology, but do not constitute it. Besides, historical theology also presupposes the activity of scholastic or doctrinal theology. For it is scarcely to be expected that we should understand the order according to which an organism is progressively formed, if we are ignorant of the perfection and internal ordering of its constitutive parts. Likewise, how could we hope to understand the order to be found in the growth of the kingdom of God in the past, if we do not begin by using the light of doctrinal theology to attain a clear and penetrating view of its state of existence at the present time or if we do not use theological data in an attempt to foresee its future definitive state?

Positive or historical theology is the result of the confrontation of the highest data of faith and of doctrinal theology with the historical data which centers around the contingent flux of history. Its light is that of a reason that is steeped in faith and its point of application is to be found in time. It explains the past by the present, since the past is orientated towards the present; and the present by the past, since the former is the offspring of the latter. One theologian has remarked: "It [historical theology] comments on revelation and its actual data by the documents of the past." [10] The remark is true, but not complete, since historical theology also comments in turn on the concrete form in which revelation manifested itself in former ages and does this by a full understanding of its present and actual status. Even this view must be expanded, for what historical theology must explain is not merely the growth of revealed doctrine, but the growth of the entire kingdom of God. Let us say, then, that historical theology comments on the present actualities of the kingdom of God by means of its past actualities and its future destiny, and vice versa comments on its past actualities by means of its present state of realization.

9. The Method of Historical Theology

If we admit that historical theology explains the past by the present and the present by the past for the purpose of showing the continuity of the kingdom of God under the diversity of its many forms, what method of procedure is characteristic of it? Is it progressive, regressive, or both of these together? It should be remembered that we have given to doctrinal theology the task of establishing or at least reviewing in the course of each of its treatises the theological places which afterwards it intends to treat doctrinally. Accordingly, we have seen that doctrinal theology is composed of a topological exposition as well as a doctrinal one; and we noted that in its topological exposition its normal method of procedure is a regressive one.

Historical theology likewise supposes a full and complete knowledge of revealed truth; when it begins to study the past, it considers it in the fullness of this light. Nevertheless we can not say that its method is regressive. Its entire care and preoccupation is to unravel with the help of revelation the mystery of the progress of the kingdom of God, to explain its stages, and to disengage the meaning of its successes and its failures. It clarifies the past by the present; it investigates how God has realized in ages long past that plan of salvation which is so dear to Him that to accomplish it He sent His only Son to the cross. But it also clarifies the present by means of the past; it makes us see how in the actual state of the kingdom the Holy Spirit makes use of the conflicts and agreements to be found in the past. In the strictest sense, then, historical theology does not tend to go back into time, but to descend from the past to the present; and it continually inquires into the capabilities of the present in regard to the future. Accordingly, its method is primarily a progressive one.

10. *Historical Theology and the Purgative, Illuminative, and Unitive Ways*

The task of historical sciences insofar as they are concerned with religious events is only a preparation for theology; it is a phase for research, for the accumulation of documents, for erudition, and in large measure for the dissipation of one's energies: it entails much labor, much asceticism, but gives little life-giving light. On the other hand doctrinal theology begins by demanding for each of its treatises the establishment or at least the review of the appropriate theological places. This phase, too, is an enquiry, but one that is definitely determined, for it is controlled by faith, makes use of the regressive method, and demands to be continued by a doctrinal treatment. Moreover, even in this stage the threshold of theology has been crossed. Nevertheless, we can say that our minds, as long as they continue on the path of documentary research, have not yet left the sphere of inquiry, that they still remain on the level of effort and asceticism.

The supreme work, however, of doctrinal theology is to manifest by a doctrinal treatment the internal order of the revealed mysteries. In so doing, it takes in the entire extent of the universe of essences insofar as these are knowable under the light of revelation,[11] for it is "as it were an impression in us of the divine knowledge." [12] With this stage, then, our minds quit the purgative way and enter on the illuminative path, which leads it from light to further light. But the mind still has before it the task of exploring the entire extent of the universe of time insofar as this is knowable under the light of revelation. Here, precisely, is the task of historical theology. By remaining docile to the teaching of Divine Wisdom, it applies itself to the discovery of the succession according to which the history of salvation has been conducted; under such an illumination it can not fail to reach a high degree of understanding in its attempts to untangle the order and the meaning of events. Thereby is consummated in some way the "circular" activity of our minds; for we begin by an inductive study of history and of the concrete; and now in historical theology, we return again to the same concrete history, but this time by way of application, of "resolution"; for our minds in some measure are now able to consider these events in the light of eternity.

We can say, then, that historical theology is a "complete theology" in the way in which Bergson calls that mysticism complete which is able without losing God to return to the world;[13] or better yet it is comparable to that perfection of divine knowledge, which, as Saint Thomas teaches, permits it to descend to singulars.[14] Such a knowledge is a peace-giving state of attainment and introduces our minds to a kind of unitive way. For it unites eternity and time, and with respect to the latter tends to embrace in one look all the vicissitudes of history.

11. *The Need for Historical Theology*

Whether we admit it or not, the progress of historical sciences, by giving us a more exact and minute view of the many authentic or errant forms which religion has taken in the course of the centuries, arouses a multitude of problems. And the very sciences which have given rise to these problems are themselves unable to solve them. For their task is not to furnish an ultimate explanation; this is the duty of theology in its positive or historical aspects as distinct from its systematic or doctrinal aspects. If such problems are not resolved, if we do not rise from the level of the confusing erudition of these sciences to that of the light and nourishment of theology, these sciences will be nothing else than thorns without roses, on which faith can severely wound itself. Without historical theology we would, when faced with the difficulties that arise through the history of religions, of the Old Testament, of the Church, of schisms, heresies, and dissidences, have to suffer in silence or "make progress by misdirection." For viewed from any standpoint other than that of God, history is a tragedy which leads us to heartbreak and despair.

12. *Historical Theology and the Education of Children*

This is an opportune time to consider the education of children, for it is to them that we teach the Old Testament and the history of the Church. It can not be doubted that it would be a serious error to think it necessary to teach them everything, for truth can be borne only by those souls who have been gradually prepared for it: "It is beyond your reach as yet" (John 16, 12). Nevertheless, the father, mother, or priest who teaches children must be sincere. What he now teaches as the truth must not have to be retracted later. Even when it is better to be silent about the difficulties to be found in Scripture in connection with the origin of things or to pass over in silence the terrible ravaging of evil to be found on each page of the Bible and the history of the Church, we must never deny them. Hence if the teacher does not wish to trouble the souls of these small children nor yet wish to distort historical truth or fall into what we have called "progress by misdirection," then there is no way open to him but to descend instinctively to the root and ultimate explanations, to the solutions which he carries in his own heart and which are his most precious possession and which resolve the problems to the satisfaction of his own mind. Only then will he be able without falsity or mental reservation to perform his duty of teaching the children who trust him.

There is scarcely a mother or a father, there is not a catechist, who does not realize that the children he teaches constantly oblige him to make use of this ultimate secret of his heart. Whether it be a question of historical or speculative truth, children will without fail demand the highest and most supernatural explanations and keys, and these must be given to them (this increases the difficulty) in imagery. Nevertheless, it is these loftiest of supernatural explanations that must be given them with the greatest joy, for the paradox of Christianity will always consist in this: that the highest revelations are destined to be given to the humblest of beings.

13. *Historical Theology and Adults*

The progress of scientific disciplines concerning the origins of man, the history of religions, Scriptural exegesis, and the history of the Church causes grave problems in the mind of every educated person. So great are these problems that such persons are powerless to resolve them by their own efforts; they thus become a peril to their faith. It is no solution at all to solve them by arresting the progress of these studies. The only thing that can be done (but it is a real solution, a real progress, and a real advance) is to show them, through the light of revelation, principles of explanation so lofty that the faithful will never more experience a desire to deny or even to gloss over in silence any authenticated fact, even the slightest.

14. *Saint Thomas and Historical Theology*

We have said that there is no true and complete theology where there is no argumentation and explanation which depend on the principles of faith. As a consequence, we shall not find the thought of Saint Thomas on the nature of historical theology in those passages where he recalls that theology—he is speaking of systematic theology and more precisely of the topological exposition that is a prerequisite for it—finds its support in the authority of canonical Scripture and of the Fathers of the Church; [15] nor yet shall we find any help in passages where he points out that one can treat the mystery of the Trinity either by citing authorities or by trying to discover what the Trinity is in Itself.[16] We can not even turn to his *Quodlibet*, 4, 9, 18, where he explains that one can carry on a theological discussion either for the sake of establishing through the use of authority the fact of the revelation of certain mysteries (*an ita sit*) or for the sake of showing the ultimate explanations of such mysteries (*quomodo sit verum*). The first method of discussion is only preparatory and is not yet that nourishing science which alone in the eyes of the Angelic Doctor deserves the name of theology.[17] Indeed, what is to be learned in all the texts we have just alluded to is the distinction between the two states of doctrinal theology: the topological and the doctrinal stages.

Nevertheless, there is no difficulty in finding in Saint Thomas indubitable traces of historical theology; we can find in him the efforts of a mind which has steeped itself in the faith in order to give an ultimate explanation of the progress of the kingdom of God in time, of its constancy even in its diversified stages, of the value of each of these stages in relation to the salvation of man, and of the significance of the refusal of grace, varying, as it does, according to the diversity of time and other circumstances in which it takes place. That would be a valuable labor which would assemble, coordinate, and fully explain these texts of the Saint, and thereby constitute a solid core of authentic historical or positive theology. For our purposes it will be sufficient to have suggested the topic and to use some of these indications as illustrations, without, however, searching for them at any great length or without stressing their importance. They will be sufficient to show that on the level of historical theology (and this is the level also of the Fathers) nothing is less true than the statement that "the notion of history is a stranger to Thomism."

Let us recall, first of all, those texts where Saint Thomas gives us a view of the progressive development of divine revelation from the first age of the world on; [18] let us note, too, other texts where he treats of the varying degrees of

awareness of revelation that can be found not only among
the faithful of different ages but even among the faithful
of the same time and the same race.[19] Here and there, because of the findings of historical sciences, we may have to
modify some of his remarks, but the illuminating power of
his principles, his theological "keys," as shown in these
articles, remains unchanged.

Another series of texts bearing on positive theology treats
the Old Law, which appears in the course of time as a
transition between the law of nature and the New Law.[20]
Here he explains the permanent quality of certain precepts
of the Old Law (the moral precepts) and the temporary
character of other precepts (the ceremonial and judiciary
ones).[21] Here, too, he notes the mysterious and anticipatory
presence of the New Law in the womb of the Old.[22] It is
in these texts, too, that he insists on the completely spiritual
and consequently definitive character of the New Law; the
capital text in this regard is that where the error of Joachim
of Flora gives him an occasion to point out the spiritual
plenitude of Pentecost.[23] Thereby he destroys at the root all
those unceasing attempts to orient history towards a Mes-
sianism of the Spirit, in which the revelation of the New
Testament and the conception of the Church would be surpassed, as the passible Body of Christ has already been
surpassed. In one place Saint Thomas attempts to show
why it was suitable that the Old Law should have been
given in the time of Moses.[24] Whatever may be thought of
the reasons he advances for his position, it is at least indubitable that his argumentation does not pertain to systematic theology, but to historical or positive theology,
which alone, in his thought, is capable of rejoining the concrete.

In treating of the Incarnation, Saint Thomas is led to

relate the coming of Christ to the ages that preceded it as well as to those that followed it.[25] Basing his thought on revelation, he shows that there should be a certain growth in the interior of history, and that the Son of God should come at the plenitude of time (Gal. 4, 4). With Christ, who is the source of salvation, begins the era of the diffusion of that grace which was created to fill all time. The sixty-first question of the third part of the *Summa* is a veritable summary of positive or historical theology. Saint Thomas gives us therein the meaning of the entire history of the sacraments, of their appearance immediately after the fall, of their modification under the law of nature, the Mosaic Law, and the New Law, and their final disappearance in the life to come. It is easy to see the importance of such a "key" for the theologian who seeks to unlock by it the data of the history of religions. The final view of this particular question of the *Summa* is especially rich, for it shows us the double and antithetical march of history—towards a deepening darkness as well as towards a more brilliant light.[26] No less precious as aids in defining the historical attitude of humanity in the presence of the realities of salvation are those texts which deal with the different forms of infidelity which correspond to the different stages of the successive unfolding of divine revelation before and after Christ.[27] Finally we should not forget that some of the data of historical or positive theology which are dispersed throughout the *Summa* reflect, as always in Saint Thomas, the more or less common doctrine of the Fathers and are in no way opposed to their teaching; moreover, in the final analysis they are founded on Scripture itself. Saint Thomas, then, if he is read with the intention of constructing an historical theology, gives us not only that, but other treasures as well.

15. *An Example of Historical Theology: Abraham*

We have seen that historical or positive theology requires an explanation which depends on revealed data and which treats of religious facts insofar as they occur in time. It is clear that it is able to embrace more or less vast periods of time, to consider more or less complex ensembles. It is no less clear that in certain cases it attempts to explain these facts from the highest possible viewpoint by using the highest kind of principles, while in other cases it can choose to attach itself to events and to follow step by step the fluctuations of history. We shall give here two examples to correspond to these two different types of explanation. Although there are thousands of others that might be given, they will suffice to give us an idea of the liberty with which historical theology can choose the level of its activity and of its point of view.

The first example is to be found in a study made by Raïssa Maritain and first entitled *Histoire d'Abraham ou la sainteté dans l'état de nature*,[28] but later called *La conscience morale et l'état de nature*.[29] That this study has not received any special attention from exegetes nor from speculative theologians seems to us to be a clear indication that it is above the level of research of the first and outside the sphere of activity of the second; in other words, it is an authentic work of historical or positive theology.

The problem that is discussed in this study is at once easy to grasp and yet extremely difficult to resolve: that of the conduct, often scandalous in our opinion, of the saints of the Old Testament. The response to the problem which is given in this study is no subterfuge but the only true solution—one which we can give even to small children. It consists in making us see the mystery of the development of the moral conscience in the womb of humanity.

But first let us repeat the problem in the author's own

words: "Saint Augustine remarked concerning the lie of
Rebecca: 'It is not a lie, but a mystery.' We dare to say:
it is doubtless a mystery, but it is also a lie. The conduct
of the saints of the Old Testament is certainly a tissue of
mysteries, but their lives are also filled with actions which
neither their conscience nor God has reproached them for,
even though these actions are now prohibited as grave sins
by the teaching of Christ and His Church. Lying, deceit,
harshness, and cruelty in regard to one's enemies are perfect
examples of such actions, as well as concubinage, incest,
and polygamy. Divorce as well as polygamy was permitted
by Moses. We are not speaking here of those faults which
were already recognized as faults in the time of Abraham
or of Moses, even though such faults were culpably committed by some of the saints of the Old Testament who
afterwards were sorry for them and did penance as David
did. For by such recognized and expiated faults, those saints
take their place in the multitude of sinners whom the mercy
of God has raised up and sanctified. . . . But what interests us in this study is the coexistence of the upright
conscience of just men with actions that today are prohibited as an offense against God. We touch here one of
the great mysteries, that of conscience as it exists in the
successive diverse states of humanity and of sanctity." [30]

And here, too, in a few words, is the solution to this
problem: "The state of nature for humanity in general is
comparable to that of infancy for the individual man.
Reason and will are present; so likewise is God, who pre-
scribes what man must do. But by the loss of innocence
reason has been reduced to its natural nakedness and now
begins its activity by becoming aware of the world. God
accordingly tempers his demands and proportions them to
some extent to human experience. The state of nature is

not a state of pure nature, since nature is wounded, though
it does not know it. Grace, to be sure, is present and active,
but since it is a vital and moving impulse, it, as it were,
disguises itself in nature, since nature is the first principle
of motion and operation in creatures. The human conscience sees but dimly and confusedly. Light is there from
the first, but it is pale and shadowy, as the universe itself
was on the first day of creation according to Genesis, since
the luminaries in the firmament of the heavens whose purpose it was to separate day from night were not created
until the fourth day. The human conscience is still too close
to the great elemental instincts, for example, to the instinct
of self-conservation and the propagation of life. To satisfy
these instincts innocent ruses were used; the great person-
ages of the Bible employed them and their actions in so
doing were not imputed to them as sinful.[31] . . . A complete knowledge could have been given to the human race
from the beginning and conserved and passed down to each
of us; but it does not seem that God acted in this way in
creating the world. . . . God acts as a gardener who plants
a seed in the ground and not a mature tree loaded with
fruit.[32] . . . After the fall Adam doubtless resembled those
men whom we call primitives but who nevertheless possess
great gifts, as that of the knowledge of the existence of a
Master of all things and a knowledge of the duties of religion." [33]

We are here led to a point of view which is extremely
elevated and thus given key principles which disclose the
intelligibility of the moral problem for an immense part of
history; these principles enable us to see the origin of the
moral conscience, the particular character it had after the
fall, and its gradual progress under the law of nature and
of the patriarchs to the Law of Moses and beyond.

16. *Another Example: The Greek Controversy on the Knowledge of Christ*

The positive theologian, however, can limit his field of investigation and, while still giving an ultimate explanation with the aid of faith, can closely follow the fluctuations of history, as for example Father M.-B. Schwalm has done in his two studies—unfortunately never completed—in which he disengaged the providential intention which made itself manifest in the controversies of the Greek Fathers concerning the knowledge of Christ.[34]

Three texts of the Gospels gave birth to this extraordinary dispute which lasted over a long period of time. The first text is that of Saint John (1, 14): "And the Word was made flesh, and came to dwell among us; and we had sight of his glory, glory such as belongs to the Father's only-begotten Son, *full of grace and truth*." On the other hand, there is the text of Saint Luke (2, 52): "And so Jesus *advanced in wisdom with the years*, and in favour both with God and with men," as well as that of Saint Mark (13, 32): "But as for that day and that hour you speak of [the day of the Last Judgment], they are known to nobody, not even to the angels in heaven, *not even to the Son;* only the Father knows them."

Granted that these texts recall at each moment the innermost reality of the Incarnation, we can well ask ourselves what heated intellectual drama it was in which these remarks on the grandeur and the abasement of the Saviour were able to endure a redoubtable conflict where the spirit of truth was face to face with the spirit of error, and eventually arrive at the doctrine of a triple created knowledge in the holy soul of Christ—the beatific knowledge, the infused knowledge, the experimental knowledge. This is what Father Schwalm attempts to show, by putting us in the presence of the oscillations of theological thought as it was secretly directed by the Spirit of God biding His time in the Church.

By gropings and stumblings, a doctrine was constructed. Athanasius affirmed vigorously that progress is impossible in the Word considered precisely as the Word; as far as the human nature of Christ is concerned, he admits that there can be progress, but not the same kind as is found in a mere man; he is of the opinion that the human nature of Christ was really ignorant of the day of the Last Judgment. Cyril of Alexandria, for his part, affirms—and this is a real doctrinal progress—that in the soul of Christ, which from the beginning was full of grace and of truth, there exists an inborn wisdom which is incapable of growth; however, he does not deny Athanasius' notion of a progress in Christ's knowledge; like Athanasius too he believes that Christ was in ignorance of the last day. Cyril, then, enriches the question of the knowledge of Christ, but leaves it unsolved. Augustine, and after him John Damascene, teaches that Jesus was too closely united to the Word to be truly ignorant of the last day of that humanity which He came to save by His Blood.[35] Finally in the synthesis given by Saint Thomas Aquinas, there are rejoined Cyril's notion of an innate knowledge which is perfect from the beginning with Athanasius' idea of a knowledge that is acquired and susceptible of growth.

This doctrinal progress, which is not achieved except through setbacks, is presented to us on the one hand as being immersed in time and on the other as explained by the highest causes. For the work of Father Schwalm is not that of a mere historian but that of a positive theologian.[36] He shows us the Holy Spirit using the faith of His Doctors, correcting and completing one of them by the other, and leading them to a purpose which they sense but can not

formulate. "The intuitions of the human spirit are fragmentary and vague, its reasonings proceed obliquely by
way of comparison in an attempt to find a middle term
which will unite two other terms. . . . The human spirit
advances among the ruins of its errors with an irregular
movement over a fatiguing road. The Spirit of God sup-
ports this way of acting where progress is ceaselessly inter-
mingled with errors and reactions. The Spirit of God bides
with patience in His Church; He watches over her, keeps
her in balance, and upholds the faith by this perpetual
tugging of antithetical truths exaggerated to the point of
error. The Spirit of God is served by these antagonistic
mentalities which were born with the Church and which
will not cease till the end of time.[37] . . . In these doctrines
the Fathers did not see problems that were merely speculative, mysterious, and troubling; they were difficulties in
which was concerned not only the interior Christ who
speaks to souls, but the historical Christ who is survived by
the interior Christ, and the celestial Christ of whom the
historical Christ is a presence.[38] . . . In all this debate
about the growth of Jesus, Christ is certainly not regarded
as a mere hero whom historians can dissect. Is it not He in
His role of Master who is teaching us in the midst of these
witnesses who attest to tradition? These witnesses listen to
the heretics and compare their new voices with the echoes
of the faith that comes from the past but is actually present
even now, with the echoes of Jesus Christ as these are heard
in the testimony of the Apostles. Is it not Christ whom
these Doctors question when they attempt a new solution?
They propose their solutions modestly, with their ears alert
to the voice of their predecessors. In all this it is a case of
Jesus attested by the Twelve and the Twelve attested by
Him. It is, in some sense, a "socialized" Christ who speaks
and whom we try to hear either through His witnesses or

His Doctors; it is these who develop His thought and communicate it to the faith of His Church." [39]

The theological key which is given to us in the above
citations is the patience of the Spirit of God in His Church;
it is, in other words, the use He has deigned to make of the
faith, of its gropings and errors, and of heresies themselves
for the purpose of making the Christological doctrine more
intelligible.

17. The Nature of Positive Theology According to Father Schwalm

A later study of Father Schwalm, entitled *"Les deux
théologies: la scolastique et la positive,"* [40] attempts to
give a precise definition of the object of positive theology.
To the question, What is the object of scholastic theology?
Father Schwalm replies that it "restrains itself from following step by step the varying stages of defense and development of the dogma which it considers. This kind of re-
straint, which is proper to a metaphysical view of things,
keeps it outside of time and movement in the region of
universal causes, pure essences, and the first qualities of
beings." [41] Nevertheless revealed data are actually spread
out and in contact with many cultures. The steps of this
resulting development escape the scrutiny of scholastic
theology precisely because of its own proper method. [42] Are
we then to forego any such science of the concrete? To do so
would be to blind ourselves. The development of dogma "requires from us a religious attention to the divine meaning
of things and demands that we constantly remember the
omnipresent God who is the proper light of the theologian.
This light illumines the concrete as well as the abstract; it
clarifies time and its changeableness as well as essences and
their immutability." [43] Here, then, in opposition to that of

scholasticism is the object of positive theology: the sphere of temporal succession.

Nevertheless, there still remains the question as to how positive theology is distinguished from the historical disciplines. To solve this, Father Schwalm opposes documentary positive study to theological positive study. The former arises from textual and literary criticism and from history itself. Once he possesses these documents "the historian's sole object is limited to those things of which his documents speak; to see the facts, to grasp the causal links between them, and to set them forth with as much clarity and sincerity as he can—such is the specialized program of a documentary positive study. It strives to realize this program by an observation, analysis, and comparison of documents; afterwards it synthesizes the findings of its two preparatory criticisms in a third work which attempts to penetrate the real by making the past relive. . . . Such a procedure is not theology, but remains history, for a purely historical method can never result in a theology." [44]

What, then, is meant by a theological positive procedure? The answer to this can be found in the following page of Father Schwalm's article: " ' If you do not believe, you shall not understand.' This old saying of Isaias, which was applied by Saint Anselm to the understanding of divine things, is just as true for the science of doctrinal developments as it is for the consideration of the metaphysical profundities of dogma. Those who possess the faith consider the scattered and fragmentary documents of doctrinal epochs under a light which emanates directly from the Supreme Intelligence who governs the development of dogma. This light is in the interior of our souls and falls on those objects whose exterior guarantee is the ever-living teaching power of the Church. The teaching of the Church gives us the present-day expressions of faith which have actualized the

original virtualities of revealed data; thereupon, without
pretending to see, for example, that the Apostolic Fathers
have professed our explicit formulas on the hypostatic
union (to do that would be historical madness), we nevertheless shall be able to recognize our own faith in Jesus
Christ in the famous words of Saint Ignatius of Antioch
concerning Jesus Christ, the only Physician, who is both
corporeal and spiritual, born and not born, who has come
from God and has also come from Mary. Our actual
present-day faith recognizes itself in that formula, but not
yet with the precision that it has in the metaphysical
formula based on the notions of nature and person. This
latter formula will come some four hundreds years later.
The content, then, of an ancient dogma is understood by
us through the actual faith of today; more than this, the
same procedure enables us to discover the logical consequences and the normal way of assimilation by which the
philosophical notions of nature and of person were incorporated into ecclesiastical dogma. For we see them
elaborated by Saint Cyril of Alexandria and Leontius of
Byzantium and approved by the Councils. In this way, from
the viewpoint of an intelligent faith we retrace the rational
pattern of this long development. This pattern includes and
surpasses all the fragments of life and epochs which are
manifested in the documents. Although these documents
speak to us only by material and empirical data, by those
sensible and natural signs which are always inadequate to
express the supernatural, and although there occur in these
documents intervals of darkness and long periods of silence,
still our faith in the development of dogma allows us to
consider them in a complete synthesis in which the minutiae
of textual, literary, and historical criticism take on a new
dimension and a higher life. They appear in this synthesis
as incomplete and distant monuments, as milestones on the

broad and sacred path which has always been followed by
the Church in its comments on the gospel. In other words,
we give to the incomplete data of our erudition and criticism a coordinated view of the stages which mark the
progress of dogma in the Catholic Church. To documentary
and purely historical criticism is added a still higher critique,
which penetrates the divine meaning of these doctrinal
stages and notes their continued unity despite all differences
in language and time. . . . This linking of the successive
developments of sacred doctrine to the texts which contain
their first principles or which mark the various stages in
this development does not constitute a departure from the
field of the positive, from that, namely, which is sensibly
manifested in time and in space. But it will be a supernatural positivism, for the observation and the criticism of
the theologian consider the monuments of revelation
and of dogma under the light of faith.[45] . . . If we were
to seek for a Scriptural motto for positive theology, we
should remember that at all times there is verified in every
detail of each doctrinal stage the continuity of the revelation given by Jesus and entrusted to the care of the Apostles.
The motto, then, which we are seeking would be: 'I am
with you all through the days that are coming, until the
consummation of the world.'" [46]

18. Reflections on Father Schwalm's Teaching

Our agreement with these beautiful texts of Father
Schwalm is so complete that we could not omit giving
them greater precision on two points. First of all, it must
be clearly understood that scholastic and positive theology
do not differ formally but only materially. Strictly speaking,
they are not two theologies, but one theology which, in the
light of reason elevated by faith, attempts to manifest either
the speculative order or the historical order respectively of

The Wisdom of Faith

Christian doctrine. Secondly, the subject matter which positive theology considers under the light of a faith controlled
by the teaching power of the Church is not only the somewhat reflexive problem of the development of Christian
doctrine, of the preparation for and the formulation of
Christian dogma, as well as the activity of the teaching
power of the Church, of its social functioning, and its role
in the approbation or condemnation of solutions proposed
by theologians, but also consists in the much larger problem of the development of Christian reality itself, of the
history of salvation for the human race in all its stages both
before and after Christ and in all its aspects, personal and
collective, doctrinal and cultural as well as moral. In a word
it is the history of the City of God, the history of its inhabitants, of its activities, and of its values; it is the history
of its conflicts with adverse forces, "of its pilgrimage between the persecutions of the world and the consolations
of God." [47]

19. An Outline of Ecclesiastical Disciplines

In the article which we have just cited Father Schwalm
was already forced to distinguish between the establishment
of theological places and the work of positive theology. The
former has as its purpose the determination of theological
notes, that is, of the doctrinal quality of propositions taught
by the teaching power of the Church, whereas the purpose
of the second is to study under divine illumination the successive stages and concrete moments of the supernatural
organism of which the Holy Spirit is the soul. [48]
In other words theological places must be investigated
and clarified from a doctrinal point of view; this is why we
have maintained that the establishment of them constitutes
the first phase of doctrinal theology, that of topological

exposition. On the other hand, positive theology has for its ultimate purpose to investigate and clarify historically the order of succession in the kingdom of God. In both there is had documentary research conducted under the light of faith, but in the one case that research is directed towards doctrinal intelligibility, in the other towards historical intelligibility.

We add here an outline of the various ecclesiastical disciplines which we have enumerated so far:

1. Positive religious sciences (these imply recourse to documents insofar as they manifest a phenomenological content):

    a. Historical sciences:
        1) of non-Christian religions
        2) of the Jewish people
        3) of the history of the Church and of dissident Churches.

    b. Exegetical sciences:
        1) of the Old Testament
        2) of the New Testament.

2. Theological sciences:

    a. Doctrinal theology:
        1) Topological exposition (this includes recourse to documents insofar as they manifest a doctrinal content)
        2) Doctrinal exposition.

    b. Historical theology (this includes recourse to documents insofar as they manifest a providential content).

The various subdivisions of doctrinal theology have been given in the table which we considered above.[49]

In the article which we have already mentioned,[50] Father Cavallera maintains that the notion of a document is the real but confused idea which is presupposed in all those disciplines which are called positive. Documents, however, are concerned in three places in the outline which we have just given: in positive religious sciences, in topological exposition (to which many give the title of positive theology); and in historical theology (which, in our opinion, alone deserves the name of positive theology).

It is clear that the name of positive theology does not belong to positive religious sciences, for they are below the level of theology. But can we say that the stage of topological exposition deserves that title? It does not seem so. On the one hand, it precedes all theological explanation; on the other, even though it uses documents and to this extent is positive, the purpose of its investigation is the doctrinal intelligibility of the "revealable," and not its historical intelligibility. Accordingly we can say that neither the title of theology nor that of positive belongs to it perfectly. On the contrary, historical theology is truly a theology, that is, an explanation given by reason under the illumination of faith. And it is truly positive: for it is the supreme intelligibility of facts which are attested to by the documentation from which this theology derives them. On every count, then, historical theology fully deserves the title of positive theology.[51]

7. Some Themes of Historical Theology

As we have conceived it, historical theology supposes an attentive, profound, and comparative knowledge of the Scriptural data concerning the progressive realization of the divine plan for the salvation of the human race. Besides this, its purpose of explaining the past by the present, the seed by the plant, demands an extremely penetrating and subtle knowledge of revelation in its most advanced stages; in other words, it needs to know doctrinal theology, which it utilizes retrospectively for the sake of illuminating the successive stages in the kingdom of God. We can say that one of the principal tasks of historical theology (it has a multitude of secondary ones) is to manifest the fundamental identity in the course of these successive stages of that Church which began immediately after the fall and which will at the hour appointed by God pass over to the timeless hereafter.

In order to confirm all this in the minds of our readers, we shall now try (we make no attempt to be complete and have relied entirely on our memory) to propose some themes which historical theology should develop.

1. *The Fall of the Angels and the Fall of Man*

The fact of the fall of the angels and the fact of the creation of man mutually illuminate each other in an extraordinary way, provided we remember to apply to them the principle that God would never permit evil to exist in His work unless He were sufficiently powerful to make that evil the condition or the point of departure for some extraordinary good. In other words, He would never have permitted the fall of some of the angels except for the betterment and elevation of men.[1] Not only do these two facts mutually explain each other, but they give us the key which unlocks the mystery of a Church composed of both angels and men.[2]

The same fecund principle is used by Saint Paul to explain the entire drama of the disobedience of the Gentiles on the one hand and that of Israel on the other (Rom. 11, 32), while it permits us to understand in the fall of Adam and the loss of the entire state of innocence, the condition for the birth in the universe of a redemptive Incarnation, in which God Himself would be substantially united to a created nature.[3]

It is remarkable that the mystery of original sin, that is, of the transmission to all the descendants of Adam of a sin which belongs to them and of which the consequence is death,[4] has been clearly revealed to mankind only in the mystery of the Redemption of Christ: "A multitude will become acceptable to God through one man's obedience, just as a multitude, through one man's disobedience, became guilty" (Rom. 5, 19). We could not support the complete revelation of our misfortune without despair unless we also had the complete revelation of our even more extraordinary deliverance. "It is dangerous for man," says Pascal, "to know his misery without knowing the Redeemer who can heal him of it." [5] And God knew this far better than did Pascal.

The permission of the fall of the angels in view of the creation of man; then the permission of the fall of man in view of the Redemption by Christ: these are the two columns that support the entrance way which opens into our historical time.[6]

2. "The Eternal Silence of the Infinite Spaces. . . ."

To conquer the dizziness which arises from the spectacle of our tiny planet suspended in an infinitude of space, number, and time, Pascal suggests we consider the exaltation which is aroused in us when we contemplate the mystery of human intelligence. To the infinity of space, let us oppose the far greater infinity of thought: "In terms of space, the universe comprehends me and engulfs me as though I were but a point; but in terms of thought I comprehend it." [7] "Should the universe destroy him, man would still know that he is nobler than that which kills him, for he would know that he was dying and he would recognize the power that the universe has over him. But the universe would know nothing at all." [8] "All bodies, sky, stars, earth and its kingdoms, are not equal in value to the least spirit; for the latter knows all these things as well as itself; while bodies know nothing." [9]

It is certainly a sure and decisive step to illuminate the infinitude of quantity by the infinitude of quality. Moreover, this illumination may be made from different angles. Pascal himself used the viewpoint of the dignity of reason and in the quotations above he plays the role of philosopher. Above this, however, there is the staggering viewpoint of the Christian: "The unimaginable heavens have no other duty than to mark the site of an old stone where Jesus slept three days." [10] Beneath the viewpoint of philosophy, it is possible without leaving the level of science to oppose to the immensity of quantity the incomparable value of quality. The earth is unique, for it bears life. Pierre Termier stood in amazement that for more than a billion years the earth by a sort of "merciful event" has maintained, without our being able to understand how, a condition of extraordinarily delicate equilibrium which permits the survival and development of life.[11] More recently Father Teilhard de Chardin has in his turn opposed to the vastness of the geometric view the ordered complexity of the elements; from the former point of view the earth is sickeningly insignificant; the second point of view, however, gives us a complete reversal of values. The millions of galaxies, each of which is formed of millions and millions of stars, appear to be composed of hydrogen, that is, of a nucleus and an electron, the simplest structure that we know; the stars, then, are but laboratories of atoms, while the earth is, as it were, a laboratory in which are to be found ever more complex molecules. It is as though one were to look at a landscape after reversing a pair of binoculars. It is the earth, then, that bears the fortune of the universe and man who bears the fortune of the earth.[12]

3. *Man's Condition on His Entry into Historic Time* [13]

The first sin had carried with it the loss of the supernatural gifts of grace which filled the heart of the first man; it likewise carried with it the loss of the preternatural gifts, that triple strengthening which grace had given the soul, the reason, and the whole man. Thereafter the soul no longer controlled the body with the result that death came into the world; thereafter, too, man's reason ceased to have full dominion over passion with the result that the troubles of concupiscence came into existence; and man himself ceased to have the full mastery of that earth which had been offered to him [14] as a paradise; hence the existence to-day of conflicts between man and exterior nature. Besides all this, man was also wounded and afflicted in his free will and in his natural inclination towards the good.[15]

Now that we have recalled the above data, it still remains possible to imagine in different ways the concrete condition of man at the moment when he entered historical time. In this regard the data of human palaeontology can orientate our choice.[16] Without any intention of exhausting all the possibilities, let us consider two important points of view in this matter.

In the first perspective, the beings which prehistory presents to us as possessing certain characteristics that are clearly simian—but who nevertheless were capable of making tools, kindling fire, and even of burying their dead—are regarded as the descendants of the first Biblical couple and as being in the full sense of the word our brothers. How, then, is their miserable condition to be explained? Three hypotheses can be advanced to answer this difficulty.

The point of departure of the first two of these hypotheses is the same. It consists in thinking that through original grace the first man had from the beginning been in possession of a complete and perfect body structure; similarly he had a complete and explicit possession of human qualities on the level of science and culture.[17] Granted this point of departure, one must then have recourse to a process of degradation to explain the appearance of prehistoric races.

The first hypothesis admits that after the fall human perfections and acquisitions, whether bodily or cultural, continued to exist and were transmitted to a certain extent by generation and education.[18] In this case it would be necessary to suppose that the first human beings after the fall lived in a state of civilization that was relatively advanced; this first hypothesis continues by supposing that after the time of these privileged generations there occurred the great migrations which plunged whole multitudes of human beings into the night of a progressive degeneration which was nothing less than a process of bestialization capable of modifying their skull structure, their orbital arch, and so forth.

This is the type of explanation which Pierre Termier seems to prefer. He thinks that nomads who have left no trace of their existence have lived, for example, in Chaldea or Egypt at the same time as other portions of humanity were in the stage of development of the lower palaeolithic age. He is likewise of the opinion that a scientist can not affirm that evolution is never regressive; for the history of the origins of life shows us three distinct events: regression followed by disappearance, sudden appearance, and slow evolution. But to close one's eyes to any one of these facts would be to abandon anything like a scientific method.[19]

Similarly, the second hypothesis admits that the state of achievement in regard to human qualities—both bodily and cultural—was one of the privileges of the first man; this state was compromised by his sin and rapidly lost by his descendants. Abandoned by the gift of innocence and crushed under the weight of the universe which afflicted him, man quickly fell to the lowest condition possible to him and approached the regions of animality. His organism, which was still plastic and capable of alterations, was reduced to an anatomical state close to that of the primates; thus suddenly degraded, man with his immortal soul entered the night of prehistory. He had first to touch the abyss of his misery before he could learn to understand by the progressive use of his intelligence and the mysterious help that began to come to him from the cross of Christ how to climb back to the surface of the ocean of reality by an extraordinary and, this time, ascendant evolution. According to this hypothesis it is no longer necessary to suppose that after the fall there existed in some parts of the earth advanced civilizations. Moreover, the majority of the reasons which are customarily given in support of a progressive evolution can be retained in this explanation.

The point of departure of the third hypothesis is a little different. It imagines that the gift of innocence was an eminent substitute for the bodily and cultural developments which the two preceding hypotheses had given to the first man. It supposes that these qualities were not given to man in their perfection and completeness from the beginning, but that he had to acquire them progressively by bringing all reality under his control and imprinting on it the image of God which he bore within himself. At the time of the fall when grace deserted him, he did not, then, remain bodily and culturally developed and evolved and perfected (as the first hypothesis supposes); nor was he left corporally and culturally degraded and wounded (as the second hypothesis would have us believe). Rather he was left to make the abrupt discovery of the initial indigence of a human nature that was as yet undeveloped but endowed with an astonishing plasticity and with latent and unused virtualities which began to be aroused through contact with a now hostile universe and through the first loving inspirations of the redemptive grace of Christ.

Must we say that the evolution of such a nature (in the eyes of the theologian the human nature which is considered in this hypothesis as well as in the two preceding ones is a fallen nature, but already, by anticipation, redeemed) necessarily took place in one direction? Must we not recall at this point, with Bergson, that the essence of any vital tendency is towards a pluri-dimensional self-development? It is generally admitted today that the Neanderthal man who was at first considered to be the link between the anthropo-simian forms and Homo sapiens appears to be rather the end of a race, the finish of one branch of evolution, which, by a progressive reduction of its variability, approached its own extinction; moreover, it is also generally admitted that the men who preceded the Neanderthal man by perhaps some seventy thousand years had certain characteristics that were closer to present-day human forms.[20] The stigma, then, of bestialization would appear to be "recessive characteristics."

In this third hypothesis it is no longer necessary to suppose a purely regressive evolution (as in the first hypothesis) nor a sudden and initial bestialization of some sort (as in the second hypothesis). Hence the problem that it poses is nothing else than a theological problem. "When we consider the state of innocence and grandeur which was Adam's by reason of the gratuitous and sanctifying gifts given him, can we think that this was the state of a nature still imperfect in the order of development and experience, and that Adam, because he was in some kind of elevated peace, kept for the future his powers of progress and those immense virtualities which he had not yet utilized?" [21]

The suggestion contained in this question is attractive. The second chapter of Genesis allows us to conjecture an evolution, since it shows us man placed in a paradise "as a point of departure for his progression in the natural order and for his education." [22] Why would the state of innocence have been incompatible with the possibility of a corporal, intellectual, and moral development? "Nothing prevents us from imagining that the body of this man, while pure from every trace of degradation, was closer to the primitive types of which prehistory and anthropology speak than to the evolved types which the canons of Egyptian and Greek artists have led us to regard as the exemplars of the human form. Provided we remove from his body the stamps of degeneracy which can affect primitive types, we can say that his body was akin to that of primitive man even though the time interval between the two may have been immense. As far as his intelligence is concerned, we should say that because of the stable harmony and the perfect subordination which human nature enjoyed as a grace at the dawn of its creation, it must be conceived as possessing an incomparable force and strength and vitality, along with energies of development on which no wound had yet been inflicted. This virgin intelligence found itself in an unimaginable state of simplicity and inexperience as far as human modes of knowledge through notions and ideas were concerned. Nevertheless, his notions and ideas were rich because of their immense rational virtualities. To assure the peace and joy of paradise, which were the spiritual privileges of the state of integrity, it suffices for us to think that divine inspiration could without opposition extend from the higher reason to the outermost fringes of sensibility, thereby directing at each instant the activity of his natural faculties. Moreover, the same inspiration could elevate him to a very high form of contemplation, but one that was ignorant of itself. In this respect it would differ widely from the contemplation that is given to a soul accustomed to and initiated in the work of reflection. Thereby divine inspiration could give him an understanding, the notional state of which would be singularly disproportionate to such an illumination. His free will would be intact, naturally and supernaturally turned towards God. The primitive state of his concepts—and concepts are no measure at all of the power or the grandeur of liberty—would in no way prevent full moral advertence nor remove responsibility from the decisions of a man in whom human nature had a completely new vigor and who enjoyed an ease and a mastery over his actions that surpass everything which our present weakness is able to imagine." [23]

In this hypothesis, then, the sight which we are given of man after the fall would not be that of an abrupt degeneration of an initial human culture, but a primitive, though human, culture suddenly deprived of the protection of the gifts of integrity which had at the first guarded it.

We have, however, still to consider the second great point of view in regard to the origin of man. In this view, the beings which prehistory tells us had certain simian characteristics but which were capable of kindling fire and using instruments were not descended from the first Biblical couple and were not our brothers. Accordingly, it is of little moment that they appeared at different points on the earth and at different moments of time. To explain their existence there is no need to have recourse to monogenism; polygenism is entirely admissible.

From this point of view two hypotheses can be proposed to answer certain questions. Were these prehistorical beings men in the philosophical sense? Did they have a spiritual and immortal soul? But before these questions can be answered, others must be asked. Does the act of kindling and feeding a fire necessarily involve an intellectual activity? Is it really possible to explain the ordered use of fire as an instrument without recourse to intelligence? The same questions may be asked about the construction of tools. Man doubtless constructs them because he has an intelligence; he can perceive the universal notion of purpose since he is able to perceive the causes of being. He knows the intelligibility of the means in its purpose and that of the instrument in its destination. But a bird can build its nest without knowing the notion of purpose; it suffices that the bird have an image of the end.[24] In the case of the superior animals, we find that their more complex and supple knowledge can produce a sort of empirical reasoning. It has been shown that among the chimpanzees there is found a kind of preparation and need for instruments, even a certain need for ornamentation.[25] If it is supposed that all creation is shot through with a divine motion that invites it to surpass itself, why could we not imagine that it leads to beings who, without being men in the philosophical sense, and who, therefore, did not possess a spiritual and immortal soul, would, however, pertain morphologically to the human species? They, of course, would not pertain to the race of Homo sapiens, but their psychological faculties would extend much farther than those of the chimpanzee; thus we would be able to explain the activity of the lower palaeolithic types. The first man in the philosophical sense of this term, the first creature possessing an immortal and spiritual soul and which belonged morphologically to the race of Homo sapiens and which was elevated by God to a supernatural state, would come after such beings.[26]

According to the second hypothesis, the beings of the lower palaeolithic age are in a true philosophical sense men. God infused a spiritual and immortal soul into their bodies, which, from the viewpoint of an evolutionist, were yet incompletely distinguished from animality. Must we, then, suppose that during a number of generations this soul remained in them as it does in an infant or an undeveloped being, imprisoned in an organism that is incapable of giving it access to the external world? Or should we rather suppose that the soul began to operate from the very first generation? It matters little what we answer to these queries, for the only serious problem lies elsewhere.

This problem can be stated thus. By these hypotheses we are in the presence of a race of true men who preceded Adam. They are pre-Adamites,[27] but not pre-men; monogenetic or polygenetic, as you will, they were engaged in an evolution but were destined to disappear completely. Their supreme purpose in the eyes of the theologians who support this hypothesis might be, for example, to mark in the future City of God the place of pure nature. Here below they were the initial term leading eventually to the supernatural elevation of the first Adam, who is the father of all our present human race. Afterwards there occurred the catastrophe which marked the entry of Adam and his descendants into the dramatic and mysterious evolution at the end of which appeared the "second Adam."

We do not maintain that all five of these ways of conceiving the origin of man are of equal worth, nor do we think that it is impossible to increase their number. It suffices to point out that—at least at first glance—theology leaves us the right to choose among them.[28] But from the point of view which interests us here, the essential point is to perceive the key that opens the locks of the entire problem and without which a Christian would always work in vain, no matter how gifted or learned he might be. That key principle is this: when there is question of the appearance of the world, of life, of the human soul, of sanctifying grace, or of the first Adam, we must consider that it is more than anything else a movement of descent by which God, breaking with what has preceded, inaugurates a new order that is superior and discontinuous to what preceded; only after considering this can we contemplate the movement of ascension by which a pre-existing being approaches in a continuous manner its proportioned ends or prepares under the influence of an elevating motion an order which surpasses it. Such is the principle which Saint Thomas considered in its supreme application and which permitted him to clarify the different aspects of the mystery of the "second Adam." It is immediately, he writes, not progressively, that the Body of Christ was assumed by the Word: "In the mystery of the Incarnation we must not consider that there is an ascent, as though something which already existed progressed to the dignity of the [hypostatic] union; this was the position of the heretical Photinus; but we must consider it as a descent by which the perfect Word of God assumed the imperfection of our nature." [29] Similarly it is immediately, not progressively, that Christ came into possession of sanctifying grace: "In the mystery of the Trinity we must consider the descent of the divine plenitude into human nature rather than a progression of an apparently pre-existing human nature to God." [30]

4. *The State of the Law of Nature*

The state of the human race after the fall was that of the law of nature. Millions of men lived under its regime. Indeed it was completely abolished only after the death of Christ; however, it still subsists in certain of its aspects in places where the gospel has not yet penetrated. The task of the historical theologian in regard to this law of nature will be to recall first of all the major principles which ruled the economy of this law. Then it must relate these principles with historical reality; thereby it will make these principles fertile and cause them to produce secondary principles which, being more immediate and containing concrete data, will be capable of clarifying the religious condition of different human groups.

What, then, are the major principles of historical theology in relation to the state of the law of nature? First of all, it is presented to us as a re-beginning which commences at the lowest point of man's catastrophe. But it is not a return to the state which had been lost; across a night of sorrows it is a journey towards a land of incomparable promises.[31] The light which appears on the horizon of history is not the remembrance of the happiness of the first Adam, but the hope in the Redemption which the second Adam would come to bring.

"It is he who has made, of one single stock, all the nations that were to dwell over the whole face of the earth. And he has given to each the cycles it was to pass through and the fixed limits of its habitation, leaving them to search for God. And yet after all, he is not far from any one of us" (Acts 17, 26–27). If He has permitted the Gentiles to follow their own ways, He has nevertheless "not left us without some proof of what he is" (Acts 14, 16). From the beginning, grace was offered to men, whether they lived in caves or were lake dwellers, no matter what the disgrace of their condition or their structure. The only requirement was that they should be men, beings endowed with a spiritual and immortal soul and descendants of Adam. Grace prevented them, secretly invaded their hearts, and acted after the manner of those instincts of nature under which it hid itself.[32] A mysterious and persistent dialogue took place between each man and that God who we know does not hate anything which He has created, who loves souls, and who closes His eyes to the sins of men provided they repent of them (Wisdom 11, 23–26). He is the God who sorrowed over Nineveh, that great city in which there were more than a hundred and twenty thousand men who did not distinguish right from wrong (Jonas 4, 11); He it is who by His Word enlightens every man (John 1, 9); it is He, too, who wishes that all men should be saved and should come to the knowledge of truth (1 Tim. 2, 4); nevertheless, He never reaps where He has not sown (Matt. 25, 14). It follows that from the fall on, each man found himself either in the state of refusing divine grace and hence implicitly in the state of rejecting the Redemption of Christ, or in the state of accepting grace; in this case, implicitly he has received the Redemption of Christ. Without doubt grace was not yet given with a fullness comparable to that which it has after the Incarnation and which the sacraments of the New Law dispense: "The Spirit . . . had not yet been given to men, because Jesus had not yet been raised to glory" (John 7, 39). Nevertheless, it was already the grace of Christ, the grace merited by Christ through His cross: "Salvation is not to be found elsewhere; this alone of all the names under heaven has been appointed to men as the one by which we must needs be saved" (Acts 4, 12). It is by anticipation that the Redemption penetrated to the first centuries of history, as the sun illuminates the fields before it actually rises.

More obscurely than the Mosaic Law, but just as truly, was the age of the law of nature orientated towards the redemptive mediation of Christ. Every offering and every sacrifice which was not perverted by hypocrisy, idolatry, or devil-worship but which truly mounted towards heaven, was accepted by God insofar as it was the beginning (though for the most part this was only implicitly known) of an as yet imperfect rite which would receive its full meaning on the day on which Christ would "enter, once for all, into the sanctuary; the ransom he has won lasts for ever" (Heb. 9, 12).

It was to permit some obscure recognition that grace came by participation in the future and visible mediation of Christ that grace—in some of its forms and notably in the justification of infants—was given in dependence on visible signs and external rites which theologians call sacraments. These sacraments were rudimentary ones; unlike the sacraments of the New Law, they were not the instrumental means and causes of grace; they were but practical signs designating the subjects on which God in His mercy promised to bestow grace, if He found them disposed for it. The specific constitution of these sacraments was not the object of any precept, but was left to human initiative. The same interior instinct which urged men to honor God also indicated to them what sensible things they should use in their divine worship.[33]

The entire substance of revelation, although it was to become progressively more explicit in the course of time, was already contained in the two fundamental truths that God exists and that He is the Remunerator of those who seek Him (Heb. 11, 6). To believe the first of these truths in a supernatural way under the secret grace of faith was already to believe implicitly in the mystery of the Trinity, while to believe the second in the same way was already to give assent to the mystery of the redemptive Incarnation.[34]

Here, then, are some of the major principles which ruled the economy of the law of nature. And here it would be wise to reintroduce the revealing view of Saint Thomas which we noted above on the meaning of human history: the human race progresses at the same time in both good and evil. On the one hand, each day sees it plunged deeper into darkness and sin. But this only constrains the divine mercy to condescend all the more to the miseries of men.[35] The more the night deepens, the more clearly shines the light. This continued up to the time of the Incarnation, nor has this law of progressive tension between the light and the darkness, between truth and falsehood, between holiness and perversion, yet ceased. Rather it has now entered its definitive stage in which history tends on the one hand to the Antichrist and on the other to Him whom the Antichrist precedes; this tension will increase "until the fabric [of the world] in the end gives way." [36]

But the work of positive theology has only begun. The confrontation of the large views of these major principles with the facts of history permits it to disengage a multitude of secondary views which have a double value. For one thing, they clarify history, since they underline the importance of certain events and organize its data. Secondly, they help us become aware of the concrete manner in which the plan for the salvation of humanity was realized. They discover for us the apparent powerlessness, the bewildering setbacks, the at times astounding retaliations, and above all the extraordinary patience of divine love. All of this, we think, is the task of theology.

One of these secondary views shows us, for example, the importance in the first ages of the precepts of adoration and obedience. "The two sins which were most severely condemned and punished in the state of nature were those of disobedience and idolatry, for faith and obedience were the first foundations for God's education of the human race." [37] Others of these secondary views can come from the signification to be given to the magic and the myths of the peoples who lived at the dawn of our civilization. It has been proposed [38] that we make in this regard a distinction between two phases or two states of the human race: the state of magic, in which the sensations, images, and ideas of men are nocturnal, that is, enveloped in the fluid and crepuscular psychism of the imagination; and the logical state, in which imagery and ideas are in the sunlight, that is, enveloped in the luminous and regulated psychism of the intellect. This proposal seems to us to be able to clarify not only cultural problems, but all the questions concerning the existence of a substantial continuity of the Church from the first ages of the world up to our own time.

To attempt to propose such an enlightening explanation it would be necessary to follow closely the evolution of different peoples under the law of nature, examining both their primitive and civilized conditions in the hope of finding the key to their beliefs and their institutions. We were never able, for example, to understand the choice of circumcision as a rite of consecration to God except by the light

of the pages written on that subject by Father Lagrange in
his *Etudes sur les religions sémitiques.*[39]

5. Israel

Everything which relates to the destiny of Israel belongs
to historical theology. This includes the time of its election
and of its fidelity, its first exile and its first return; it also
includes the fatal hour when it contemned the Messias, that
hour which made of two peoples—the Jews and the Gentiles—but one people, the Christian one (Eph. 2, 14). It
likewise includes the time Israel was broken up in the great
dispersion. The keys which Saint Paul gives us in chapters
three and four of his Epistle to the Galatians and in chapters nine to eleven of his Epistle to the Romans not only
open to us the meaning of the destiny of Israel, but also
show us the meaning of the history of the Church herself
and that of the religious history of the entire human race.[40]

6. The Incarnation

From the point of view of His "ordered power" it does
not seem to us that God would ever have permitted the
loss of the state of innocence, if He had not been ready to
succor us by some marvellous remedy. And this already gives
us some enlightenment on the mystery of the redemptive
Incarnation. But the question of the providential suita-
bilities of the time and place chosen for the realization of
the Incarnation (it is a question which ancient writers had
already proposed) is surrounded by a mystery so vast that
it seems to expand almost to infinity and before our very
eyes the dimensions of time and space.

The truth which the Fathers and the Doctors have found
in this connection with the aid of Holy Scripture is that
the human race is ordered by the God of love to pursue an
ascending course which began on the day of the fall and

which will end on the day of the Last Judgment; and to do this in the face of formidable shocks and terrible catastrophes together with the confrontation of the forces of evil which, as we have seen, daily grow more powerful.

In this ascending course can be distinguished two important stages. The purpose of the first stage is to conduct humanity through the regime of the law of nature and the privileged Mosaic Law to a state of perfection so high and so pure that through the desires of the best of their members, it can attract to itself the Divine Word. At the very instant of the Annunciation, when there is contracted the perpetual marriage of the Word with human nature, what waits on the free consent of the Virgin is the assent of the entire human race.[41] When "the appointed time came . . . God sent out his Son on a mission to us. He took birth from a woman, took birth as a subject of the law" (Gal. 4, 4). This is the summit of all history. It is not the summit, however, in the sense that the Incarnation marks the point of decline of the kingdom of God, its progressive extinction, and its gradual slipping down into darkness; but in the sense that for the great mass of humanity which heretofore had dwelt in darkness and in the shadows of death and which now can gather around Christ its Head, it begins an ascending movement which, though not continuous and even held back by terrible forces, bears a resemblance to the activity which makes a field grow until harvest time. "We have all received something out of his abundance, grace answering to grace" (John 1, 16). We have received this grace in order, as Saint Paul says, that we might "realize our common unity through faith in the Son of God, and fuller knowledge of him. So we shall reach perfect manhood, that maturity which is proportioned to the completed growth of Christ. . . . We are to follow the truth, in a spirit of

charity, and so grow up, in everything, into a due proportion with Christ, who is our Head" (Eph. 4, 13 and 15).

Of these two stages of progress in the kingdom of God,
the first is above all qualitative, since it rises from the imperfect to the perfect and ends with Christ, who is the
Head; the second is principally quantitative, since it diffuses
the perfection of Christ in space and time and invites men
to fill up in their own flesh "the debt which the afflictions
of Christ still leave to be paid" (Col. 1, 24) and to increase
without measure the Church, which is His Body. Both of
these stages are noted with precision by Saint Thomas, who
expresses his admiration for the mystery of the divine power
which has in different ways willed the salvation of all time,
past, present, and future,[42] and of all places, by recapitulat-
ing them around Christ.

We know that in times now past there were innumerable
multitudes who immediately after the fall began the advance towards the New Law, by slowly emerging from their
"nocturnal" regime of knowledge and of conscience. We
know that there are five continents cast adrift on a planet
of a stellar system which, with a billion others, forms our
galaxy. But this imperceptible planet carries on it the human
tragedy. It is to this planet that has been sent the Angel of
the Incarnation and on it was planted the cross on which
the Son of Man draws all men to Himself. Henceforth our
true center of gravitation is not the sun nor the stars; it is
not even our own universe of phenomena, which does not
have a "Christian atmosphere," [43] for, since the loss of our
preternatural gifts, we feel in ourselves our disaccord with
that universe. But our center of gravitation is an Infant in a
manger, a cross on which Love is crucified; in the future it
will be the glorified Body of Christ around which "the
eagles will gather" (Matt. 24, 28).

But is it possible that some of the other worlds are inhabited? If so, how are they related to the Incarnation? The theologian is not taken by surprise by such imaginations. He can answer them by hypotheses—for example, that of the angels or that of the islands; for the spiritual beings that may exist on other planets would pertain to a supernatural order that remained at first without Christ, as did the angels, but which ultimately would be incorporated into the universe of Christ. The angels, who at first received grace only from God, now receive it from Christ; from the beginning they were disposed as points on a circumference of which Christ would one day be the center. Or these spiritual inhabitants of other planets may have belonged from the first to the supernatural order of Christ, who would have been implicitly known to them in the mystery of God and His Providence. In this case they would be somewhat similar to the men who lived in past centuries under the law of nature or to those who live today on some forgotten island of the Pacific.[44]

7. Christian Origins

It is part of the work of historical theology to recall that the Christian revelation which was entrusted to the early Church was not something lifeless like an ingot of ore but something vital like a mustard seed, which conserved its identity only by growing in the sunshine of God. This revelation contains certain fundamental truths which we expect to find formulated in the New Testament—for example, those concerning the mystery of Christ, of the Last Judgment, of heaven, and of hell. We would not at all be scandalized if we found no teaching in Scripture concerning secondary truths which are either presuppositions to the former or deductions from them. Our surprise, therefore, is all the greater when we discover, far more explicitly than we had at first imagined possible, precious and valuable

texts relating, for example, to the privileges of the Blessed
Virgin, to the Particular Judgment, to purgatory, and so
forth.

One would likewise be doing the work of historical theology by recalling that the Apostles received from the
Saviour a double power of jurisdiction. The first of these
was extraordinary and unable to be transmitted, since it was
destined to be used only for the work of founding the
Church; moreover, in respect to this power the Apostles
were all equal. The other power of jurisdiction was permanent and able to be transmitted, since its purpose was to
foster the diffusion of the Church; in this respect Peter held
the Primacy. Such a view of the dynamism of the Church
gives us the key to certain facts which might otherwise
appear to be troublesome. By it, for example, is explained
the fact that Saint Paul was able to resist Peter to his face,
since he was equal to Peter in the apostolate (Gal. 2, 11).
Similarly it is through this key that an explanation can be
found for the fact that awareness of the Primacy, though it
always remained explicit in the Roman Church, was able
to be somewhat [45] hidden in the Orient, since the Church
had passed from the regime of the Apostles to that of
bishops, with the result that awareness of the Primacy had
to be rediscovered at the end of a dogmatic progress which
the Easter schism unfortunately interrupted.

As far as the permanent jurisdiction is concerned, historical theology, in reply to the misunderstandings that
stem from the East and from Protestantism, would show
us, among other things, what place the Roman Primacy
ought to take. It would show us how the Council of the
Vatican was led to consider the Primacy first of all in its
surest and most eminent exercise, that in which there is
required an absolute assistance from God, while its more
frequent exercise implies forms of assistance which, though

they are certainly divine, are inferior and less rigorous. Historical theology would also point out how the Vatican
definition has thrown back an extraordinary and henceforth
unforgettable light on the *Thou art Peter* of Matthew
(16, 18) and the *Feed my sheep* of John (21, 17). It was
in this way, too, that the definition of the Immaculate Conception of the Blessed Virgin gave a sudden and unheard-
of emphasis to the gospel phrases that relate the angelic
salutation.[46]

8. The History of the Church

Rather than attempt to propose a chain of problems pertaining to historical theology about the Church, it will be
more simple to say that all these problems, after they have
been studied in their profundities by doctrinal theology,
would be taken up again from the viewpoint of historical
theology for the purpose of freeing all the light which is
contained in them. The Church succeeded the state of
innocence, which can be considered as the age of the Father,
the age of a religion without an intermediary. The Church
was born in the age of Christ, who was first waited for in
signs and figures and then manifested in the flesh in the
midst of men. At Pentecost the Church entered the age of
the Holy Spirit, in which the grace of Christ is poured out
from the Head to the entire Body.

In this last age the Church began her life in a persecuting
era which was hostile to the growth of a Christian culture.
Then it entered the "sacral" era of the Middle Ages, where
she tried to found a political city reserved for her children
alone. In this era the practical theme which seemed most
important to the majority of men of good will was that
"human things ought to protect divine things." It was in
this era, too, that there arose the Papal States, the Inquisi-
tion, the Crusades, the use of interdict. Finally, the Church

passed to a new era in which she must continue her growth alongside of hostile forces, as the wheat must grow by the side of the cockle. In this era the most important practical theme would seem to be that it pertains "to divine things to protect human things."

Since the Church has lived under such completely different circumstances, how would she be able to manifest always more explicitly her own proper mystery as well as the mystery of her relations with various cultures? The opposition between the *My kingdom is not of this world* (John 18, 36) and the *Give back to Caesar what is Caesar's, and to God what is God's* (Matt. 22, 21); between the *Thou must needs be submissive* (Rom. 13, 5) and the *They adored the beast* (Apoc. 13, 4); and the meaning of the *Like lambs among wolves* (Luke 10, 3) open to us new profundities. It seems possible to disengage the great tendential laws of the Church's growth which are hidden in Scripture and which were glimpsed by Saint Augustine and Saint Thomas. According to these laws, the more the Church becomes incarnated, the less carnal does it become, that is, the less it is bound up with the destiny of a particular people; and the more visible it becomes, the less political and military it becomes, that is, the more differentiated it is from the State.[47]

9. The Actual Condition of the Gentiles

The continued existence, after two thousand years of Christianity, of innumerable peoples who have not yet been evangelized and of large religious groups such as the Buddhists and the Confucianists, draws our attention to the fact that the Church which was born of the great visible missions of the Incarnation and of Pentecost is missionary by its very essence. But the missionary activity of the Church must be followed in each of its stages and must be distinguished from the impurities which political ambitions have introduced under its standards. It must be constantly directed back to its own light, to its divine liberty.[48] Without these precautions, we would not be able to give a judgment concerning the salvation of the Gentiles, some of whom have perhaps accepted baptism in order to obtain temporal advantages, others of whom have perhaps risen up against a certain kind of preaching to protect their legitimate political independence. Without such precautions we would confuse the Church with something that is in no way the Church. Such a study, however, goes beyond the limits of mere historical sciences as well as the limits of speculative theology. It supposes an application of the light of doctrinal theology to the data of history; it is, in other words, the work of historical theology.

In a general and yet precise way, the problem of the continued existence of pre-Christian religions poses at the same time the problem of the Gentiles who came after Christ and of the possibility of their being saved by implicit belief in the mysteries of the Trinity and the Incarnation. To these problems the answer would seem to be that the individual conditions for salvation are the same for all Gentiles who are invincibly ignorant of the Gospels, whether they lived before or after Christ; nevertheless, the status in which the Gentiles find themselves has changed. Before Christ, an implicit belief in these truths was a normal state; after Christ, it is an abnormal one. From this point of view, Saint Thomas had every reason to make a definite distinction between the Gentiles who preceded Christ and who were called by their state only to an implicit belief in the Trinity and the Incarnation, and the Gentiles who came after Christ and who are called by their state to an explicit belief in these mysteries.[49]

10. The Condition of the Dissident Churches

Not only the two-thousand-year-old obstinacy of the Jewish people, but also the spectacle of the enduring and apparent success of such formidable secessions as Islam, the Byzantine schism, and Protestantism obliges us to reflect anew on the *Leave them to grow side by side till harvest* of Matthew (13, 30) and the terrible remark of Saint Paul (1 Cor. 11, 19) that it is necessary that divisions should exist.

It has become more urgent than ever before to make a constant and careful distinction between the sin of heresy and the patrimony of heresy; we must see the great dissident Churches as beset by a double movement. The first of these springs from the determinism of the original break with Rome and seems to condemn these Churches to be separated forever from the life which continues in the true Church; the other, however, through the secret solicitation of the Spirit which enlightens every man, tends to join the best members of these Churches to the life of the true Church. The ways in which this is achieved are often enough surprising and remain the secret of God; the most beautiful of these ways are those of love and of mystical impulse.[50]

That God permits His Church to remain in a mutilated state in millions of souls, and perhaps until the time of the harvest, opens up to us unheard-of perspectives of the profundities of the divine permissions of evil and of the utilization of evil by love.

11. The Condition of the Atheists

For the first time in the history of the world a prominent place in the forestage of human activity is occupied by a disastrous and conspicuous group of important atheistic cultures inspired by an atheistic humanism. The sight of these groups forces us to scrutinize the divine plan with a faith full of fear and love, for a number of questions trouble our hearts because of this condition. Is it possible, for example, for a true faith to continue to exist, especially in children, under the shell of an atheistic education and culture in much the same way as it not too infrequently happens that a practical atheism can be cloaked over by the appearance of a Christian culture? Is God now commencing to redivide and regroup humanity, in spite of the barriers of their adverse views, for the sake of the great feast to which many will come from the East and the West while the sons of the kingdom will be rejected (Matt. 8, 11)? [51]

12. *The Inspired Prophecies*

The main lines and the master ideas of historical theology are sketched in Scripture especially in the visions of Daniel concerning the advent of the kingdom of the Son of Man; in the prophecies of our Lord concerning the destruction of Jerusalem, the supreme mission of the Apostles, the end of the world, and the second coming; in the revelations of Paul on the destiny of Israel, the activity of the Antichrist, and the final triumph of Christ; and finally in the book of the Apocalypse.

In regard to this last document, we may say that the reading of this sealed book, the comparison of its teachings with the eschatological teachings of the other books of the New Testament, the interpretation of its prophecies, and the disposition of its many scenes—these things pertain to historical theology for a double reason, since it is a question of situating in time a writing whose content itself reveals the meaning of time.

By joining together all the prophecies of the New Testament we find that we can represent the Church as ex-

periencing in the course of its Messianic pilgrimage from
the first coming of Christ to His second an initial period of
expansion which will be crowned by the conversion of the
Jews and which shortly thereafter will reach its greatest extension. There will follow a period of contraction and of
apostasy in which the Antichrist will appear. In this period
the Church will gain in heroism what it has lost in extension. At this point Christ will come again.[52]

13. *The Church Eternal*

From what we have seen in this chapter, we can say that
the Church is present throughout the length of history.
Gathered together immediately after the fall in the shadow
of the cross of the Christ who was to come, she maintained
her substantial identity in the midst of transformations as
profound as those successive ones of the law of nature, the
Mosaic Law, and the New Law. It is true to say that,
although the Church is not without sinners, it is without
sin, for we belong to her by reason of the supernatural gifts
we possess and not by reason of the sins we have committed.
Seen in this way, the Church appears incomparably more
pure and yet incomparably more vast than we could ever
have imagined.

We can follow the mounting curve of the destiny of the
Church to the point beyond time in which she will exist in
the fullness of her growth.[53] In this stage the hierarchy will
no longer be of need. What we believe even today will
then be seen by all, namely, that the greatness of the hierarchy is completely at the service of the greatness of love
and that the profoundest of the characteristic elements of
the Church—one which is stronger than death, which resists
the encroachments of time, and upon which the Church is
centered and grouped today—consists in her charity and in
the inhabitation in her of the three Divine Persons.

14. Interdependence of Doctrinal and Historical Theology

Throughout this attempt to place the Church in time we have seen doctrinal theology and historical theology aid each other and react one upon the other. We have received a sort of experimental proof that they are, not two theologies specifically distinct, but the application to two different spheres of the work of our reason insofar as it depends on the data of revelation and is sustained in its progress by faith.[54]

15. Rewriting "The City of God"

We have enumerated in the order of their appearance in time some of the themes which historical theology might treat of from different points of view, at one time soaring aloft in the sky of principles, at another time hovering close to the ground of history. In the final analysis we have thereby given to theologians the opportunity to rewrite *The City of God*, to furnish an ultimate explanation under the light of revelation of the birth, growth, and outcome of the gigantic drama in which two antagonistic cities oppose each other, the City of God and the City of Evil. Both of these are mystical,[55] that is, both of them are specified by an immediate relation to an ultimate end, to heaven or to hell, to a love of God even to hatred of self or to a love of self even to a hatred of God.[56] The theologian, however, would consider them purely and formally in themselves, since he would force himself to give no attention (he is more able to do this than was Saint Augustine) to the lot of human cities which are specified by an immediate relation to intermediate ends. He would not consider, then, the common good of a temporal, political, and cultural order, for what concerns these human cities should be treated by the theologian only in the measure in which they are capable of being attracted in opposite ways by the two great mystical cities, either towards the heights or towards the abysses of human destiny.

As Paul Claudel has rewritten the *Divine Comedy*, so the theologian must rewrite *The City of God*. There can be no doubt that the point of view of Dante is unsurpassable. "Alone among all the poets he has painted the universe of things and of souls, not from the point of view of a spectator, but from that of the Creator, by attempting to place them in the framework, not of the *how*, but of the *why* and by judging them to a certain extent or rather by allocating them through their relations to their final ends. He has understood that in this visible world we do not perceive complete beings, but, in the phrase of the Apostle Saint James, a certain beginning of the creature, passing signs, the eternal meaning of which escapes us. He has attempted to give a complete history of the times in the midst of which he lived; he has traced for us the definitive form it took, by following it from its contingent origins up to the immutable outcomes as conceived by the Wisdom of God. He has spelled out for us one of the pages of that *Liber Scriptus* which is mentioned in the Mass for the Dead." [57]

Nevertheless, the complete synthesis of medieval sciences, of its astronomy, cosmography, geology, geography, and history, has been disrupted; with its disruption also fell the imagery which had been forged by the poets to speak to the people of the things of the other life. [58] The result has been a prolonged religious crisis which is less a crisis of the intelligence than it is of the imagination. "If men continue to sustain hope and if we continue to tell them that the realization of this hope can not take any of the forms which they think it should take, they will finally revolt and maintain that their hope itself is illusory." [59] Hence arises the pressing need to attempt from the point of view of Dante, but on the basis of a completely different scientific imagery a new poetic creation of the universe, in which, for example, continents will take the place of the little republics of Italy. Such is the task ahead of poetry. But let us cease the consideration of this to return to theology.

The point of view of Saint Augustine is likewise unsurpassable. We can only put ourselves in the school of this master; thereby we shall immediately experience how difficult it is to be a student of such a teacher without constantly being in danger of betraying him by a lack or an excess of fidelity to his teaching. In all truth it is not so much necessary to rewrite what he has already written as to write as he would do were he alive today. "A philosopher who is worthy of the name," writes Bergson, "never says more than one thing; he keeps on trying to say what he has not yet expressed exactly. . . . Had a given philosopher lived many centuries before his actual life, he might have been concerned with another philosophy and with another science; he might have expressed himself in other formulas; he might have posited other questions; not a chapter, perhaps, of his books would have been the same as the ones he actually did write; yet he would have said the same thing." [60] If we respect on the one hand the metaphysical value of the first principles and on the other the transcendence of Christian revelation, these words can be applied to the theologian. The principles, the lofty data, the master definitions of *The City of God* are lasting things.

Only the material of the book must be changed. For one thing, doctrinal theology has not ceased to progress; and for another, fifteen centuries of the history of Christianity in the world, fifteen centuries of the history of the gift of God that has been entrusted to the greatness as well as to the misery of men, have produced new facts. Continents have been discovered; depths of cruelty and horror have been unveiled; historical and prehistorical studies have, during these last centuries, made great strides forward. If our wisdom is far from that of an Augustine, our information is none the less immense. Though the difficulties of the enterprise may seem to be insurmountable, they will not be so when the task has received sufficient preparation or when there is born into the world the genius destined to accomplish this labor. The principal task in this work will be less the assembling of materials than it will be putting them to work, choosing the most formal points of view that will be capable of illuminating and fecundating the data of history.[61] Since it is based on revealed principles, it is evident that there is no need to wait until an examination is made of all the facts in order to have a great and certain positive theology.

It was the scandal provoked by the sack of Rome under Alaric and by the imminent collapse of the empire at the very moment when it seemed likely to become Christian, which led Saint Augustine to concentrate all the light of revelation and all the fire of his genius on the course of history in the hope of discovering the plan of that mysterious salvation to which men of every epoch of history are invited. Thereby he deliberately introduced into theology the dimension of time. The growth of the scholastic synthesis and the extraordinary developments which have taken place in historical sciences at a time when the meaning of the entire life of humanity is in question would seem to announce the dawn of a second blooming of historical theology, one that can be characterized as an attempt to insert the dimension or, if you prefer, the coordinate of time into the theology of Saint Thomas. In this there will be given one more proof that it is impossible to disjoin Saint Augustine and Saint Thomas; they are the flaming brands that light our way to the greatness of theology.

16. *The Theology of the History of Salvation*

The revealed truths which are the principles of theology, even though they are not evident to us during the length of our pilgrimage on this earth, were given to the Prophets and to the Apostles and then communicated to the world by means of miraculous illuminations which Saint Thomas ranks among the charisms, that is, among those gifts which are given for the common good, not the immediate sanctification of the subject who receives them (*gratiae gratis datae*). These truths were accepted by divine faith first by the Prophets and the Apostles and then by the faithful to whom they were afterwards communicated. The light of faith is more divine than the light of prophecy, for it is theological and belongs to the order of graces which immediately sanctify their recipients (*gratiae gratum facientes*). The Apostle Saint John was greater when he believed in the Incarnation than when he revealed it to the world, even though he alone had the power of revealing it; Pope Pius IX was greater when he believed in the Immaculate Conception than when he defined it, even though he alone had the power of so defining that truth. Here, then, is a new paradox of Christianity: that which is less precious is the privilege of only a few and what is more precious is given to all who are poor in spirit and is ceaselessly offered to sinners. Our Lord's observation that we should not cast pearls before swine is the one saying that He Himself has forgotten to observe.

These revealed truths are penetrated, contemplated, and experienced by the gifts of the Holy Spirit, by the gifts of knowledge, understanding, and wisdom, which are, as it were, the flowers of intellection on the branch of love or, to use an expression of Saint Paul, the eyes of the heart (Eph. 1, 18). In turn, these truths are scrutinized by speculative and positive theology, which rests its discursive work on the knowledge of a faith previously illuminated by these gifts.

Leaving aside what concerns doctrinal theology and the internal order of the revealed, let us return for the last time to a consideration of historical theology. As we have just seen, there are many different ways of obtaining knowledge of the order of succession in the divine mysteries: prophetic knowledge, the knowledge of simple faith, the knowledge of a faith illuminated by the gifts, the knowledge derived from theological reasoning.

The Promethean hope of Leon Bloy was to be able to obtain prophetic knowledge, to be able to snatch from the hands of the Prophets of the Old Testament the miraculous key which permitted them to unlock the meaning of an entire history in its progress towards the drama of the Redemption. Then, armed with this prodigious instrument for the exploration of time, he would try to the full measure of his powers to explore not only Biblical history (which, moreover, terminated at the Redemption and at the High Mass of Calvary) but universal history itself, the secret of which lies hidden ahead of us in an indiscernible but imminent future, which will bring us the end of the world, the consummation of the Redemption, and the triumphant coming of the Holy Spirit.[62] In all truth this passion which devoured Bloy was the combined result of his deep and loving theological faith, of his absolute certainty of the imminence of the end of the world, of his human gift for poetic divination, and finally of his impatience with the present, which he never ceased to foster by his continued reading of the Prophets.

It is to be noted, moreover, that the divine revelations to which faith adheres not only announce Calvary and the end of the world, but they are also concerned with what occurs between these two, with the establishment, the growth, and the vicissitudes of the Church throughout the Messianic age. In relating these divine revelations at each moment with the succession of actual facts, reason, when it is sustained by faith, readily releases new light. This, then, is historical theology. Its direct concern is to illuminate the history of salvation; it is, in brief, a theology of the history of salvation. It is not directly concerned with the history of peoples and of their cultures, but touches them only in connection with the destiny of the kingdom of God, which forms its specifying object. But the large views which it can thereby express concerning the temporal destinies of the universe permit it to proceed in all sureness to the establishment of a Christian philosophy of history or of culture or of politics. Although these perspectives of historical theology are in themselves insufficient to constitute an entire theology of history or of culture or of politics, they are nonetheless the *prolegomena* for a Christian philosophy of these matters.

The principles of theology demand to be known and penetrated in the fervor of love and the gifts of the Holy Spirit. This is true also of historical theology. It is necessary that the theologian should possess—obscurely, to be sure, but with a kind of certainty that is mysterious and inexpressible—the total meaning of the destiny of the kingdom of God from the time of the fall to that of its entry into glory; it is necessary that the theologian should be able to "suffer" in the emotion of a single indivisible moment the complete rhythm of the Church's duration, if he wishes to have the power to speak of any of its phases, of its successes or its failures, without falsifying the divine perspectives, without altering the life-spirit which pervades the entire history of the Church.

The two gifts which above the rest should inhabit his

heart are those of knowledge and understanding. It is the gift of knowledge by which the history of the universe is learned experimentally through pains, tears, and the absence of the God whom that history conceals; and it is the gift of wisdom by which the history of the universe is learned experimentally in the light, peace, and presence of the God in whom "we live, and move, and have our being" (Acts 17, 28).

8. Beneath Theology: The Wisdom of Reason

1. The Existence of a Wisdom of Reason

Can reason know anything about God? If the ox can know its master and the ass its owner, is it possible that man is unable to know his God? Is it possible that man, by reason of that image of God which is in him, of that unshakeable foundation which makes him remain man even after the fall, is no longer able to discern in the universe any traces of his Maker? Or would we rather suppose that the first work of the divine resemblance which grace gives us when it comes to regenerate man is to do away with the most reasonable of man's occupations?

It is a commonplace in certain quarters [1] to speak of philosophy as a game; when it becomes such, it will be a deadly game for those who have engaged in it. In truth, however, philosophy and, more generally, the progress of reason in search of God by means of the world is a serious matter. Although the early apologists were not entirely able to make a clear distinction between the light of reason and that of faith, they nevertheless had a great respect for reason.[2] Neither Saint John Damascene [3] nor Saint Thomas Aquinas was any more ready to believe that it was praise-

worthy to contemn reason; they were far too attentive to
Scripture to make such a mistake, since Scripture assures
us that the heavens proclaim the glory of God by signs that
are perceptible even to the ends of the world (Ps. 19, 2–5);
that in the very midst of pagan nations God is not without
His testimony (Acts 14, 16); and that only men who are
by nature unthinking could fail to rise through visible beings to the knowledge of Him who is (Wisdom 13, 1–5;
Rom. 1, 19–23). They believed that human reason even
among the Gentiles was able to come to a knowledge of
God and that among the Christians of today it can still discover in the heart of the universe the imprint of His
sovereign infinity.

The traditional Christian teaching, then, is that the
human intelligence can apply itself to the things of this
world not only to learn their phenomenological laws, to
control them, and to bend them to human desires; but that
by either a spontaneous or a philosophical exercise of itself
it can come to know their nature, their hierarchy, their contingence, and that thereby it can rise to the assertion of
the existence of the Creator by means of His creatures.

2. The Value of the Wisdom of Reason

But what is the value of the wisdom of reason? Of what
validity is its knowledge of creatures and of God? It is clear
that the knowledge which reason—either spontaneously or
philosophically exercised—can have of the ultimate causes
of the universe, of the structure of mobile being and of life,
of the different stages of life in plants, animals, and men,
is a knowledge which pertains to the domain of cultural
activities and which of itself remains on a level lower than
that of the kingdom of God. This is true even of the knowledge which it can have of God. The divine names which
men discover are able to signify the true God; and they do

this, not in a metaphorical, but a proper sense by virtue of the transpositions made possible by metaphysical analogy. Nevertheless, they attain God only under His aspect as Creator, never under the aspect of the Trinity or as Saviour; through them we are in the presence of God, but like a blind man before a rose or like an injured man who knows that someone is taking care of him but does not realize that it is his mother. The knowledge of reason tells us about our nature and the Author of our nature but leaves us in ignorance of the ultimate bases for our actual existential condition and of the mysteries of our salvation. Reason perfects us in the sphere of culture, but it is incapable of justifying us,[4] of opening to us the gate to the kingdom of God.

From the fact that the knowledge of reason is unable of itself to justify us, we should not conclude that it therefore bears no relation to our salvation.[5] For it creates favorable conditions and removes certain obstacles which might otherwise compromise our salvation. Reason prepares the ground on which grace can fall and grow more abundantly. Or, if you wish, reason is the water in the pitchers of Cana. The Saviour had no need either of the water or of the work of the servants who drew it. But if the pitchers had not been filled with water, the miracle would never have been performed.

Recall, for instance, the services which metaphysics rendered Father de Nobili during his apostolate among the Brahmins. After the first conversion of which he was the instrument, he had to discuss with one of the Brahmins the problems of creation and transmigration. "The learned men of this country, because of their adherence to the principle that nothing comes from nothing, admit three eternal things: Padi, Pajou, Passam. Padi is God, Pajou is the matter from which God produces souls; Passam is the matter

from which He forms bodies. I opposed to this position the
ordinary arguments of philosophy to prove to them that if
Pajou were not created it would itself be God; then I
pointed out to them that if Padi were not able to create
or draw something from nothing, He would not be all-
powerful and consequently would not be God, since His
action, like that of secondary causes, was limited to modifying forms. I developed this argument by various applications and comparisons, thereby convincing him.

"The next day we spoke of the transmigration of souls.
The Brahmin based his position on the variety of conditions
to be found among men, a variety which could be explained
only by admitting merits or demerits which preceded this
life. With the Platonists he held that the soul is not the
form of the body, but that it is imprisoned in it like a bird
in a cage or like a chick in the shell of an egg. To this I
replied that soul and body formed a composite which is
man; man lives, changes, operates in such a way that his
actions do not belong to his body alone nor merely to his
soul, while a bird and its cage do not have any natural relation between them. Furthermore, since sin has an infinite
malice, the differences to be found in the temporary conditions of misery in this life can not of themselves be an
expiation for sin. Finally I pointed out that the differences
between rich men and poor, between Brahmins and pariahs,
between the joyous and the sad, between the fortunate and
the unfortunate, come from secondary causes, the activity
of which God is in no way bound to suspend; indeed by
these very differences He wishes to show us how worthless
are the great riches and joys of this world in comparison
with those which He has prepared for us in the next world
and which we merit by using the good things of this life
and by patiently enduring the evil things. . . . At the end
I concluded with an argument *ad hominem:* 'You say that

God drew the first Brahmin from His head, the first Rajah from His shoulders, the first pariah from His feet, and so forth; but the first Brahmin, the first Rajah, the first pariah could not have had any merit or demerit anterior to their first production into being.' " [6]

Furthermore, it is not impossible that the purely natural notions of God and of His Providence to which the human reason can rise, should be touched by a divine ray which would elevate and transfigure them, enabling them to signify by means of the transanalogy of faith the innermost profundities of that God of whom the Epistle to the Hebrews (11, 6) remarks that to please Him one must believe under the illumination of faith "that God exists and that he rewards those who try to find him." The Saviour Himself took the water from the well of Jacob as an occasion to speak to the woman of Samaria of the waters of eternal life.

3. Christian Philosophy

In becoming Christian, philosophy does not change its nature. It continues to study what things are in themselves, to support itself on rational principles in order to investigate the proper causes of reality, and to interest itself first of all in the world in order afterwards to rise to the supreme cause that is God.[7] Nevertheless it receives from revelation a strength that was unimaginable before revelation. Philosophy becomes aware of a favorable regime which, while not modifying its essence, changes its state. It remains philosophy—that is, the rational study of beings by their ultimate causes; but it becomes Christian by reason of the lucidity and assurance with which it is now vested.

As we have seen, in the case of theology human reason is utilized by faith after the fashion of an instrumental cause; it is elevated above itself in the service of purposes which also surpass it, something like a piano when it is played by an artist.[8] As a result, reason enters into the activities of the kingdom of God and receives wings with which it can fly.[9] In the case of philosophy, however, human reason functions after the manner of a secondary but principal cause for its own purposes and in accordance with its own laws, something like a piano when it is touched by a tuner.[10] As a result, it remains on its own proper level, that of cultural activities. Nevertheless, it there receives marvellous aid from faith and obtains means by which it can progress and run along at a better speed. This influence of the Christian faith on philosophy is exercised in a double way, in an objective and a subjective fashion.

4. *The Objective Influence of Christianity on Philosophy*

In somewhat the same way as food is necessary for life, so, says Saint Thomas, the wisdom of revelation and of faith is absolutely necessary (*necessarium ad esse simpliciter*) for man in order to be able to find God, not in an indirect way only insofar as He is the hidden principle of the universe of nature, but directly as He is in Himself in the most intimate and most profound aspects of His life, in the mysteries of the Trinity, the Beatific Vision, the Incarnation, the Redemption. And just as a horse is necessary for a traveller, so the wisdom of revelation and faith is morally necessary (*necessarium ad melius esse*) if the truths concerning God—and, let us add, concerning the soul—which are naturally accessible to our reason are to be known more widely, more quickly, and more surely.[11] From this last remark, which is found more than once in Saint Thomas,[12] it follows that the illuminations of revelation and of faith can at times reach the level of the wisdom of natural reason and light up certain truths of the natural order which are of special importance or which are most severely contested.

Let us remember, however, that it is always as a visitor and as a stranger that the light of revelation and of faith descends to the level of reason. Saint Thomas explains with great profundity in the second book of the *Contra Gentiles* that even when the teaching of the theologian is partially coextensive with the area of the philosopher, the illuminations are always different in both cases; the theologian considers creatures in terms of the God of revelation, while the philosopher is interested in them for their own sake.[13]

It would take little trouble to multiply the examples of the incidence of the supernatural light on the level of philosophical reason. Thus many precepts of the decalogue are concerned with norms which in their immediate bearing do not surpass the level of the natural law: "Honor thy father and thy mother. . . ." "Thou shalt not kill. . . ." "Thou shalt not steal." [14] The Biblical revelation of creation by its insistence that there was a first moment when things began to exist contains the metaphysical notion of creation from nothingness,[15] which reason, although it did not discover it, was able to recognize as soon as it was pointed out. "Nothing could be more familiar than the first verse of the Bible: 'In the beginning God created the heavens and the earth' (Gen. 1, 1). . . . In uttering so simply the secret of His creative action, it seems that God puts us in possession of one of those enigmatic key-words, which we knew all along must exist but could never discover for ourselves, and the truth of which comes home to us with irresistible force as soon as it is gratuitously given. The Demiurge of the *Timaeus* so closely resembles the Christian God that the whole Middle Ages saw his activity as a kind of foreshadowing of creation; and yet he endows the universe with everything except precisely existence. The first unmoved mover of Aristotle is also in a certain sense the cause and father of all that is, so that Saint Thomas will go so far as to write: *Plato et Aristoteles pervenerunt ad cognoscendum principium totius esse.* But Saint Thomas never credits the Philosopher with the notion of creation; never once does he qualify as creationism his doctrine of the origin of the world; and if in fact he does not do so, it is because the first principle of all being, as Plato and Aristotle conceived it, integrally explains indeed why the universe is what it is, but does not explain why it exists." [16]

The teaching power of the Church informs us that God, the principle and end of all things, can be known with certitude through the light of natural reason by means of His effects, that is, by the visible works of creation; [17] it also teaches that reason can establish with certitude the spirituality of the soul and the liberty of man. [18] Such teaching—and it rests on Scripture—gives philosophical investigation an inestimable stimulus. The dogma of the Eucharistic presence teaches us that we should define an accident, not in terms of its actual inherence, but in terms of its aptitudinal inherence, since the Eucharistic accidents do not exist in any substance. The dogma of the Incarnation teaches us not to identify human nature and human personality, for the former alone is found in Christ.

No one can fail to see that these divine illuminations, by shining on certain truths of the natural order which henceforth are guiding posts for all philosophy, bring to philosophical research a strength the value of which can not be estimated. These illuminations in no way change the nature of philosophy, but aid it in an objective way, that is, by instructing it. This help can be given to philosophy either in a negative way by preventing errors or in a positive way by exciting the activity of philosophy and consecrating its results. In relation to the entire work of philosophical investigation, revelation shines, to use the figure of Pius IX, as a guiding star. [19]

5. *The Subjective Influence of Christianity on Philosophy*

Besides an objective influence, there is a subjective influence which Christianity brings to philosophy to purify and illuminate it. The first work of supernatural grace is to elevate man, to order him anew after the catastrophe of Eden towards his divine, surpassing, and supernatural destiny. Grace, however, has a secondary work: namely, to cure and heal the wound which was opened in the depths of man and which prevents him from accomplishing fully even that which is proportioned and natural to him. Accordingly Christian grace has two effects: in relation to the supernatural order, it is elevating; while in relation to the natural order, it is healing.[20]

According to Saint Thomas, it is clear that the wound of sin has disturbed even the ordering of human intelligence to the truth that is connatural to it. To say that "human nature since the fall is wounded more in its desire for the good than in its knowledge of the true" [21] is to recognize that human nature as a matter of fact is defective even as far as the knowledge of truth is concerned. Moreover, Saint Thomas affirms this expressly elsewhere: "It is probable that certain signs of original sin appear in the human race. For since God provides for human acts in such a way that He gives a reward for good acts and a punishment for bad acts . . . we can learn of the sin through the punishments for it. It is apparent, however, that the human race generally suffers from corporal and spiritual punishments. . . . Among the spiritual punishments, the chief one is the weakness of our reason on account of which it is difficult for man to reach truth and easy for him to fall into error; it also follows that reason can not entirely overcome man's bestial appetites, but is frequently darkened by them." [22] It follows from this text that the wound of our reason (*vulnus ignorantiae*) not only affects, as Cajetan thought, our intelligence insofar as it is the subject of prudence and insofar as it dictates in the immediately practical realm of moral conduct, where passions seek to obscure its vision; but also extends, as other commentators have pointed out,[23] to the intellect insofar as it is ordered to know speculative truth and the principles of moral law and natural right. As a result, the grace of Christ has the task of sustaining human reason in its endeavors to discover the meaning of the universe and to establish the natural foundations of moral life. From this point of view—that is, by reason of the secret and subjective influence of grace which labors to heal the wounds of our minds and our hearts—we find a new reason for affirming once more the existence of a Christian philosophy.

6. *The Encyclical "Aeterni Patris"*

The encyclical *Aeterni Patris* concerning scholastic philosophy [24] recognizes and sanctions the validity of philosophical procedure: "In all points of doctrine which the human mind can attain by its natural resources, it is clear that philosophy should be allowed to use its own methods, principles, and arguments." The encyclical declares that philosophical wisdom "has the power to clear and smooth in some way the path which leads to faith, by suitably disposing the soul of its disciples to accept revelation." There exists a whole multitude of truths which pagan philosophers had professed and which have been since consecrated by Christian revelation. It is in this sense that the Fathers have been able to say that the children of Israel received the command to take for themselves the riches of the Egyptians.

It can not be said that the first result of Christian faith is to make fruitless the noblest activities of our minds. On the contrary, as the Vatican Council teaches, "faith frees and guards reason from errors, and furnishes it with manifold knowledge." [25] The same teaching is found in the encyclical: "It is not in vain that God has caused the light of reason to shine in the human soul; the additional light of reason, far from extinguishing or putting out the vigor of the intelligence, rather perfects it and increases its powers, thereby rendering it ready for the highest truths."

There even occurs in the encyclical a mention of the double strengthening which Christianity brings to philosophical reason. Thus in regard to the objective influence of revelation, the encyclical remarks: "The splendor of these divine truths which is received in the soul comes to the aid of the intelligence and far from lessening its dignity, increases its nobility, its penetration, and its solidity." On the point of the subjective influence of revelation the encyclical says: "If, before it was enriched by the power of Christ, natural reason was able to produce such a rich harvest, now that the grace of the Savior has restored and increased the native resources of the human soul, the mind should certainly produce a much more abundant return." [26]

Not only, then, are there Christian philosophers; there is also such a thing as Christian philosophy. Catholics who have held the contrary have gone astray on this point.

7. The Problem of an Existential Christian Moral
      Philosophy

Can moral philosophy be anything more than a skeleton discipline, inadequate to its object? Can it be a philosophical norm of human activity if, in order to remain independent of theology, it wishes to ignore the concrete and existential conditions which have been imposed on human activity by the wounds of the fall as well as by the invitations and strengthening of grace? In an effort to constitute a perfect discipline adequate to its object and philosophically directive of human activity, should we not rather borrow from the higher level of theology data concerning these concrete and existential conditions of human activity as these have been produced by the fall and by grace?

What, for example, should moral philosophy think of the first moral act by which a child, after deliberately deciding the meaning of his life, chooses to make a natural act of love of God above all things? Should moral philosophy prescribe this as possible to the unaided powers of the human will? If so, then the first step of moral philosophy would be a false one.[27] If, on the contrary, moral philosophy teaches that this first natural moral act, which is the foundation of a human moral life, is not possible to the human will insofar as it is wounded by sin, and if it further points out that, nevertheless, such an act can be demanded of the will insofar as it has been touched by the healing grace which is offered together with elevating grace to every man who is induced to act freely, in this case moral philosophy will not be in error and there is nothing to prevent it from studying this first moral act from the point of view of its natural implications.[28] The question, however, still remains: In what way would moral philosophy have avoided error in this regard, had it not borrowed from theology?

The same problem can be posited in a slightly different manner. As we have explained, philosophy is of itself sufficient to attain its object; metaphysics, for example, can know God as the cause of being; the philosophy of nature can know the spirituality of the human soul. It is not, then, the object of philosophy, but the state of existence of philosophy in its human subject that gives rise to the need that philosophy has of the strength of revelation and of grace if it is to become Christian. But considering the concrete conditions produced in human activity by the wounds of sin and by the invitations and strength of grace, can we still say that moral philosophy of itself is sufficient to attain its object, that is, to direct human activity even in its own proper line of such activity? Or must we rather say that moral philosophy is Christian precisely by reason of its object, that is, by reason of those teachings which it borrows from theology concerning the concrete conditions of its object? Can we say that moral philosophy is of itself capable of being existential? Or must we hold that it is existential only insofar as it becomes Christian?

These questions have ranged Catholic thinkers into two groups, the first of which consists of partisans for an independent moral philosophy, while the second adheres to a moral philosophy that must be Christian in order to be existential. Everything that is essential to the thinking of both sides seems to have been already written; the upholders of both positions will certainly do little more in the future than to add to their case some rectifications of secondary importance. It is, then, the future that will decide between them. For our own part, we shall devote a few lines to show how the problem appears to us.

8. *The Solution to the Problem of an Existential Moral Philosophy*

We have no difficulty in agreeing that one can call moral philosophy a natural ethic constructed by reason alone, for the purpose of ordering man considered purely as an intelligent and free being to God considered purely as the ultimate end of all creation.[29] Since human nature as such was not destroyed but remained essentially the same both in the fall and in the Redemption, whatever reason can assert about the relations of man with the inferior natures of the universe, with other human natures, and with God considered as the principle and end of creation, constitutes a group of truths which, because they flow from the essence of man, are presented in a general fashion abstracting from the different states in which this essence can be or has been realized—the states, for instance, of pure nature, of fallen nature, of repaired nature.

However precious and however necessary such a natural ethic and moral philosophy may be, it can not by its very nature sufficiently attain the concrete so as to be able to constitute a practical science of human activity; by nature it is imperfect and incomplete, for it is not the essence of the human existent which acts, but the human existent itself in the given state in which it is: that of pure nature or of fallen nature or of repaired nature. Such an ethic, then, or moral philosophy, is not existential. Is it not possible, however, for such an ethic to become existential solely by the effort of observation and the reflection of human reason independently of any borrowing from revelation? Such a completion of this natural ethic by recourse to the resources of reason alone would be possible on the hypothesis that we had been created or would be yet created in the state of pure nature. As a matter of fact, however, we are not in the state of pure nature; and even if we were to succeed in constructing an existential moral philosophy for such a state, it still would tell us nothing of our true final end nor of the wounds which render us incapable of accomplishing without the help of grace the good which is connatural to us. Such a philosophy would only confuse us.[30]

All Catholics agree that there exists an existential moral doctrine. It is nothing else than theology. Its purpose is to direct the activity of the concrete man, who, it knows, was deprived from his birth of a form of supernatural life which had been prepared for him, and who was wounded in his nature but redeemed by Christ who died on the cross in order to reinstate man in a new form of supernatural life, to gradually heal the wounds of his nature, and to redestine him to the Beatific Vision. It takes into account everything which a natural ethic could know of human nature, since this nature continues to exist in its fallen but redeemed state. It teaches us in what manner, under the action of the First Cause, the activities of his human nature demand to be supernaturalized, whether substantially or modally, in order that man might be able to ascend to his ultimate end, God. It distinguishes, for example, the things which under the influence of grace should be rendered immediately to God for the sake of God, from other matters which under a similar influence should be rendered immediately to Caesar for the sake of God.

Theology is concerned with concrete human activity in its entirety insofar as it is considered as proceeding from the first principle of grace and ordered to the final end of the supernatural order, that is, to the final end of a transhuman, transpolitical, transcultural order. Nevertheless, it is not concerned with concrete human activity in all its aspects. It does not—at least directly—touch that activity insofar as it is ordered to human, political, and cultural ends. Moral theology is existential insofar as it treats of the kingdom of God; it leaves room, however, for an existential moral doctrine which would treat of things belonging to the human order.

Saint Thomas teaches that theology does not exhaust all the aspects of created being. Even when the theologian and the philosopher treat the same subject, it is under a different light. "It is clear that the doctrine of Christian faith considers creatures insofar as they contain a likeness to God and insofar as error concerning them leads to error concerning divine realities. So it is that creatures pertain to this doctrine and to philosophy for different reasons. . . . For the philosopher treats of creatures according to their natures, while the believer considers them only insofar as they are referred to God . . . hence it is not to be thought that it is an imperfection on the part of the doctrine of faith if it does not consider all the properties of things. . . ." [31] These remarks apply with equal force to the practical order. Moral theology considers the ends of the kingdom of God; there is place, then, for a moral doctrine that would consider the ends of the human, political, and cultural orders.

It is essential that we be fully aware of the double finality which can inhere in the state of fallen but repaired nature in the same human activities which under one aspect belong to the kingdom of God and under another aspect pertain to the kingdom of this world. Here below man is subject to a double movement. The first one is principally a vertical movement, the purpose of which is to turn man directly towards eternity, towards the celestial Jerusalem which is present in the womb of human history as well as beyond it. The other movement is principally horizontal; its purpose is to turn man towards the tasks which he must accomplish in the interior of time; it is concerned with the political city, with the work of culture and of civilization; its ulterior and mediate purpose, however, is also to turn him towards eternity as it is discovered this time in terms of human history. The command given to man to love God with his whole heart and his whole soul and his whole strength (Deut. 6, 5) concerns the first movement; while the precept to till the earth and to be master of everything on it (Gen. 1, 28) pertains to the second movement. It is clear that these two precepts are entirely compatible; but it is no less clear that both of them do not always advance simultaneously; it may even accidentally happen that an act of sin can occasion, or an act of virtue can prevent, cultural progress. If when Pascal was sick he had made fewer visits to relics and churches, he might have left us new inventions in mathematics or in physics; if Wagner had not loved

Madame Wesendonck, we would not have *Tristan and Isolde.* What could have happened if Racine had not renounced the theatre for God; or what could have been the result if Calderon, after he had become a priest, had renounced the theatre?

Nevertheless, it is not reflections such as these that should delay us. In appealing to this double movement to which man is subject (we have treated this matter in others of our writings [32]), we must insist that it be understood here in its most formal sense. This is not the case of a distinction which aims to oppose to each other different activities (*distinctio per oppositas res*), but one which opposes two different aspects which are capable of coexisting in the same activities (*distinctio per oppositas rationes*).

Let us consider, for instance, the activities which belong primarily to the vertical movement, the purpose of which is to turn man immediately towards eternity, to the celestial Jerusalem which is present in the womb of time as well as beyond it, of which the Deity is the center. These activities can be substantially supernatural; nevertheless, they normally offer an aspect by which they can be concerned—though secondarily and, as it were, by excess—with the natural values of human political and cultural life. It is under this latter aspect that these activities belong to moral, political, and cultural philosophy, for this is attentive to everything which treats of human things precisely insofar as they are human. But these activities belong to a philosophy that was previously illuminated in order that it might be able to recognize that these values constitute the human side of activities which are entirely supernatural and which would remain impossible to exercise without the intervention of the elevating grace of Christ. Such activities, then, pertain to a moral doctrine which has been completed by borrowing from moral theology data that concerns the ulti-

mate nature of its object; it is not, however, the same thing
as moral theology, from which it is formally distinguished.
This can be seen if we remember that it treats the same
object as does moral theology but under a different formal
light, that is, not insofar as the object is immediately referred to the things of the kingdom of God (for this is presupposed) but insofar as it is referred to the things of this
world by reason of the interior superabundance and excess
of the activity in question (and this is precisely what moral
philosophy is interested in).

This, then, is existential moral philosophy. "Although it
[moral philosophy] does not need theology in order to
obtain possession of its principles and its own proper light,
nevertheless, it is by reason of a perfective title and for the
sake of perfecting these principles and this light (this is
necessarily so, considering the conditions in which as a
matter of fact its object is found) that moral philosophy
has need of theology in order to resolve its conclusions in
its principles—completed and elevated in the way we have
discussed—of practical reason." [33]

Is it permitted to study the mystics as Bergson has done
in the *Deux sources*, not only insofar as they are the shining
stars of the heavenly Jerusalem which is the Church, but
also insofar as they represent the highest part of humanity,
the perfection of human values? Is it permitted to show
that, besides what exists in mysticism for the kingdom of
God, there is to be found therein a current of life which
alone is able to prevent modern civilization from suffering
a collapse of its purest and most precious values? If such
studies are conducted for their own sake and independently
of any specifically apologetic intention, are they to be for-
bidden to the philosopher who is eager to neglect none of
the riches that belong to human life in its proper sense?
If, on the one hand, we suppose that such studies attempt

to constitute themselves without wishing to borrow anything from the data of theology, we may well ask how they
can avoid including in themselves many serious errors. It
was miraculous that Bergson was able to maintain the lofty
position that he did, and yet he did not avoid all error.
Nevertheless, it remains true that what he attempted was
of itself legitimate: "Since everything that is human interests the philosopher, it is eminently fitting that he should
meditate on what is at the very heart of humanity, the
mystical life and sanctity. But, while all the time keeping to
his own proper standpoint and his own rightful means of
procedure, he must then have recourse, because of the intrinsic exigencies of such an object, to the information of
theology; its scientific powers are alone competent to deal
with such a theme; for the reality which he is studying in
this case is not purely natural and is moved by principles
which are superior to reason alone. If the unbelieving
philosopher can not admit these principles and in consequence the theological science which is founded on them,
his information will inevitably be deficient." [34]

To take a contrary case, how can we forbid a philosopher
to study from the point of view of the human values they
emphasize the meaning of the consequences of that special
and well-characterized form of atheism which proceeds from
a previous rejection of Christianity? Yet how could we expect him to be free from misunderstanding and errors, if he
followed an independent moral philosophy conducted without any borrowing from the data of Christian doctrine? [35]

Let us now turn our attention to those activities which
belong primarily to the horizontal movement, the purpose
of which is to turn man immediately towards the tasks of
time, towards the exploitation of his human virtualities,
towards the political city, towards the work of culture and
of civilization. Substantially these activities are human and

their study pertains to philosophy. But in the existential state of fallen and redeemed nature, they offer a supernatural aspect which moral philosophy, since it regulates our activity, can not disregard without falling into error and of which it has no knowledge except by borrowing from theology.

Granted the weakness of human nature since the fall, moral philosophy has need of being strengthened by grace, not, of course, in order to make progress in technology or, as Saint Thomas puts it, in order to build houses and to plant vineyards, but in order to attend to the highest values of civilization; to continue to make explicit the data of natural and international law; to illuminate and spiritualize the work of culture; and to discover and make prevail on the level of family, political, and international life the consequences of the dignity of the human person which was partially veiled before the gospel revelations came to illuminate that dignity.[36] Would a moral philosophy be existential if it were unaware of the need and reality of this strength given to it by grace?

Moreover, there can be no doubt that human, political, and cultural ends can and should be sought after for their own sake as ends having their own value, and not as mere means to the supernatural life. Nevertheless, they are not ultimate ends but intermediate ones, and as such they must be referred even in the interior of time to the supernatural realities of the kingdom of God which are their final end. They are supreme in their own order, but not purely and simply so. How, then, could a philosophy take into account this necessary subordination of human, political, and cultural ends to supernatural ends, if it ignored the existence of these supernatural ends? And if it did not take account of such a subordination, how could it be existential?

So we see that in the case of activities that are super-

natural in themselves but abounding in human virtualities
and in the case of activities that are natural in themselves
but referred to the supernatural either by the way they are
produced or by reason of their orientation, we find ourselves in the presence of a world of dynamic and concrete
values which are existential and properly human and which,
as such, are directly of interest, not to theology, but to
philosophy; but which retain so close a connection with the
supernatural world on which they depend and towards
which they are orientated that moral philosophy can understand them only by accepting its presuppositions from
theology.[37] Notwithstanding this, philosophy is not absorbed
by theology. If it accepts the help of theology, it does not
do so in order that reason should function after the manner
of an instrumental cause for the sake of the values of the
kingdom of God, but in order to function as a secondary
cause for the sake of values that are properly human but
existentially in dependence on the kingdom of God. In this
case reason does not receive, as it did in theology, wings
with which to fly. Nor does it receive even that simpler aid
it obtained in speculative philosophy, by which it was better
able to proceed on its own level. Let us say that it receives
wings in order to descend to the moral terrain of existentiality
where it properly belongs.

"Moral philosophy adequately considered is first and
foremost," says Jacques Maritain, "a factual philosophy.
The believing philosopher, like the theologian, turns his
glance not towards an abstraction of human nature, but
towards our wounded nature—the scientific notion of which
he has already received from the theologian. But he is interested in our wounded nature, like the novelist and unlike
the theologian, for its own sake: and the notion of a
wounded nature awakens in his wisdom other echoes than
those that are stirred in the theologian. The same may be

said of the notion of nature redeemed. In the light of these notions he can study the problems which are his own, for instance of concrete psychology and of character, or the history of philosophy, or political philosophy, or the philosophy of the world and of culture, the historical development of the enigma of the human being and the phases of man's factual situation which are typical for different moments of civilization; or yet again, transcendent psychology. Of course the problems of natural spirituality and those of natural pre-mysticism, even those which touch on supernatural spirituality and the mystical transformation of one nature into another, with all that that involves of human values and of human aspirations which have been saved, and human reasons for living that have been broken, are doubtless theological problems first of all. But they are all philosophical problems also, and offer formal aspects which are of special concern to the philosopher of manners and customs, and sharpen his curiosity concerning concrete nature." [38]

From what we have said, philosophical activities are to be ranked among the activities of civilization and these we must now consider.

9. *The Principal Activities of Civilization*

What is meant by the word *culture* or *civilization?* [39] The word civilization, *civilitas*, comes from the word city, *civitas*. This simple remark contains a very important lesson. Since the city pertains by its nature to the natural order, it would be wrong to introduce supernatural elements into the definition of the concept of civilization. Only natural religion, understood as representing the movement of man's speculative life towards the First Cause and the movement of his moral life toward the Sovereign Good, is included in the definition of civilization as the part is included in its whole.

The Church, which is supernatural, is the salvation of the nations, but she does not pertain to the same order of things that the nations do; the Church is likewise the salvation of civilizations, but in her own nature she is not of the same order as are the civilizations she saves.

The word *civilitas* has always been used to denote some relation to the city: the science of government (Quintilian); the equality of civil rights (Cassiodorus); the virtues of urbanity, sociability, refinement (Suetonius). The word is found in this last sense in Saint Thomas, who recalls the myth of Orpheus persuading men to abandon their savage state for a civilized life.[40] Civilization, then, is opposed to savagery and barbarism. It is the good, the appearance of which is possible only in a city, in a society; in brief, it is the full blossoming of a properly human life.

It is not an overly difficult task to point out in what this blossoming of human life consists and to determine, though only in a summary fashion, the different elements of civilization. Truly human life can reach its summit of growth in the speculative and in the practical orders, the latter order including the sphere of morality (*moralia, agibilia*) as well as the sphere of the arts (*artificialia, factibilia*).

The development in the speculative order is nothing else than the life of the intellect when it seeks to understand the proximate or ultimate causes of things and desires to take its rest in the contemplation of the highest of these causes, that is, in the contemplation of God, of whom we must say, not that He has existence, but that He is Existence. The development of the practical life can be made in two distinct spheres of activity: that of morality and that of art.

To the sphere of morality pertain our free acts insofar as they are related to our last end and hence insofar as they bring us nearer or farther from that last end, which is the Sovereign Good towards which we should always strive as far as our condition as men allows us. This sphere of morality is divided into three parts, which are clearly distinguished one from the other: individual morality, economics and politics. In each of these God must appear not only as the object of special obligations but also as the ultimate reason for all other obligations.

Saint Thomas gives a profound explanation of the meaning of this triple division.[41] Man, he says, is by his nature social, for in order to live he has need of many things which it would be impossible for him to procure by his unaided efforts. Man's nature, then, demands that he be a member of a society which would enable him to live. The family takes care of his fundamental needs: birth, nourishment, education. The State bestows on him supplementary goods which permit him to experience the fullness of life in both the material and the moral orders. Man, then, is a member of the family society and the political society. It is certainly exact to say that under one aspect man can be identified with the family and under another aspect with the State; insofar as one considers these aspects, it can be seen that individual morality is resolved into family morality, and this latter into political morality, which then becomes the only morality. Man, however, since he has an immortal soul, can not pledge his entire being to the family, for this is only a temporal society; similarly, the family, which is charged with the care of the primary human goods, can not be resolved into the political society, since this latter is concerned only with supplementary goods. Accordingly there is another aspect according to which man remains independent of the family, and the family in turn independent of the State. This, then, is the reason why there are three divisions in moral philosophy and three distinct sciences to study them.[42]

The first division is concerned with individual moral life. It includes all the independent activities by which each individual man achieves his true end or loses it. The second division includes everything concerning domestic or economic life; in other words, it is interested first of all in the interior life of the family, the relations between parent and child, between husband and wife, between master and servant; secondarily it is interested in the art of acquiring wealth in the measure in which this is necessary to provide for the necessities of the family.[43] The third division is concerned with political [44] and international life. Since before everything else it is necessary that the State should exist, peace is the first of all values in the order of political realizations. Then it is necessary that the State should progress towards its end, which is a life lived in accordance with virtue. But since man is weak and heroism is rare, a virtuous life can not be lived by all unless there exists a sufficiency of material goods.[45] This is the reason that the arts which pertain to the acquisition of wealth are dependent on moral political philosophy insofar as this wealth is necessary for the good of the State.

The ancients distinguished two arts for acquiring wealth, the first of which made wealth an end in itself. Far from esteeming this first art as an element of civilization, the ancient thinkers regarded it as detestable, since they maintained that it had its origin in the malice of men who did not want to live in accordance with virtue but in accordance with their own whims and for the sake of pleasure. Moreover, they held that it was this art which had invented the principle of the fecundity of money and had countenanced monetary manipulations. The ancients noted that since artificial riches can increase indefinitely, the art of acquiring them eternally remains with work to do; accordingly, men were led to prostitute the highest things in order to make of them instruments of gain: justice was rendered, medical care given, war conducted, intelligence and thought used for the sake of money and still more money—"Money, it answers every need" (Eccles. 10, 19). This art, which the ancients removed from all economy and from all politics because it led to the corruption of both, is precisely that which capitalism has baptized as political economy.

Nevertheless, increase in wealth can be sought, not as an end or for the sake of pleasure, but as a simple means to the necessities of life. In this case its rule and measure is service to human life. Such an art, it is clear, is in strict dependence on a true economic and political philosophy and indeed can be called a part of such a philosophy. It would not, however, be an integral part of that philosophy but an auxiliary part insofar as it furnishes economics and politics the instrument which they need in order to attain their ends. Unfortunately, Aristotle informs us that already in his time most men who were occupied in economics and politics conducted themselves by the principles of the first art we discussed.[46]

To the domain of art pertain those voluntary activities which are ordered to the production of an external work, to the making of an object. The purpose of this external work may be mere utility. In this case one would be dealing with the useful arts, which could be either servile or liberal insofar as they are ordered to the conservation of life (medicine, for example) or to the acquisition of objects necessary for life (agriculture, manufacturing, commerce, and so forth). On the other hand, the purpose of the external work can be to enclose and, as it were, imprison in itself a little of that spiritual radiance and splendor which is found in its perfection only in God. In this case we would be dealing with the arts of the beautiful, the fine arts.

From what we have said, we see that in all there are six elements of civilization, which can be reduced to three headings: the speculative life, the moral life, the artistic life. Although supernatural religion remains beyond civilization, natural religion is included in it; it is represented by the highest stages of the speculative and moral lives. All of what we have said can be summed up in the following outline:

Civilization is the development of human life, that is, of human activities which include:

A. Speculative activities (which seek the proximate and ultimate causes of things and especially their supreme cause, which is the pure Act of being; this constitutes the speculative life, which embraces the sciences as well as wisdom or philosophy);

B. Practical activities, which are ordered either to
   1. moral life, which directs to their last end—that is, the Sovereign Good—
      a. the individual (individual moral science)
      b. as well as the fundamental human societies, namely:
         1) the family (economic philosophy)
         2) and the State (political philosophy);
   2. or to the artistic life, which produces either
      a. works of usefulness (the useful arts, whether liberal or servile)
      b. or works of beauty (the fine arts).

It must be remembered that the word *civilization* can signify either the act of civilizing or the state of that which is civilized.[47] The definition which we have given of this word contains room for this double sense, for the expres-

sion "development of human life" can be understood either
as an evolution or as the result of such an evolution. Since
the development of a truly human life brings about the
establishment of a social order, we are able, by emphasizing
the second of the senses which we have just seen the word
civilization can have, to define civilization as the natural
social order. "Social order" as here used signifies not only
the moral values of the economic and political order which
are directly procured by the family and by the State, but
also those goods whose existence is conditioned by life in
society: science and philosophy, for example, the philosophy
of individual morality, and the arts which the State is supposed, not to control, but only to foster. The phrase which
the swallows of Stello utter to men, the scientist, the meta-
physician, and the artist cry out to the State: "Protect us
but do not touch us." [48]

If now we compare Christianity with civilization, we can
say that civilization is the development of life insofar as it
is merely human, while Christianity is the development of
life insofar as it is divinized by grace. Or if we take the second definition of civilization, we can say that civilization is
the natural social order, while Christianity is the order of
the supernatural society, of the City of God, in which man
becomes a fellow citizen of the saints, the angels, and the
Divine Persons.

When the influence of Christianity is exercised on a
civilization, that influence is not felt equally in all the
branches of the civilization in question. While Christianity
affects the whole, still it directly touches only the most
spiritual of the activities of civilization, those which lead the
soul to God—wisdom, for example, or moral philosophy.
Moreover, the influence of Christianity is received in an
imperfect and precarious way. To be exact, civilization
taken as a whole is Christian only by reason of a tendency

or movement which leads it to a kind of exceptional human clarity and transparency which alone can confer on it a closeness to divine grace.

Certain activities of civilization are more subject to the influence of grace than are others. After Saint Thomas remarks that the wound of sin has made it more difficult for us to know the truth which is connatural to our intellects, he adds that we are weaker still in desiring and accomplishing the good which is connatural to us.[49] From this we see that in a Christian civilization activities of the speculative order will be purer than those of the prudential order, that, for instance, philosophy will be more Christian than politics.

When we use the term *Christian civilization*, we do so with all the reserves which we have discussed. We mean to say that there is a Christian philosophy, a Christian economics, and a Christian political philosophy, and not just that there are Christians who treat of philosophy or economics or politics. And there is a Christian art, which is such far more by reason of its spirit and its inspiration than by its subject matter. But there is no such thing as Christian mathematics or Christian technology. There are only Christians who do work in mathematics, in technology, or in the thousand other necessities of daily life. Divine grace which such men bear in their hearts leaves intact such activities and all the thorny problems that accompany them. Grace touches these problems, it is true, but only to make them bring forth roses for the kingdom of God.

9. The Vital Structure of Christian Knowledge

The only thing left for us to do is to add by way of conclusion a few remarks concerning the vital structure of Christian knowledge.

1. The Different Degrees of Christian Knowledge

In our attempt to define theology and to assign it a place in the hierarchy of knowledge, we have been led to distinguish and to characterize briefly the different presences of the light of faith in the human soul, presences which we can call the degrees or stages of Christian knowledge. According to the way in which it is touched by the light of faith, our intelligence is established on different levels of knowledge, different spheres of cognition, which are mutually and formally distinguished from each other. These levels include the sphere of mystical or apophatic knowledge, which supposes the conceptual data of faith but which does not use such concepts as a formal and ultimate means to its knowledge; the sphere of the simple knowledge of faith, which uses concepts and judgments as a formal means of attaining its object, but without discourse and after the manner of intuition; the sphere of theological knowledge, which is entirely dependent on faith, but which is also discursive; the sphere of positive religious disciplines; and finally the sphere of speculative and practical philosophy.

Nevertheless—and this is the point on which we wish to insist at the conclusion of our essay and which gives coherence to everything we have said—these different spheres of Christian knowledge are closely connected; a vital bond links them together. If one of these spheres is misunderstood or rejected, by that very fact the entire vital structure of Christian knowledge is placed in peril of dissolution. The relationship of solidarity which exists among these levels of knowledge is the result of the presence in each of them of the light of divine faith. Their specific differences arise from the different ways in which the light of this faith is present in them.

Accordingly, we can see that all these degrees of Christian knowledge must exist simultaneously in the Church taken as a whole. Nevertheless, as long as our pilgrimage on earth continues, the weakness of our condition makes it impossible that they should coexist simultaneously in each Christian taken individually. There are only a few privileged souls among the faithful in whom all the degrees of Christian knowledge can grow and increase to some degree of fullness, and even in such souls this occurs only successively and in alternation.[1]

2. Mutual Exclusion of These Degrees of Knowledge

In order to emphasize at one and the same time the profound kinship of all these different knowledges, their specific differences, and finally the difficulty of exercising them simultaneously, let us examine the case of an intelligence which is faithful to the light of faith but whose focus of attention is successively shifted in order to enter one by one each of the spheres of knowledge accessible to it.

If we begin by considering the knowledge of simple faith, we see that at the first moment at which it is received in the soul, the light of Christianity gives the soul the things which have been revealed as well as the power of knowing them; this latter is nothing else than theological faith, which makes the soul adhere to the mysterious profundities of revelation and which is the root of all justifying endeavors. The believer is encompassed with notions and with revealed propositions in which are expressed what he believes God has done for him; they contain the doctrines of creation, salvation, and of the last things. His faith employs these propositions in an intuitive, not a discursive, manner. Faith is intent on adhering to their content, not on making an inventory or study of them.

If we turn now to a second stage, that of mystical knowledge, we must suppose that at this point the divine light attains its greatest intensity in the believer. We must suppose that faith, deepened by charity, is no longer content to make the soul adhere to the truths which have been revealed, but begins to make it experience that the truth of these revealed propositions is greater than can be expressed in such judgments; it elevates the soul on the wings of love and the gifts of the Holy Spirit to such heights that the soul bows down in a speechless contemplation in which all concepts cease their activity. We are in the sphere of mystical knowledge in the act of its supreme activity. All the dogmas remain, but like the stars at midday. In all truth, there is no other case in which the dogmas are so necessary a prerequisite, so effectively present as here. The very light which eclipses them strengthens them in an extraordinary way; for when it passes, they remain still shining from its splendor.

When Saint John of the Cross was engulfed in the "mid-day" of God which is the "midnight" of faith, how would it have been possible for him to think distinctly and successively of each of the mysteries of the infancy or of the Passion of the Saviour? He had been sent to instruct the world about an ineffable contemplation, and those who read his works have no right to forget this fact. Nevertheless, when the dazzling spectacle of unity gave him a little respite, he clearly recalled each of the Christian mysteries and, as it were, was intoxicated by them: at Baeza he carried in his arms the Infant Christ from the crib; at Avila he sketched his vision of the Crucifixion; he was inflamed with love by his contact with the Eucharist.[2] A mystical contemplation which, at the moment it opens and uncloses itself, is not ready to permit the appearance—enclosed in it like petals in a rose—of each of the mysteries of the gospel is not a Christian contemplation. We would have to de-essentialize mystical contemplation, if we wished to oppose it to Christianity. This is what Karl Barth and Aldous Huxley have both equally done, the one to give up mystical contemplation for Christianity, the other Christianity for mystical contemplation.[3]

In its superconceptual and speechless grasp of the Deity, orthodox contemplation confusedly includes Christ, the Church, and the entire world. "My mind," says Saint Catherine of Genoa, "was fixed on the abyss of the Trinity, but my memory was fully occupied with recalling the necessities of Holy Church and of all the faithful."[4] These are the truths which are manifested distinctly when the mind returns from the ecstasy of love and descends again towards the world, the welfare of which is the mission of this soul. These truths existed before the contemplation; they were all the time underlying the contemplation; then they re-

appear in the foreground illuminated by the fires of contemplation to leave the ways to contemplation open to the
soul and to excite the soul to new visitations. Is it not said
of the disciple of Christ that "he will come and go at will,
and find pasture" (John 10, 9)?

We can turn now to theological knowledge. In rediscovering clearly, distinctly the truths of faith, the mind of the
believer feels the spontaneous and ineluctable need to relate
them to each other, to order them among themselves, and
to illuminate them one by another, at least in an initial and
rudimentary way. It is the spur of theology urging the mind
on. It is possible that in an individual Christian there will
be slight possibility for progress on this level. Nevertheless,
there is never any authorization to deny or even to contest
the legitimacy, the suitability, and the necessity of the work
of theology. If a so-called "spiritual" would pretend to
forbid—and not just to an individual but as a general rule—
theological investigation for the sake of better safeguarding
the sovereign purity of the faith or of mystical contemplation, he would thereby give irrefutable proof of a tendency—
inadvertent, perhaps—to substitute for faith and for Christian mysticism something that is neither one nor the other
but only a facsimile.

If, finally, we consider the case of the inferior disciplines,
we observe that every human being adopts, however confusedly or provisorily, a certain historical explanation of the
origin and destiny of Christianity; and that each man carries
with him either hiddenly or openly a philosophy. If this
man is or becomes a believer, he is forcefully made to realize
that the Christian mind demands rectification even on these
levels of its investigations and that the light of faith must
descend even to these regions where—often in a remote

way—are nourished the choices which are either hostile or favorable to faith.

3. *Impossibility of a Simultaneous Existence of These Knowledges in the Individual*

From what we have said, we can perceive not only the close connection that exists between these different Christian knowledges but also the difficulty of exercising them simultaneously. The source of the entire vital unity of Christian knowledge is found in theological faith; when that is uprooted, the Christian mind is also destroyed on all its levels of activity. Faith, then, must coexist with each of the other Christian knowledges, even when the simultaneous existence of these other knowledges is impossible.

When mystical contemplation deepens the desire of faith and elevates it by the impulse of love to an ineffable knowledge of its object, the concepts of faith, however active they remain in themselves, pass to the background in such a way that all exercise of meditation on particular mysteries and, a fortiori, all exercise of theology and of the philosophical and historical disciplines is suspended. Nevertheless, even in this light the concepts of faith are not destroyed but hidden; with these concepts are also hidden their powers of illuminating the levels of theological knowledge, of positive religious knowledge, and of Christian philosophy. When the concepts of faith reappear in the foreground, these disciplines can expand again immediately.

The silence of mystical contemplation is alone capable of conferring authenticity and profundity on the lower Christian knowledges. It is like the extraordinary silence of the Coliseum which does not abolish the noise of the city, but on the contrary condenses within itself the clamor of the

city, of the centuries, of the world, in order to reveal thereby
the supreme drama of human history.

4. *The Simultaneity of these Knowledges in the Church Taken as a Whole*

We have mentioned that all the degrees of Christian
knowledge must coexist simultaneously in the Church taken
as a whole, even though it is impossible for them so to exist
in each individual Christian. It is impossible that the
Church should ever be deserted even for one moment by
faith or by mystical contemplation. Doubtless, she could
continue to exist should she be momentarily deserted by
theology or the lower Christian disciplines, but she would
then be in an unnatural state, which might well become
fatal for many of the Church's children. By the demands of
her very nature the Church must be represented on all these
different levels. Time has been given to her in order that
she might advance in them.

She advances slowly. At one time in the East and at another in the West, now in the North, now in the South,
she takes a step forward to make her theology more explicit
or to disengage the notion of a positive religious science or
that of Christian philosophy. One who has grasped the way
in which the Church advances would think it useless to
attempt to draw a title to glory from a statement such as
this: "The question of the relations between theology and
philosophy was never posited in the Orient." [5]

5. *Christian Knowledge in Christ and in the Church*

The Church in her entirety is precontained in Christ,
and the knowledges of the Church are precontained in an
eminent manner in the created knowledges which here
below filled the intelligence of Christ. According to Saint
Thomas Aquinas,[6] besides the supreme form of created

knowledge, the Beatific Vision, there existed in Christ in an eminent degree knowledge by connaturality through the gifts of wisdom, understanding, and knowledge. Added to this, He had an infused knowledge similar to that of the angels which He could use in a discursive manner, as when He explained to Simon Peter that though kings demanded tribute from their subjects, their sons were exempt from paying it (Matt. 17, 24).[7] Finally, he possessed an acquired knowledge which permitted Him to understand the events of the world as they took place before His eyes. This knowledge grew as He advanced in age. This knowledge was so ready for use that it was always complete and full; even in the case of this knowledge, Christ was ignorant of nothing that He should have known at a given place or time.[8]

This is the grand doctrine of Saint Thomas towards which the speculations of the Greek and Latin Fathers on the knowledge of Christ converge and in which they find their consummation. In recognizing that in Christ there exists below the Beatific Vision the mystical knowledge of the gifts as well as discursive knowledge, this doctrine shows us clearly the term towards which here below the intelligence of the Church taken as a whole tends, as a curve approaches its asymptote. The intelligence of the Church is still in the sphere of faith, not of vision; nevertheless, even now her intelligence also has the privilege of conciliating in her the simultaneous exercise of infused contemplation and of the discursive knowledges. In this way, the divine plan which directs the Incarnation brought it about that there should be found consecrated and eternalized in Christ and His Church—because they were made up of beings which were by nature complex—the mystery of the differentiations and degrees of knowledge.

Footnotes

CHAPTER 1

[1] *Mystical Theology*, Chapter 1, Numbers 1 and 2 (*P.G.*, III, cols. 997 and 1000).

[2] *Ibid.*, Chapter 3 (col. 1033).

[3] *The Divine Names*, Chapter 2, Number 9 (*P.G.*, III, col. 648). This is the passage (which Saint Thomas loved to cite) about Hierotheus, "who not only learned but also suffered divine realities."

[4] There is an ecstasy in the order of knowledge which is produced when a being exists in abnormal conditions caused by an excess of pleasure or anger. On the other hand there is also a kind of ecstasy that is proper to love. See *Summa Theologica*, I–II, 48, 3. It is from this second kind of ecstasy that mystical theology flows.

[5] *The Divine Names*, Chapter 4, Number 13 (*P.G.*, III, col. 712). The translation is taken from *Dionysius the Areopagite on the Divine Names and the Mystical Theology* translated by C. E. Rolt (New York: 1920), pp. 105–106.

[6] Saint Thomas Aquinas, *Expositio in Dionysium De Divinis Nominibus*, Chapter 4, Lesson 10.

[7] "A man should so love God that he should leave nothing for himself that is not ordered to God. When, however, he loves things that are equal to or below him, it is sufficient that he tends towards them in such a way that he seek not his self interest alone, but also that of others; nor should he order himself completely to such objects." *Ibid.*

[8] *The Divine Names*, Chapter 2, Number 9 (*P.G.*, III, col. 648).

[9] *Summa Theologica*, I–II, 28, 2.

[10] *Ibid.*, I, 1, 6, ad 3.

[11] *Ibid.*, II–II, 45, 2. See also Saint Thomas, *De Divinis Nominibus*, Chapter 2, Lesson 4. The citation from the *Summa* in the text is taken from *Summa Theologica* translated by Fathers of the English Dominican Province (New York: 1947), II, 1381.

[12] See Charles Journet, *The Dark Knowledge of God* (New York: 1948), p. 74.

[13] Vladimir Lossky of the Confraternity of Saint Photius in his *Essai sur la théologie mystique de l'Église d'Orient* (Paris: 1944), pp. 23–25, does not hesitate to create such an opposition. None of the texts of Saint Thomas dealing with mystical wisdom is used by him. In support of his position he appeals to the *De Potentia*, 7, 5, ad 2, where there is a discussion of a distinction made by Dionysius himself in his *Celestial Hier-*

archy; this distinction, however, does not concern mystical theology but only that theology which uses concepts (whether negative or positive). On this text of *De Potentia*, see the following chapter, note 11; consult also Journet, *Dark Knowledge*, p. 71.

[14] Henri Bremond, *A Literary History of Religious Thought in France*, tr. by K. L. Montgomery (New York: 1930), II, 436.

[15] See Journet, *Dark Knowledge*, pp. 81–88.

[16] See Charles Journet, *L'Église du Verbe Incarné* (Bruges: 1941), I, 162.

[17] Instead of considering the growing consciousness of the profundities of the dogma of the redemptive Incarnation, we could have given the example of the realization of the profundities of the dogma of grace and its sanctifying effects on the human will; this was the path chosen by Augustine, Bernard, and the German and Spanish mystics and thrown open by them to all Western mysticism.

[18] "It was the greatness of the Renaissance of the twelfth century that it discovered in the treasury of Christianity resources which had not yet been fully exploited." Dom Wilmart, *Auteurs spirituels et textes dévots du moyen-âge latin*, p. 59; see also pp. 63 and 506.

[19] If we may be permitted to complement the penetrating and respectful article of Madame M. Lot-Borodine, "*De l'absence de stigmates dans la chrétienté antique*," which appeared in *Dieu Vivant*, 1945, No. 3, pp. 83–89, we would say that while the absence of stigmatics is to be explained by the attention given to the dogma of the redemptive Incarnation precisely under the aspect of Incarnation and while the later appearance of such stigmatics is to be explained by the consequent attention given to the same dogma under its redemptive aspects, still this second consideration does not abolish but rather presupposes and prolongs the first.

Moreover, if we might change to a certain extent the perspective of that article, we would say that God permitted the fall of man for the sake of a Redemption destined, not to restore man to the state of Adam from which he had fallen, but to place him immediately in a Christological state which, even in its initial stages here below, is incomparably superior to the state of Adam. The first head of mankind was purely human and non-stigmatized; the Head of the new humanity, even in the midst of His sufferings, was already the Word made flesh; of Him, moreover, we can say that He was stigmatized that He might afterwards enter into His glory. We can, therefore, also say of ourselves that we must first be crucified with Him in order afterwards to be glorified with Him.

We need scarcely mention that we are here considering the stigmata of the saints, not insofar as they are extraordinary phenomena which even in their highest forms are only preternatural (on this see "*Le point de vue théologique sur les sueurs de sang et les stigmatisations*," *Études Carmélitaines*, October, 1936, p. 171), but insofar as they signify the essentially supernatural mystery of the compassion of the Church with Christ suffering.

[20] This is a discovery that is ever ancient and ever new. Louis Massignon compares "the martyrs of the first centuries, claiming on the day of their condemnation the absolution and the reconciliation of the apostates, adul-

terers, and murderers who according to the discipline of the time were ex-
communicated for life, with the co-sufferers with Christ in later centuries,
who, whether stigmatized or not, interceded with God for sinners—both
the former and the latter acted by a mystical substitution as members of
Christ." The same author emphasizes "the importance of atoning compassion in the comparative history of mysticism. Wherever outside the visible
Church (to be more exact, outside that part of the Church which is completely formed) are to be found special victims offering themselves humbly
to God for the salvation of others, a Christian may see there a secret activity
of the Holy Spirit, a precursive sign of that Pentecost which is not yet perfected for all men." *L'expérience mystique et les modes de stylisation lit-
téraire*, No. 4 of "Chroniques du Roseau d'Or," p. 155.

21 Jacques Maritain, *The Degrees of Knowledge*, tr. by Bernard Wall
and Margot R. Adamson (New York: 1938), p. 361.

22 *Ibid.*, p. 361. The mystical quality of the spirituality of Bérulle has
recently been the subject of much discussion.

23 *Ibid.*, pp. 361–362.

24 See *Summa Theologica*, I, 1, 5, ad 2.

CHAPTER 2

1 "Because Sacred Scripture considers things precisely under the formality
of being divinely revealed, whatever has been divinely revealed possesses
the one precise formality of the object of this science." *Summa Theologica*,
I, 1, 3. The translation is taken from *Summa Theologica* tr. by Fathers of
the English Dominican Province (New York: 1947), I, p. 2.

2 This phrase is to be found in the Prologue of the *Summa Theologica*.

3 Saint Thomas teaches that the principles of demonstration can either
be considered in themselves—and then they will pertain to the habit of
understanding—or insofar as they cause the conclusions—and then they
will pertain to the habit of science. See *Summa Theologica*, I–II, 57, 2,
ad 2. Similarly when revealed truths are considered in themselves, they
pertain to faith, but when they are considered as the cause of conclusions,
they pertain to theology. To explain one revealed mystery by another, for
example, to explain the mystery of Christ's permanence in the Eucharist
by the mystery of His coming in the Incarnation, is the highest achievement of theology.

4 *Exposition of the Orthodox Faith*, Book I, Chapter 8 (*P.G.*, XCIV,
col. 812).

5 *Élévations sur les mystères*, 12e semaine, 7e élévation.

6 See the Vatican Council as cited in the *Enchiridion Symbolorum*
edited by H. Denziger, C. Bannwart, and I. Umberg, 24th edition (Barce-
lona: 1946), Number 1795.

7 See *Summa Theologica*, II–II, 1, 7. There is no difference in level
between the *theologia unita*, which treats of the unity of God and the
theologia discreta, which treats of the Trinity.

8 Theology is to be understood here in the sense in which Dionysius uses
it in most of his treatises and which Saint Thomas at the beginning of the
Summa Theologica expresses by the term *sacred doctrine*.

[9] *The Divine Names*, Chapter 13, Number 3 (*P.G.*, III, col. 981).

[10] It is under one of its aspects that the notion of wisdom is affirmed of God and under another of them that it is denied of Him.

[11] In Chapter 2, Number 3 of *The Celestial Hierarchy* (*P.G.*, III, col. 141), the Areopagite notes that Scripture refers to the Hierarchy in both a positive and negative way. Moreover, he says that it is this second way that is the more suitable, for we know only that the Hierarchy exists in a way that is not like the mode of existence of anything else and we are ignorant of its supersubstantial indivisibility. If, then, in the case of divine realities negations are true and affirmations are inadequate, it is better for us to represent such realities by gross rather than by noble images. This text is commented on by Saint Thomas in the *De Potentia*, 7, 5, ad 2, which can be thus summarized: While Dionysius says that negations are true, he does not say that affirmations are false, but that they are inadequate. The affirmation that God is wise is true in the case of God insofar as the perfection signified is concerned; in some way or other wisdom exists in God. But as far as the limited mode is concerned which wisdom always has in this life, wisdom can be denied of God in an absolute sense.

[12] *Pensées*, Number 862 in the standard edition by Brunschvicg, 3 vol. (Paris: 1904).

[13] *Ibid.*, Number 353.

[14] Since the time of Abelard theological procedure in the West takes its point of departure in the antithetical process of *Sic et Non*. Accordingly each article of the *Summa Theologica* of Saint Thomas can be viewed as a resolved antinomy.

[15] To this level belongs the now lost *Outlines of Divinity* where the Areopagite explains, as he himself tells us in his *Mystical Theology*, Chapter 3 (*P.G.*, III, col. 1033), "those conceptions which are most proper to the affirmative method, and . . . in what sense God's holy nature is called single and in what sense trinal, what is the nature of the Fatherhood and Sonship which we attribute unto It; what is meant by the articles of faith concerning the Spirit . . . ; in what manner Jesus being above all essence has stooped to an essential state in which all the truths of human nature meet; and all the other revelations of Scripture whereof my *Outlines of Divinity* treat." The translation of this passage is taken from *Dionysius the Areopagite on the Divine Names and the Mystical Theology* translated by C. E. Rolt (New York: 1920), pp. 196–197. To this level also belongs the theological treatises dealing with the Divine Names in which theologians explain how God can be called goodness, being, life, wisdom, power, and so forth. The negative way is frequently used in such treatises.

[16] See *Summa Theologica* II–II, 1, 2.

[17] A. Gardeil, *Le donné révélé et la théologie*, 2nd edition (Juvisy: 1932), pp. 144–145.

[18] See *Summa Theologica* I, 1, 9.

[19] *Ibid.*, ad 2. The translation is taken from *Summa Theologica* tr. by Fathers of the English Dominican Province (New York: 1947), I, p. 6.

[20] *Mystical Theology*, Chapter 3 (*P.G.*, III, col. 1033).

[21] Book I, Chapter 11 (*P.G.*, XCIV, cols. 841 and 844).

22 Homily on the Transfiguration of Our Lord, Number 8 (P.G., XCVI, col. 560). A little farther on is found this beautiful text: "A person who has come to the summit of love and in some sort has gone out from himself knows the Invisible. Flying through the dark cloud of corporeal things, with his soul established in peace, he fixes his attention in the most penetrating manner possible on the Sun of Justice, never, however, becoming surfeited by this sight." Ibid., Number 10 (col. 562). Concerning this text let us note that we know God who is invisible and this in spite of the darkness of corporeal things that is interposed between us and Him. This is the traditional teaching and not the Palamite doctrine which Vladimir Lossky attributes to the Saint in "La théologie de la Lumière chez saint Grégoire de Thessalonique (Palamas)" in Dieu Vivant, 1945, number 1, p. 111. According to Palamas' doctrine the triune God would be as near to our senses as He is to our minds.

23 The Divine Names, Chapter 1, Number 4 (P.G., III, col. 592).

24 Scholia for the Book of The Divine Names (P.G., IV, col. 192).

25 Saint Thomas, De Divinis Nominibus, Chapter 1, Lesson 2 towards the end. Nevertheless, even according to Saint Thomas, another interpretation is possible. "Just as," he says, "when I see a living being, I can say that I see life insofar as I perceive manifestations of that life, so will it be in the divine vision. The splendor of the new heaven, the new earth, and the glorified bodies will be such that it can be said that we shall see God by their means as it were with our bodily eyes." In Evangelium S. Matthaei Commentaria, Chapter 5, Number 2; see also Summa Theologica, I, 12, 3, ad 2. The same teaching is already found in Saint Augustine: "Wherever we turn the spiritual eyes of our bodies, we shall see even in the world of bodies the incorporeal God who rules them." The City of God, Book 22, Chapter 29.

It was, we believe, in the name of these magnificent remarks of Saint Augustine and Saint Thomas, that the monk Barlaam, in some degree at least, should have met the challenge of Palamas according to whom we shall see the glory of God with the eyes of our flesh.

26 This whole controversy is detailed by Martin Jugie in his two articles "Palamas (Grégoire)" and "Palamite (controverse)" to be found in the Dictionnaire de Théologie edited by A. Vacant, E. Magenot, and E. Amann (Paris: 1923 and on). The same author has also discussed the controversy in his Theologia Dogmatica Christianorum Orientalium (Paris: 1926–1933), I, pp. 431 ff. and especially II, pp. 47 ff.

27 Homily on the Transfiguration, Number 2 (P.G., XCVI, col. 548).

28 Ibid., Number 13 (col. 565).

29 Sermon on the Transfiguration (P.G., XCVII, col. 949). See also a preceding remark made in the same sermon (col. 941).

30 Vladimir Lossky in his Essai sur la théologie mystique de l'Église d'Orient (Aubier: 1944), p. 221, writes: "The Transfiguration was not a phenomenon circumscribed by time and space; there was no change at this moment in Christ, not even in His human nature; there was only a change in the consciousness of the Apostles, who received for a brief time the faculty to see their Master as He really was, shining with the eternal light of His divinity."

But if it were true that at the moment of the Transfiguration the Body of Christ was not really changed, if it were true that it did not pass from a passible state to a glorious state, if it were true that Christ's Body was constantly transfigured and glorious, then we would have to conclude that the passible state of Christ, the suffering and the death of Christ, were illusions, since they consisted only in appearances. Thereby we would rejoin the very ancient error of Docetism.

Moreover such an opinion on the Transfiguration was certainly not the unanimous teaching of the Oriental Church. Speaking of that mystery, for instance, Saint Cyril of Alexandria remarks that Christ was then "transformed by an excellent and divine splendor." *Homily on the Transfiguration* (P.G., LXXVII, col. 1011). Basil of Seleucia is of no other opinion: "While the disciples considered what had taken place, suddenly Christ was transformed before them. His appearance changed, and clothed in a tunic of light, He afforded them a brilliant sight." *Sermon on the Transfiguration of the Lord*, Number 2 (P.G., LXXXV, col. 457).

[31] See *Summa Theologica* III, 8, 1, ad 2.

[32] Father Schwalm in his *Leçons de philosophie sociale* (Paris: 1910), I, pp. 104–106, has decried the error of those who would reduce collective personalities to fictional persons: "The error is clear: a collective being does not exist separated from the individuals which compose it; nevertheless it is distinct from those individuals taken separately. It is a whole, subsisting by itself, having the nature and the operations of a whole, as Saint Thomas tells us. Hence a social personality is not fictional, but something real." To be entirely precise we must say, as Cardinal Zigliara has already done, that only perfect societies properly deserve the name of person. See the remarks in *Nova et Vetera*, 1936, p. 63.

[33] *Summa Theologica* I, 29, 3 and ad 4.

[34] *Ibid.*, III, 48, 2, ad 1. The translation for this and the preceding citation is taken from *Summa Theologica* tr. by Fathers of the English Dominican Province (New York: 1947).

[35] *Ibid.*, III, 19, 4.

[36] See the articles in *Nova et Vetera*, 1941, pp. 214, 432, and 442; 1942, p. 62.

[37] The Fourth Council of the Lateran has defined it as "a union of charity in grace." See Denziger, *op. cit.*, Number 432. Also see the remarks in *Nova et Vetera*, 1936, pp. 67 and 85.

[38] We are not speaking here of transcendental perfections—truth, goodness, wisdom, and so forth—which are in God formally and eminently.

CHAPTER 3

[1] See Charles Journet, *L'Église du Verbe incarné* (Paris: 1941), I, 149.

[2] See Number 3 of Cajetan's commentary on *Summa Theologica*, I, 1, 4.

[3] "The machinery of controversy," says Paul Claudel, "and the enormous apparatus of catechetics are the strange but blessed paths—coast roads, bridges, passes, tunnels—all of which lead to Rome . . . their only purpose is to bring us to a consent that will be as free as grace itself is, free

as any agreement between man and man." *La messe là-bas* (Paris: 1919).

⁴ Following Aristotle, Saint Thomas distinguishes enunciative discourse which the scientist uses from the forms of discourse which the orator and the poet use who attempt to lead us to consent to what they say "not only because of what is proper to the thing under discussion but also by taking into account the dispositions of their listeners and by attempting to move their feelings." *In Libros Perihermeneias Expositio*, Book I, Chapter 4, Lesson VII, Numbers 5 and 6. See also M.-R. Gagnebet, O.P., "Le problème actuel de la théologie et la science aristotélicienne," *Divus Thomas* (Piacenza), 1943, p. 265.

⁵ In the *Prologue of the Sentences*, 1, 5, Saint Thomas describes from different points of view the various modes of procedure to be found in sacred doctrine which he calls theology (in the wide sense of any consideration about God). If, for example, one considers its principles, the credibility of these is guaranteed us by the accounts of miracles (historical mode); the truth contained in these principles is often given to us under the veil of metaphors, symbols, and parables (hence the metaphorical mode). If one considers the use which theology makes of these principles, it will be seen that it adopts different methods of procedure in accordance with its varying intentions of destroying errors (argumentative mode), of directing morals (preceptive mode in the Mosaic Law, mode of threats and promises in the Prophets, narrative mode in the historical books), or of leading to contemplation by studying the different senses of Scripture, etc.

⁶ Saint Thomas, *Prologue to the Sentences*, 1, 5, ad 3.

⁷ It is necessary to assign a double cause to the manifestation of revealed truth. First there are the prophetic graces which are ordered directly to the instruction and the salvation of one's neighbor; secondly, there are the sanctifying graces which are directly ordered to the progress of the soul which receives them and which, by their superabundance, overflow and lead to the instruction and the salvation of the neighbor. See Saint Thomas, *Summa Theologica*, I–II, 111, 1.

⁸ This is the problem which is posited by Saint Thomas in his Prologue to the *Summa Theologica*.

⁹ "When Saint Thomas asks [in the *Summa Theologica*, I, 1, 1] 'Whether sacred doctrine is a science,' his question really means this: Is it possible that Christian teaching which embraces more than one function and more than one mode and which includes with Scripture other forms or acts, should be in one of its functions a science; in other words, in one of its modes is it possible for Christian teaching to have a scientific quality?" M.-J. Congar, O.P., "Sur la théologie," *Bulletin Thomiste*, 1938, Number 8, p. 499. Saint Thomas himself uses the phrase "Theology which pertains to sacred doctrine . . ." in *Summa Theologica*, I, 1, 1, ad 2.

¹⁰ See Saint Augustine, *Defense of Baptism against the Donatists*, Book I, Chapter 8 (*P.L.*, XLIII, col. 43).

¹¹ See *Summa Theologica*, II–II, 39, 2.

¹² Taken from the article "*Schisme*" in the *Dictionnaire de Théologie Catholique*.

¹³ Saint Thomas in *Quodlibet*, IV, q. 9, a. 18 says: "One kind of disputation has as its purpose the removal of doubt concerning the existence

of a thing; such a disputation in the realm of theology makes especial use of authorities whom the opponents will accept. . . . There is however in the schools also a magisterial disputation the purpose of which is not to dispel error but to instruct the students by leading them to an understanding of the truth which is being discussed. . . ."

[14] Father Ferdinand Cavallera, in connection with the expressions positive doctrine and scholastic doctrine, refers to the eleventh rule of orthodoxy of Saint Ignatius: "To praise positive and scholastic doctrine; for, as it is characteristic of the positive Doctors such as Saint Jerome, Saint Augustine, Saint Gregory and others to arouse the affections and to lead men to love and serve God our Lord with their whole strength, so the principal purpose of the scholastics like Saint Thomas, Saint Bonaventure, the Master of the *Sentences*, and those who have followed them is to define and to explain according to the needs of modern times the things that are necessary for eternal salvation and to attack and clearly point out the errors and false reasonings of the enemies of the Church. . . ." The same author, after emphasizing the extremely varied use of the expression positive theology, concludes that it is "the notion of documentation that is the real but confused notion that underlies all these different uses; it alone can justify the application of the same name to so many disparate realities." "La théologie positive," *Bulletin de Littérature Ecclésiastique*, 1925, p. 21.

[15] Saint Thomas in *Summa Theologica*, I, 1, 3 uses the phrase "divinely revealed" (*divinitus revelata*) or "divinely revealable" (*divinitus revelabilia*). "The word *revelabile*, like *scibile*, *credibile*, *sensibile*, *amabile*, was formed to designate a certain order of objects; in this case . . . [it signifies] everything that is able to be known by the light of revelation. This equivalence is given by Saint Thomas himself in Article 4, when he uses the phrase 'prout sunt divino lumine cognoscibilia.' " Congar, *Sur la théologie*, p. 496.

CHAPTER 4

[1] See *Summa Theologica*, I, 1, 8.

[2] "By setting out from things which we know by adhering to the First Truth, we pass on to the knowledge of other realities in a manner that is proper to us, that is, by a discursive process from principles to conclusions." Saint Thomas, *In Boethium de Trinitate*, 2, 2.

[3] ". . . the principles of a demonstration can be considered apart, without the conclusions being considered at all. Again, they can be considered together with the conclusions, since the conclusions can be deduced from them. Accordingly, to consider the principles in this second way, belongs to science, which considers the conclusions also: while to consider the principles in themselves belongs to understanding." Saint Thomas, *Summa Theologica*, I–II, 57, 2, ad 2. The translation is taken from *Summa Theologica*, tr. by Fathers of the English Dominican Province (New York: 1947), I, 829. "The faithful can be said to have the science of those things which can be concluded to from the articles of faith." Saint Thomas, *De Veritate*, 14, 9, ad 3.

4 *Prologue to the Sentences*, 1, 3, 2, ad 3.

5 *In Boethium de Trinitate*, 2, 2.

6 "It matters little whether the mediate predicates (which are explained by predicates that are immediately revealed) are themselves formally or only virtually revealed. . . . The light of virtual revelation can give a scientific explanation of a truth that is formally revealed by means of another truth that is equally formally revealed." M.-R. Gagnebet, "*La nature de la théologie spéculative*," *Revue Thomiste*, 1938, pp. 234 and 238. The author gives several examples of cases in which Saint Thomas finds the scientific explanation of one dogma of faith in another dogma. The same teaching is found in M.-J. Congar, *art. cit.*, *Bulletin Thomiste*, pp. 500-503.

7 Like metaphysical or mathematical deduction, theological deduction proceeds from a reality known under one notion to the same reality known under another notion; it supposes a real identity of meaning and of conceptual progress and consequently it supposes an homogeneous development and growth. See Saint Thomas, *In Boethium de Trinitate*, 6, 1, ad 3. On the real homogeneity of the formally revealed which is the object of faith and of the virtually revealed which is the object of theology, as well as for the specific distinction between faith and theology, see F. Marin-Sola, O.P., *L'évolution homogène du dogme catholique* (Fribourg: 1924), I, 36-38; 65-67.

8 For example, if one admits that the Holy Spirit does not proceed by way of intelligence but by way of love, one can thereby deduce—and it is revealed—that He is not generated and can not be called a son. See Saint Thomas, *Summa Theologica*, I, 27, 4. Another example would be this: If one admits that the sacramental characters are participations in the sacerdotal power of Christ and that as such they are reducible to spiritual qualities of the second class (*potentiae*) and not of the first class (*habitus*), one can thereby deduce—and this too is revealed—that they can not be lost. See Saint Thomas, *ibid.*, III, 63, 2 and 5.

9 Jacques Maritain, *Science and Wisdom*, tr. by Bernard Wall (New York: 1940), pp. 236-237.

10 These words are taken from Saint Augustine, *De Trinitate*, Book XIV, Chapter 1, Number 3 (*P.L.*, XLIV, col. 1037). The Saint explains in this place that while faith is necessary for all men, the science which fosters faith in the good and defends it against the impious is not the possession of all. This science is, according to Saint Thomas, sacred doctrine (see *Summa Theologica*, I, 1, 2, *sed contra*); more precisely it is theology.

11 "Whatever the truth you treat of, it is difficult not to enter the sphere of theology, since it is the center of all truths." Pascal, *Entretien avec M. de Saci*.

12 The attacks of Luther and Erasmus have been summarized by M.-R. Gagnebet, "*La nature de la théologie spéculative*," *Revue Thomiste*, 1938, pp. 645-674.

13 *In Boethium de Trinitate*, 2, 1.

14 *Ibid.*

15 *Ibid.* One can read at this point the profound and well-weighed teach-

ing of Saint Thomas on the virtue of studiousness and the contrary vice of curiosity in *Summa Theologica*, II–II, 166 and 167.

[16] In *Boethium de Trinitate*, 2, 1, ad 7.

[17] *Ibid.*, ad 7.

[18] Some examples of such directive intuitions would be our concept of the Incarnation, which would involve the ontological causality of the sacred humanity of Christ and ultimately of the sacraments; likewise the conception of the dependence of our activity on the motion of God which is as profound as the dependence of our being on the Being of God; the concept according to which the Body of Christ and the Church are really identical or according to which the words *society* and *authority* can be applied to the Church and to the State in an analogous, not a univocal manner; finally the manner in which it is necessary to conceive the relations of nature and of grace—for instance, to what point must we descend in man to find this nature which grace does not destroy but perfects?

[19] "I gain devotion in such reading and by it I can more easily ascend to speculation. The heart is there enabled to grow in devotion; and the mind, by the merit of this devotion, is raised to the highest levels." *Life of Saint Thomas* by William de Tocco, Chapter 22.

[20] Canonization Process of Naples 1319, Deposition of William de Tocco.

[21] Father Gagnebet in his article *"La nature de la théologie spéculative,"* pp. 16 and 17, speaks of theology insofar as it is the systematization or the science of those things which order us to the fruition of God and places this systematization under the name of Augustinianism (although to our mind it coincides, in the measure in which it is legitimate, with the practical part of theology). And when Father Gagnebet says of this systematization or science that it is strengthened by mystical wisdom, we think this should be applied to all theology which is eminently speculative and practical, and even more speculative than practical. As far as the wisdom of Saint Augustine is concerned, we have seen that it is the pure gift of wisdom operating with a sovereign liberty and utilizing all possible means among which must be enumerated theology in its inchoative state. "With Saint Augustine, by the very degree to which it is absorbed in the discursive movement of a higher wisdom which is not in itself discursive, theology is still, in relation to its own proper and human mode as a science, in a state of imperfection." Jacques Maritain, *The Degrees of Knowledge*, p. 372.

[22] Noële and Robert Boulet, *Romée* (Paris: 1936), p. 782.

[23] For other examples see Marin-Sola, *L'évolution homogène*, I, 300 ff.

[24] The notion of relation can be found realized in its place among the other categories of being; such would be, for example, relations of equality, similitude, fatherhood and sonship, and so forth. These are accidental relations. But the notion of relation has exceptional privileges or properties. First of all, the notion of relation continues to exist even when it is deprived of all reality and thus passes into the purely logical world. These are logical relations or relations of reason. We can see this, if we consider the relation between the idea of being and the idea of nothingness or

between the idea of genus and the idea of species. Secondly, the notion of relation continues to exist when the process is reversed by intensifying its reality until its reality is made to coincide with that of the Absolute. This, however, can be known only by revelation, for it is a mystery of the Christian faith. There are, then, in God relations of paternity, of sonship, of procession; and they are subsistent relations.

25 *Sermon XXIX,* Number 16 (*P.G.,* XXXVI, col. 96).

26 In connection with the axiom that two realities that are identical with a third reality are also identical with each other, Aristotle had already remarked that the saying is true when the two realities are identified both in reality and in the mind (*re et ratione*) with the same third reality, but that it is not valid when the two realities which are really identified with the same third reality nevertheless differ from it in the mind and are opposed, not to this third reality, but to themselves by a relative opposition. There is one and the same road between Athens and Thebes, but one can begin it either at Athens or at Thebes, in which case there is a real opposition. Between the road taken in itself and the road considered as beginning at Athens, there is a real identity but also a distinction of reason. See Aristotle, *Physics,* Book III, Chapter 3. See also the commentary of Saint Thomas on this passage, Lesson V, Numbers 11 and 13; also note the application which he makes of this text to the life of the Trinity, *Summa Theologica,* I, 28, 3, *ad* 1. Similarly we could say that the three angles of an equilateral triangle are identified in the same surface, but remain distinct by their relations of opposition.

27 *Sermon XXXI* (*P.G.,* XXXVI, col. 141).

28 *Letter to Cledonius against Apollinaris* (*P.G.,* XXXVII, col. 180).

29 "In God there are no accidents, for He is not mutable; nevertheless, not everything that is said of God is said after the manner of a substance, since there is something relative in God; the Father is relative to the Son and the Son to the Father. This relation is not an accident because the Father was always the Father and the Son always the Son. . . ." *The Trinity,* Book VI, Chapter 6 (*P.L.,* XLII, col. 914).

30 The Provincial Council of Toledo as cited in Denziger, *op. cit.,* Number 280.

31 The Fourth Council of the Lateran as cited in Denziger, *op. cit.,* Number 432.

32 Cited in Denziger, *op. cit.,* Number 703.

33 On the intervention of the teaching power of the Church and on the importance of her definitions, see Marin-Sola, *L'évolution homogène,* I, pp. 173 ff.

34 See footnote 10 of this chapter.

35 *Proslogion,* Chapter 2 (*P.L.,* CLVIII, col. 227). Saint Anselm is thinking here of a new proof for the existence of God which he intends to propose and the key to which he believed himself to have found in his meditations on the aseity of God. In the *Monologion,* however, he attempts to gain an understanding of the Trinity; he attempts, therefore, a theology, and that of the highest kind—a Trinitarian theology.

36 At times Saint Augustine seems to explain this text by referring to a

passage from a lower faith to a higher one. See *Sermon XLIII* (P.L., XXXIX, col. 1830) and *Sermon CXXVI* (P.L., XXXIX, col. 1994).

[37] Claudel, *La messe là-bas*.

[38] *Christ the Savior* tr. by Dom Bede Rose, O.S.B. (St. Louis: 1950), pp. 629-630.

[39] Saint Thomas, *Summa Theologica*, I, 19, 2.

[40] *Ibid.*, III, 1, 1.

[41] *Ibid.*, III, 1, 3, ad 3.

[42] *Ibid.*, III, 65, 1.

[43] *Ibid.*, I, 27, 1.

[44] *Ibid.*, I, 27, 3.

[45] *Ibid.*, I, 27, 5, ad 3; 34, 2, ad 4.

[46] *Ibid.*, I, 27, 3.

[47] *De Deo Trino et Creatore* (Turin: 1943), p. 67.

[48] See *Summa Theologica*, I, 32, 1, ad 2. To put the Augustinian and Thomistic theology of the Trinity on the level of metaphor would be to misunderstand these arguments from fittingness. This remark touches the fundamental reproach which, in his *Le Rôle de l'analogie en théologie dogmatique* (Paris: 1931), pp. 295-311, T.-L. Penido makes against the otherwise valuable *Études de théologie positive sur la Sainte-Trinité* by Th. de Regnon (Paris: 1892-1898).

[49] *Letter CXX*, Chapter 1, Number 2 (P.L., XXXIII, col. 453).

[50] *Ibid.*, Number 3 (col. 453).

[51] Isaias 7, 9 according to the Septuagint version.

[52] *Letter CXX*, Chapter 1, Number 3. This passage is at the center of the reflections of Pascal, who himself refers to the *Letter*: "The reason would never submit, if it did not judge that there are times when it ought to submit. It is right, then, that it should submit when it judges that it should do so." *Pensées*, Number 270 in the edition of Brunschvicg. "To submit and to use reason, this is what true Christianity consists in." (*Ibid.*, Number 269).

There is first of all a use of reason whereby it shows us that it is not unreasonable but highly reasonable to believe the suprarational mysteries of Christianity; this is the level of the motives of credibility. Then comes the submission of reason, which under the impulsion of divine grace believes these mysteries; this is the level of supernatural faith. Finally there is a new use of reason when it seeks to understand better what it believes—*fides quaerens intellectum*; this is the level of theology.

The second quotation from Pascal which we gave above was misprinted in the small edition of the *Pensées* edited by Brunschvicg in 1912 and read thus: "To submit is to use the reason." Nevertheless it too expresses what Saint Augustine and Pascal held to be true. The submission of faith is an adherence of the intellect when it is profoundly stirred by the divine impulsion. To submit is not to betray my intellect. Rather it is the supernatural use which God makes of my reason when it assents to His infinite Truth.

[53] *Letter CXX*, Chapter 1, Number 4 (cols. 453-454).

[54] *Ibid.*, Number 5 (col. 454).

[55] *Ibid.*, Number 6 (cols. 454-455).

[56] *Ibid.*, Chapter 2, Number 7 (col. 455).

[57] *Ibid.*, Number 8 (col. 456).

[58] *Ibid.*, Chapter 3, Number 13 (cols. 458–459).

[59] *The Trinity*, Book XV, Chapter 28, Number 51 (*P.L.*, XLII, col. 1098). The translation is taken from *Basic Writings of Saint Augustine* ed. by Whitney J. Oates (New York: 1948), II, p. 877.

[60] Henri de Lubac, *Corpus Mysticum, L'Eucharistie et l'Église au moyen âge* (Paris: 1944), p. 269.

CHAPTER 5

[1] See Chapter 3, footnote 14.

[2] "Holy Scripture and Tradition are not primarily collections of arguments to be used in scholastic disputations and in defense of contested conclusions; primarily they are something given us to be studied, known, and loved for their own sake; all further speculations would be vain unless they led us to a better knowledge of what is contained in Scripture and Tradition in all the aspects of its religious intelligibility." M.-D. Chenu, *Une école de théologie* (Le Saulchoir: 1937), p. 55.

This "religious intelligibility" can be either doctrinal or historical. It is clear that topological exposition is only a point of departure. Since the purpose of doctrinal theology is to order the ensemble of revealed truths among themselves, it will create a spiritual area or perspective in which each of the doctrines and documents of Scripture and of Tradition can spontaneously assume their full dimensions. And, as we shall point out later (see Chapter 6, Number 11), theology will not reach its completion except by becoming historical and descending to the successive events of salvation in order to explain them.

[3] Some of these places manifest the revealed deposit in an absolute and irreformable manner: the Sovereign Pontiff alone, or united with the bishops dispersed throughout the world, or united with the bishops assembled in Council. Others of these places manifest the revealed deposit only in a prudential way: the Fathers and the Doctors. And we need not mention that whoever does the greater, can also perform the lesser.

[4] "The Catholic theologian must choose between two methods: the first is historical and progressive; it reconstructs theology by setting out from the original primitive data as these are found in documentary sources. The second method is regressive; it begins with the historical term of the evolution of Tradition; this it regards as something already acquired and through it goes back to the sources." Ambroise Gardeil, "*Idée d'une méthode régressive*," *Revue Thomiste*, 1903, p. 19. The author cites the story of two explorers, one of whom traced the Congo back to its sources; the other, wishing to make better time, set out from the watershed and likewise found himself at the Nile.

[5] "With the help of God our Lord and to the best of our ability, we shall attempt to show . . . the reason why the Trinity is the one true God. . . . But we will first have to show by the authority of Holy Scripture that this is a matter of our faith." *The Trinity*, Book I, Chapter 2, Number 4 (*P.L.*, XLII, col. 822).

6 *In Boethium de Trinitate, Prologus.*

7 *Quodlibet,* 4, 9, 18.

8 *In Boethium de Trinitate, Prooemii explanatio.*

9 *Ibid.* This text is borrowed from *De Utilitate Credendi,* Chapter 11, Number 25, where Saint Augustine contrasts three general attitudes of the human mind, understanding, faith, and opinion: "What we understand, we owe to reason; what we believe, we owe to faith; what we think [opinion], to error" (*P.L.,* XLII, col. 83).

10 *In Boethium de Trinitate, Prooemii explanatio.*

11 Cited in Denziger, *op. cit.,* Number 1796. The translation is taken from Dom Cuthbert Butler, *The Vatican Council* (New York: 1930), II, p. 265.

12 J. Mansi, *Sacrorum Conciliorum Collectio,* L, col. 84-85.

13 Analogy can be used on the occasion of a revealed proposition the meaning of which is metaphorical (God sleeps) or on the occasion of a revealed proposition the meaning of which is literal (God generates).

14 We can distinguish here the domain of teaching from that of research.

In the domain of teaching: 1) the Church has legislated that professors in seminaries should teach philosophy and theology according to the method, doctrine, and principles of the Angelic Doctor, *Code of Canon Law,* Canon 1366, 2; 2) she prefers that the teaching be faithful on all points to the methods, doctrine, and principles of Saint Thomas and for this purpose has proposed the twenty-four theses as "safe directive norms"; 3) she permits a teaching whose fidelity to Saint Thomas is understood in a larger sense. On this last point see the article *"Jésuites"* in the *Dictionnaire de Théologie Catholique,* cols. 1041–1042.

In the domain of research: 1) the Church earnestly desires that research in the ceaseless work of understanding and extending Christian philosophy and theology should be based on a strict fidelity to Saint Thomas and should use the weapons prepared by him. The more one experiences the urgency of the problems of our time and the need to extend and renew the way in which the Christian mind grasps reality, the more one realizes that this task can be done only through Saint Thomas. 2) Nevertheless, as long as the faith is safeguarded, each one, though at his own risk and peril, is free to found a theological system by the aid of a philosophy other than that of Saint Thomas. But each one is also warned that such an enterprise is dangerous. 3) This danger becomes greater as one separates farther from Saint Thomas in those points in which his philosophy is nearest to natural, simple intelligence which constitutes the philosophical propaedeutic of common sense.

15 Strange as it may seem, laymen were the first and almost the only ones, according to the statement of Pius XI in September, 1938, to protest against anti-Semitism. They did this not only in the name of the natural law but also in the name of the supernatural vocation of the people of Israel. (On another level, is it not remarkable that it was not Bossuet, but a layman, Fustel de Coulanges, who best understood the role of religion in the political practices of the Romans?)

In our own times, we know of several strictly theological views (for example, the role of the gifts of the Holy Spirit in prayer, the nature of the theological work of Saint Augustine, the interpretation of difficult passages in Saint John of the Cross) which have been accepted by many theologians with full recognition, although these views were due (by a sort of super-abundance on their part) to laymen who nevertheless firmly desired to remain faithful to their vocation, which is to give testimony to the faith on the temporal level.

16 The same remarks hold for theological systems. From the first the science of theology is accompanied by opinions and hypotheses. As a science, there can be no doubt that it is interested only in demonstration; the criterion of its certitude is demonstration. Concretely, however, it may happen that the preoccupation and perspective which orientate its chain of demonstrations can deflect these demonstrations to different, even opposed meanings. Hence the anomaly of a plurality of theological systems, all of which maintain they are scientifically deduced. "It is the whole of theological science that each of these great systems pretends to offer together with its own hypothetical prolongations; and, as a matter of fact, each does offer this science but with greater or lesser success." M. Labourdette, "La théologie, intelligence de la foi," Revue Thomiste, 1946, p. 40.

17 The purpose of the teaching power of the Church is to give authentic declarations of the deposit of faith, which was revealed to the primitive Church by means of Scripture and Tradition. In this task the Church always has assistance. At times this assistance is infallible in an absolute and irreformable way; at other times this assistance is infallible in a merely prudential way; at still other times it is not infallible at all. On all this, see Charles Journet, L'Église du Verbe Incarné, I, 397 ff.

18 This is the place to recall the views of Father Clerissac: "When the dreamer of a great religious work is a man of great sensibility, he caresses this work as the fruit of his personal art; as a true artist he endows it with subtle exigencies and febrile impulses. But the works of God are fruits of reason and wisdom and, further, they must be such that they cannot be attributable to caprice, nor even to the genius of the human artist. Thus God gives the artist the honour of foreshadowing and announcing the work, but He reserves its accomplishment to His Church and often by more humble instruments. This trial, this law of purification of what is human and individual is imposed upon ideas as well as upon works." The Mystery of the Church (New York: 1937), p. 107.

19 "Truth, which is inaccessible to the individual, becomes accessible only to the collective thinking of many who are united in love. This characteristic makes the teaching of the Orthodox Church conspicuously distinct from the teaching of any other faith." A. S. Khomiakov, "A propos des fragments de Kireïevski," as cited in Nova et Vetera, 1945, p. 264. The opposition between the individualism of Western thinking and the collectivism of Eastern thinking is the point of departure of Soloviev's thesis in La crise de la philosophie occidentale. On this see Nova et Vetera, loc. cit., p. 263.

Father Schwalm often insisted on the social character of doctrinal elaboration. For example, in his study, "Les deux théologies: la scolastique et la positive," Revue Thomiste, 1908, p. 681, he points out: "Since it involves both a conservation and an assimilation, the development of doctrine of its nature is associated with a series of generations. As in the Church, so in this development we can nowhere say that it is the dead who are speaking; for these are resurrected and rejuvenated in the expressions used by the living. Saint Augustine still speaks to us—and his thought is also ours—on the intimate excitation and prevenience of grace; the faith, study, and piety of Catholics will always be nourished by his thoughts, without ever exhausting them. Harnack was impressed by our Augustinian mysticism, but Augustine was more than Augustine in this legacy of his soul to the soul of every Catholic. His interior religion still remains nutritive for us, only because he fed himself the pure food of the original revelation. His religion was nourished by Saint Paul, who in turn was nourished by Jesus. Hence it is that the dogmatic testimony and the moral influence of the Fathers come to us as social products. This was essential if they were to pass down to us through the course of time. Their teaching was elaborated by a continued collaboration with Christ the Revealer. The ancients did not consider us, and for the most part we do not know the ancients; nevertheless, the thoughts which they expressed circulate in the Church; from soul to soul, they transmit their impulses and excite life. Because He is always present in His Church, it is Christ, the first Author of these thoughts, who unifies their development by giving them a continued meaning which always agrees with His own."

20 The expression is found in *De Veritate*, 14, 9, ad 3.

21 Saint Thomas, *Summa Theologica*, I, 1, 2.

22 "He [a theologian] is not said to have a science of those things which he supposes, but of the conclusions which are necessarily deduced from these presupposed principles." *De Veritate*, 14, 9, ad 3.

23 *Summa Theologica*, I, 32, 1, ad 2.

24 Note some of the expressions which the Church uses: "The perpetual sense of the Catholic Church held and now holds. . . ." "It was always held in the Church. . . ." It would be inexact to say that the Church was ignorant of something which she implicitly believed. On this see Marin-Sola, *op. cit.*, I, 257.

25 "Like a kind of impression of the divine knowledge which, though one and simple, extends to all things." (Saint Thomas, *Summa Theologica*, I, 1, 4, ad 2).

26 "By a proper, though slight, participation." (Number 5 of Cajetan's commentary on *Summa Theologica*, I, 1, 4).

27 Saint Thomas, *Summa Theologica*, I, 1, 4.

28 Father Gagnebet in "Le problème actuel" (following Cajetan in his commentary on the *Posterior Analytics*, Chapter 25) distinguishes the formal subject as the being of which a science seeks perfect knowledge from the formal object (quod), which in turn is the judgment expressing this knowledge. Nevertheless in his commentary on the *Summa* Cajetan himself, speaking with less rigor, says that God under the aspect of His deity is both the formal object (quod) and the formal subject of theology. See Cajetan, *In Summam Theologicam*, I, 1, 3, number 9; I, 1, 7, number 1.

29 "Everything is considered in sacred doctrine in relation to God, either because the thing considered is God or has an order to God as to its Principle and End." Saint Thomas, *Summa Theologica*, I, 1, 7.

[30] Theology, says Saint Thomas, treats of all these things: types and realities, the works of reparation, the whole Christ, that is, the Head and His members, "but insofar as they are referred to God," *Summa Theologica*, I, 1, 7. Father Gagnebet, "*Le problème actuel*," p. 251, emphasizes this forcefully: "The first subject (the formal subject) of a science is a simple notion which does not imply any anterior notion and which is implied in all other notions of the science. But in the whole Christ there is implied the notion of the Deity who is anterior to It but who does not imply the whole Christ. It is then the Deity and not Christ as God who is the formal subject of theology. Moreover, it is important to note that there is nothing more exclusive than a formal object. If the whole Christ insofar as He is God is the formal subject of theology, then the Incarnate Word insofar as He subsists in His divine nature is the primary object of theology; the other Divine Persons become secondary objects to be considered only in Their relation to Christ. It would be necessary to explain the mystery of the Trinity, the mystery of the divine perfections, and so forth by the mystery of the Incarnate Word."

[31] Saint Thomas, *Summa Theologica*, I, Prologue to Question 2.

[32] Jacques Maritain, *La philosophie de la nature* (Paris: 1935), pp. 38–75.

[33] *Ibid.*, p. 75.

[34] "Discourse to the Society of Jesus," September 17, 1946, *Acta Apostolicae Sedis*, 1946, p. 385.

[35] "This science can receive something from philosophy . . . not, however, as though from a superior; rather it uses philosophy as an inferior and a servant. . . . The fact that it uses philosophy is not to be attributed to any defect or insufficiency in theology, but to a defect of our intellect. For by the things which are known by our natural reason, the intellect is more easily led to those things above reason which this science considers." Saint Thomas, *Summa Theologica*, I, 1, 5, ad 2.

[36] Denziger, *op. cit.*, Number 1790.

[37] *Ibid.*, Numbers 1635, 1794, 1799.

[38] *Ibid.*, Number 1169.

[39] Saint Thomas, *Summa Theologica*, I, 43.

[40] This is the way in which "the theology of the missions" is understood by Father de Menasce at Fribourg and Father de Lubac at Lyons.

From the first author we shall quote a few lines of the article "*Polarité de l'action missionnaire*," *Nouvelle Revue de Science Missionnaire*, 1945, pp. 81–87: "When it is a question of building up the Church, faith must be the foundation; and it must be a living faith. Only if there is a superabundance of such faith in the missionary, will the Church be able to expand with the degree of intensity required by the infant state which is that of the mission. . . . We are speaking of the fullness of this life of faith as a condition for a certain kind of preaching, namely, the apostolic preaching which penetrates for the first time into an inert or a hostile matter. . . . Doubtless we cannot demand that all missionaries should be contemplative to an equal degree nor apostolic from the same abundance of such contemplation; neither should we decry the role of action in the matter of the missions. But it seems to us that the tone should be set by this apostolic spirit in the sense in which this spirit is defined by theology.

. . . More than ever before, the apostolate of today should be one in which the values of the spirit and hence of supernatural faith, should hold first place; our struggle is not on a practical level, but on the level of truth. In saying this, however, let us not forget that supernatural truth is eminently practical."

As for Father de Lubac, one should read his *Le fondement théologique des missions* (Paris: 1946). It is a work of intelligence and faith, the writing of which was, moreover, an act of courage. We shall note the answers which Father de Lubac there gives to two or three questions of importance to missionary theology.

a. What is the purpose of missionary activity? Father de Lubac points out that "the charter for the foundation of the Church" is also "the charter for the foundation of the missions." And he notes that "in the person of the Twelve, the Church herself is sent." "The Church is essentially missionary because what we call her missions is nothing else than the primary means by which she accomplishes her mission. She is not, then, missionary in some of her members only who are charged with a specialized function. She is missionary in all her members who are united in a common belief. Above all is she missionary in her entire hierarchy, in her bishops and in her Supreme Pastor" (pp. 16–17). But how can we distinguish her mission from her missions? What is the difference between apostolic activity and missionary activity? "The characteristic of the missions is to bring the essential means of salvation to men who have never before had these means at their disposal. Now these means are summed up in a single one, the visible presence of the Church in the midst of men. We conclude, then, that the proper object of the missions is to bring this visible presence to men, or, in the words of the liturgy, to plant the Church in all countries where she is not yet established" (p. 46). Father de Lubac with good reason does not wish that the action of "planting the Church" should be restricted merely to the foundation of the hierarchy; nor does he wish that this planting should be opposed to the action of converting the world to Christ. If we use expressions that are different from his (p. 47), we can say that the purpose of missionary activity is to found the hierarchy insofar as this gives birth to the Mystical Body of Christ; or we can say that the purpose of this activity is to found the Mystical Body of Christ insofar as It issues from the hierarchy (the Mystical Body is here synonymous with the believing Church—see Charles Journet, *L'Église du Verbe Incarné*, I, 38 and 63). As Father de Menesce so well puts it in his article, "*La Catholicité de l'Église et ordre de la charité*," *Annuaire Missionnaire de la Suisse*, 1939, p. 13: "We pray and toil for the conversion of the infidels, and, by this very fact, for their accession to the full Christian life, for their aggregation to the Church's flock, for all the states they must pass through from conception through birth to maturity. What, then, do we mean by the adult age of an individual church? It signifies the moment a church is constituted in its integrity and in a relative independence; it is the moment when a church subsists as an interior part of the universal Church, in which there are always found the unity of the fold of Peter and the multiplicity of flocks ruled by the successors of the Apostles. Christ founded the Church in her pastors. She grows insofar as the faithful are joined to her in such a way that they constitute not a new tissue but a new part, which is informed by a hierarchy capable of renewing and perpetuating that part. Hence the purpose of the missions is to establish the Church (and the Church begins with the first person to receive the faith and baptism) but the mission is not perfected as the Church until the time when it finds itself endowed with its own hierarchy." On this point consult also the same writer's, "Sur le nationalisme des pays de mission," *Nouvelle Revue de Science Missionnaire*, 1947, p. 1: "The episcopate of itself is indigenous; when it is not so, this is a sign that the Church has not yet come to the fullness of maturity, that she has not yet acquired the essential organs which alone are capable of assuring her stability and fecundity; these organs are the Christian family and the Christian priesthood, both of which are the effects of a social sacrament. When it becomes adult, the individual church becomes an integral part of the universal Church. The mission prepares the way for this integration and then disappears."

b. What is the cause of missionary activity in the Church? The Holy Spirit is the First Cause; the theological virtue of charity is the created cause. On this answer both Father de Menasce and Father de Lubac again agree. See the remarks of Father de Menasce in *Divus Thomas* (Fribourg, 1942, pp. 199–202) on those who, because they were not sufficiently trained in theology, wished to attach missionary activity to the virtue of religion rather than to that of charity.

c. In what sense are the missions necessary? In our opinion it is not sufficient to reply to this, as some have done, that the missions are only relatively necessary, that is, that they are necessary only that the divine plan of salvation for the world may be better accomplished (*ad melius esse salutis*). Rather we must say that the missions are absolutely necessary, just as the promulgation of the gospel is absolutely necessary (*ad esse simpliciter novae legis*), if men are to be snatched from an abnormal condition in which the salvation of Christ is accessible to them only by desire and in an inchoative, imperfect, and dangerous manner. It is necessary if they are to be removed from the state in which, under the best of conditions, they can be saved by the Church but in which they themselves do not become saviours of the world in and through the Church of Christ.

[41] See below, Chapter 6, Number 1.

[42] The word is derived from the Greek term meaning *herald*.

[43] Etienne Gilson, "*Michel Menot et la technique du sermon médiéval,*" *Les idées et les lettres* (Paris: 1932), p. 98.

CHAPTER 6

[1] For this expression see Denziger, *op. cit.*, Number 1681.

[2] Here, then, we are opposing science and wisdom. Historical theology is more than a science; it is also a wisdom. History can also be called a science, but in the modern meaning of that word, not in Aristotle's.

[3] The distinction between positive theology, the purpose of which is to give an explanation—more exactly to give a certain kind of explanation— and historical disciplines has been expressed by Father Cavallera, *art. cit.*, p. 29, in the following words: "Positive theology, because it is a theology,

should not be purely and simply identified with the history of dogmas, of
doctrines, or of theology. It is not content with giving information. . . .
Its purpose exceeds this and yet it is obvious that it attains its purpose only
by utilizing the data of these historical disciplines." M.-D. Chenu writes
in turn in his *Une école de théologie*, p. 63: "Historical exegesis and the
history of dogmas, as their names suggest, are the work of history; as such,
they are conducted in all sincerity and loyalty in accordance with their
own methods and procedures and under their own light; scriptural, patristic,
symbolic theology, in brief everything which deserves the name of positive
theology, is developed, on the contrary, under the light of faith and in
accordance with the criteria of faith, since it is in a proper sense a true
theology. . . . The consideration of formal objects is one of the most
valuable possessions of Thomistic pedagogy; the distressing confusion of
ideas, methods, and vocabulary among the better theologians during the
course of the Modernist crisis once more emphasized the worth and the
need of this consideration." As a matter of fact, in both of the above texts
the phrase *positive theology* seems to mean what we have termed the
topological phase of doctrinal theology rather than historical theology,
which in our opinion alone deserves to be given the title of positive
theology.

4 See Olivier Lacombe, *L'Absolu selon le Vedânta* (Paris: 1937), p. 372.

5 See P. de Menasce, "La théologie de la mission selon M. Kraemer,"
Nouvelle Revue de Science Missionnaire, 1945, p. 251; also see his article
"Islam et universalisme," *Annuaire Missionnaire de la Suisse*, 1940–1941,
pp. 9 ff.

6 We need not mention that the history of the Councils, the history of
dogmas, the history of theology itself can be studied from higher points of
view. See below, footnote 36 of this present chapter.

7 "In the case of textual criticism, one can not without endangering the
faith prefer the Syriac manuscript of Sinai, at least if one understands it in
the sense that Jesus was the true son of Joseph." M.-J. Lagrange, *La
méthode historique* (Paris: 1904), p. 17.

8 Taken from the *Bulletin de Littérature Ecclésiastique*, 1901, p. 92. The
passage is cited by Father Gagnebet, who rightly wished to apply to the
positive theologian what Father Lagrange remarks of the exegete. See
Nature de la théologie spéculative, p. 244.

9 Pius XII, *Divino Afflante Spiritu*, Acta Apostolicae Sedis, 1946, p. 310.
The translation is taken from the Vatican translation as published by the
National Catholic Welfare Conference.

10 F. Cavallera, *art. cit.*, p. 28.

11 Note the phrases of Saint Thomas: "Insofar as they are divinely revealable. . . ." "Insofar as they can be known by the divine light. . . ."
Summa Theologica, I, 1, 3, ad 2; I, 1, 3, 4.

12 See Saint Thomas, *Summa Theologica*, I, 1, 3, ad 2.

13 Henri Bergson, *Les deux sources de la morale et de la religion* (Paris:
1932), pp. 235 ff.

14 *Summa Theologica*, I, 14, 11.

15 *Ibid.*, I, 1, 8, ad 2.

16 *In Boethium de Trinitate, Prologus.*

[17] "The hearer will be assured that the thing is so, but will not acquire any science or understanding and will go away unsatisfied."

[18] *Summa Theologica*, II–II, 1, 7; 174, 6.

[19] *Ibid.*, II–II, 2, 6–8.

[20] *Ibid.*, I–II, 98 ff.

[21] *Ibid.*, I–II, 99.

[22] *Ibid.*, 98, 2, ad 4; 107, 3.

[23] *Ibid.*, 106, 4.

[24] *Ibid.*, I–II, 98, 6.

[25] *Ibid.*, III, 1 and 2.

[26] *Ibid.*, III, 61, 3, ad 2.

[27] *Ibid.*, II–II, 10, 5.

[28] It appeared in *Nova et Vetera*, 1935, pp. 239 ff.

[29] This was published by the Éditions de la Maison Française (New York: 1942). All future references will be to this pagination.

[30] Raïssa Maritain, op. cit., p. 13.

[31] *Ibid.*, p. 15.

[32] *Ibid.*, p. 23.

[33] *Ibid.*, p. 24. Also read the pages on the origin of morality, pp. 58 ff.

[34] "*Les controverses des Pères grecs sur la science du Christ*," *Revue Thomiste*, 1904, pp. 12 ff.; pp. 257 ff. Since that time, the thought of the Fathers on Christ's ignorance of the last day has been treated, but from a more technically historical point of view by Jules Lebreton, *Les origines du dogme de la Trinité* (Paris: 1919), I, note c, pp. 512–544.

[35] The text on the day and the hour of the Judgment (Mark 13, 32) is explained by that of Acts, 1, 7: "It is not for you to know the times and seasons which the Father has fixed by his own authority." By a decree of the Holy Office, of June 5, 1918, we are assured that it is not safe to teach that "it is not certain that the soul of Christ was ignorant of anything." For the decree see Denziger, *op. cit.*, Number 2184.

[36] The history of dogmas and of theology can be treated in a purely historical manner, as was indicated above in this chapter, footnote 6. The history of theology can also be treated in a theological manner by giving the history of successive problematizations for the purpose of integrating them into a doctrinal synthesis. If even one authentic acquisition could not be assimilated into a given synthesis, then that synthesis must be abandoned. Finally one can study the history of theology, not for the sake of the progress of doctrinal theology, but for itself from the viewpoint of historical theology.

[37] M.-B. Schwalm, *Les controverses*, p. 267.

[38] *Ibid.*, p. 13.

[39] *Ibid.*, p. 33.

[40] This appeared in *Revue des Sciences Philosophiques et Théologiques*, 1908, pp. 674 ff.

[41] *Ibid.*, p. 691.

[42] *Ibid.*, p. 693.

[43] *Ibid.*, p. 695.

[44] *Ibid.*, p. 697.

[45] *Ibid.*, pp. 699–701.

[46] *Ibid.*, p. 701.

[47] Saint Augustine, *The City of God*, Book XVIII, Chapter 51, Number 2 (*P.L.*, XLI, col. 614). In assigning to positive theology as its specific task the study of the activity of the Church's teaching power alone and in this field making positive theology study this activity especially from its sociological aspects to such an extent that this theology should be defined in the final analysis as the supernatural sociology of dogma, Father Schwalm seems to us to limit the object of positive theology unjustly. In our opinion the object of this theology is the development of the work of salvation in time, insofar as this development can be known by us through revelation as this is proposed by the Church.

[48] M.-B. Schwalm, *Les deux théologies*, pp. 695 and 701.

[49] See above, Chapter 5, Number 11.

[50] See above, Chapter 3, footnote 14.

[51] To a certain extent we can apply to positive theology the following passage from Father Chenu's *Une école de théologie*, p. 61: "It is, then, on the level of history that the theologian operates. His data are not the natures of things nor their timeless forms; his data are the events which are part of an economy that is linked with time, just as extension is linked to bodies; he is outside the order of essences. . . . The believer, the theologian enters this economy by faith; he seeks an understanding (*quaerens intellectum*) of a divine undertaking, more, of a series of divine undertakings. . . . This is the true world of theological contemplation and understanding; it is concerned with the undertakings of a free God who, according to His own will, conducts this immense and undefinable history in which He Himself plays the primary role."

Father Labourdette, *art. cit.*, p. 29, distinguishes positive theology 1) insofar as it, once it has been constituted in its own proper dimensions, takes account of the concrete development of revelations and of the progress of dogmatic formulas; and 2) insofar as it is utilized by systematic theology. His first division can be reduced to what we have called the "history of theology"; and the second to topological exposition. The history of theology, however, can be utilized not only by systematic theology but also by historical theology.

CHAPTER 7

[1] See Saint Thomas, *Summa Theologica*, I, 23, 6, ad 1.

[2] If we ask ourselves what are the a priori possibilities among which the exegete or the theologian of history must choose when he reads the narration of the creation of man, we can say that there are two possible hypotheses. Either God can be regarded as creating the soul and infusing it into a body which He has transformed from a clay image or from a vegetable organism or from an animal organism. Or we can say that He has immediately created from nothing the whole man, body as well as soul. In a sense this latter hypothesis is the simpler.

If we hold that God first created the universe in an unformed state and then little by little used its energies to force it to surpass itself, so that an inferior order would be elevated to produce the penultimate disposition for a higher order (in other words, so that the mineral would prepare the way for vegetative life, the latter for animal life, and this last for man), we have a spacious view that can find its ultimate speculative explanation only in the Thomistic notion of instrumentality. Provided we remember that we are dealing only with a priori possibilities, we can even imagine that the first two human souls were infused into an embryonic body, for example, into twin cells.

In the course of a wonderful synthesis (*Summa Contra Gentiles*, III, 22 and 23) Saint Thomas writes: "The ultimate end of all generation is the human soul; matter tends to this soul as to its ultimate form. Accordingly the elements exist for the sake of the compounds and these in turn for the sake of living things; among living things plants exist for the sake of animals, and these for the sake of man. Man, therefore, is the end of all generation. . . . The celestial body by its operation is directed towards this ultimate form which is the human intellect. This celestial body, therefore, in generation is not a principal cause acting by reason of its own form, but it acts according to the form of a higher agent which is intellectual and is related to this agent as an instrument to its principal cause." And Pascal remarks: "All things come from nothing and are directed to the Infinite. Who could imagine such astonishing progression? Only the Creator comprehends these marvels; no one else can do so" (*Pensées*, Number 72). We have only to extend in time this evolving process at which Saint Thomas and Pascal were so amazed to understand that it is not only qualitative but also successive and chronological. On the text of Saint Thomas see the remarkable commentary of A. Gardeil, "*L'évolutionnisme et les principes de saint Thomas,*" *Revue Thomiste*, 1896, pp. 215 ff.

³ See Saint Thomas, *Summa Theologica*, III, 1, 3, ad 3.

⁴ "The injury caused to the human race by the sin of Adam consists in the transmission not only of the death and bodily pains which he incurred but also of his very sin; for all men are born afflicted with this sin. This is certainly the thesis of Saint Paul, but it is not explicitly found either in the Old Testament or in ancient Jewish theology. . . . Man was deprived of the privileges which Adam had enjoyed; it was impossible, however, to determine whether the loss of these privileges had the nature of a sin. In order to affirm this, it would be necessary to have a precise idea of these privileges which essentially consisted in a friendship with God; besides we would have to know that God had decided to clothe all men with the same privileges in such a way that the absence of grace in the sons of Adam would be a true privation. Add to this that we would have to conceive Adam as the responsible head of the human race, who was constituted by God as the depository of these supernatural gifts in such a way that his sin would be the sin of all. But these notions of grace, of the Divine Life, of the supernatural Providence which God had for all men are truths which we learn only by the light of the Redemption. It is in opposition to Christ, who is the source of grace, that we can best understand Adam, who is the source of sin. . . . The complete doctrine of original sin, then, is a Christian one, which the Old Testament could suggest only in a vague way." M.-J. Lagrange, *Epitre aux Romains* (Paris: 1916), pp. 114 and 118. See the definition of the Second Council of Orange as cited in Denziger, *op.*

cit., Number 175; also the canon of the Council of Trent as cited in Denziger, *op. cit.*, Number 789.

Let us recall, too, that the notion of sin is verified, not univocally, but analogously when it is applied to inherited or original sin and to committed or actual sin. This consideration alone is sufficient to dispose of a number of misunderstandings.

5 *Pensées*, Number 556.

6 As Michelangelo planned it, the *Last Judgment* in the Sistine Chapel should have a companion scene of the fall of the angels. See Noële and Robert Boulet, *op. cit.*, p. 65.

7 *Pensées*, Number 348.

8 *Ibid.*, Number 347.

9 *Ibid.*, Number 792.

10 Léon Bloy, *La femme pauvre* (Paris: 1937).

11 "La terre, la vie et l'homme," *Nova et Vetera*, 1929, pp. 232–239. And today the body of man appears under the microscope—though in the eyes of faith and even those of philosophy it has other qualities also—as a statistical effect which surges up for a few hours from the universe of contingence through yet another "merciful event." On this see Louis de Broglie, *Physique et microphysique* (Paris: 1947).

12 "Vie et planètes," *Etudes*, 1946, pp. 146–157. At the end of the article, where the author uses a purely scientific apparatus to clarify problems that are more and more philosophical, the considerations become a fantasy.

13 By "historical time" we mean that period which begins with the fall of man and which will terminate with the second coming of Christ.

14 We purposely say "to man." It is completely unreasonable, thinks Saint Thomas, *Summa Theologica*, I, 96, 1, ad 2, to imagine that in the earthly paradise the lions were grazing animals. Sin has changed the relationship of man to the order of the universe, but has not changed the order of the universe itself. The dream of an age of gold, when all the animals were herbivorous, figures in the book *L'évolution régressive* by G. Salet and L. Lafont (Paris: 1943).

15 See Denziger, *op. cit.*, Numbers 181 and 793. Also consult Saint Thomas, *Summa Theologica*, I–II, 109, 2; 85, 1.

16 The first stage of historical theology in similar matters is to propose different hypotheses among which science and faith can choose. Is not this what Saint Augustine—and Origen before him—so frequently did?

17 This was Saint Thomas' opinion, *Summa Theologica*, I, 94, 3.

18 Saint Thomas, *Summa Theologica*, I, 101, 1 and 2.

19 Pierre Termier, *La joie de connaître* (Paris: 1925), p. 298. See also "La terre, la vie, et l'homme," pp. 241 and 251.

20 See Alberto Carlo Blanc, "L'évolution humaine dans le cadre de la cosmolyse," *Revue de Théologie et de Philosophie*, 1946, p. 68.

21 Raïssa Maritain, *op. cit.*, p. 48.

22 *Ibid.*, p. 49.

23 *Ibid.*, pp. 50–52.

24 "An imagined, not an understood end," says Saint Thomas, *Summa Theologica*, I–II, 1, 1, ad 3. And Pascal says: "If an animal were able to

understand what it does by instinct. . . ." *Pensées*, Number 342. Nevertheless Pascal, who was a Cartesian, was woefully behind Saint Thomas in
matters of animal psychology.

[25] "In order to use these simple instruments (a lever, for example) there
must be a sort of practical and concrete 'intelligence' which flows from an
unreasoned optics and mechanics and which leads within certain limits to
an appropriate and continued use of these instruments." W. Koehler,
L'intelligence des singes supérieurs (Paris: 1927), p. 70.

[26] Pierre Termier, *op. cit.*, p. 297, did not take this hypothesis into consideration and thinks that the Chellean and Neanderthal types were real
men who did not differ essentially from us. As he says: "No one would
have thought to call them primitives, had not their anatomy possessed
certain characteristics of animals as compared to ours." The same views are
expressed in Bergounioux and Glory, *Les premiers hommes* (Toulouse:
1943), p. 96.
As a matter of fact, the general opinion among prehistorians is that the
existence of controlled fires and the discovery of tools are sufficient to
prove the presence of men. See Eugène Pittard, *Histoire des premiers
hommes* (Lausanne: 1944), p. 7. An even stronger proof is the discovery
of burial places: "There can be no question in this case of instinct; such a
practice heralds the dawn of human thought manifesting itself in a kind of
revolt against death." P. Lecomte du Nouy, *L'avenir de l'esprit* (Paris:
1941), p. 188. According to the hypothesis we are now considering, the
expression "the dawn of human thought" would signify what precedes and
announces human thought, without itself being human thought.

[27] As must be clear, there is no question here of renewing the seventeenth
century error of Isaac Peyrère, who contrasted Adam, the father of the
People of God, with the pre-Adamites, who were the ancestors of the
Gentiles.

[28] We do not think that a suitable avenue of explanation is opened up
by the opinion reported by A. and J. Bouyssonie in *Dictionnaire de
Théologie Catholique* under the article, "*Polygénisme*," col. 2536 ff. According to this opinion original sin "was the act of a more or less numerous
group rather than the act of a single couple." No better is the hypothesis
of A. M. Dubarle, *Les sages d'Israël* (Paris: 1946), p. 21; this author cites
several Catholic writers who maintain that the descent of the entire human
race from one single head does not seem to be taught by revelation. According to this theory, original sin properly speaking would not be "a mysterious transmission of culpability," but "the hereditary privation of the
good will of God which was manifest to men at first." Consequently,
original sin would be "a state of disorder, difficulty, and tension in regard
to Him" (p. 15). Original sin would be "a universal hereditary misfortune
which arose from many mutually independent sins and not from a single
sin" (p. 22). Compare this with the doctrine we gave above in this chapter,
footnote 4. On monogenism, see the text of Acts 17, 26.

[29] *Summa Theologica*, III, 33, 3, ad 3.

[30] *Ibid.*, 34, 1, ad 1.

[31] "The ineffable grace of Christ has given us better gifts than the ones

which the jealousy of the devil took from us"—Saint Leo the Great, *Sermon LXXIII*, Number 4 (*P.L.*, LIV, col. 396).

[32] Saint Thomas, *Summa Theologica*, III, 60, 5, ad 3.

[33] *Ibid.*

[34] *Ibid.*, II–II, 1, 7 and 8.

[35] *Ibid.*, III, 61, 3 ad 2; and see III, 1, 6.

[36] Jacques Maritain, *The Angelic Doctor* (New York: 1931), p. 105.

[37] Raïssa Maritain, *op. cit.*, p. 19.

[38] See Jacques Maritain, *Ransoming the Time* (New York: 1941), pp. 227 ff.

[39] (Paris: 1905), pp. 242 ff.

[40] See Charles Journet, *Destinées d'Israël* (Paris: 1945).

[41] Saint Thomas, *Summa Theologica*, III, 30, 1.

[42] *Ibid.*, III, 1, 6.

[43] Pierre Termier, *op. cit.*, p. 322.

[44] See the suggestion made in the last hypothesis of section 3 of this chapter.

[45] This lack of explicit awareness was not universal. The Eastern testimonies to the exercise of the Roman primacy have been collected by Martin Jugie in his *Le schisme byzantin* (Paris: 1941), pp. 48 ff. The theological value of these testimonies is not always easy to estimate. However, even if we take into account the Oriental custom of adulation, they still retain a certain importance.

[46] The Primacy of the Pope makes us understand the *Tu es Petrus*; the use of confession makes us understand the *Quorum remiseritis peccata*; and the offering of the Holy Sacrifice makes us understand the *Hoc facite in meam commemorationem*; without these, such texts would be understood "only half-way or not at all" (M. Becqué, "La méthode apologétique du cardinal Deschamps," *Nouvelle Revue Théologique*, 1947, p. 145).

[47] See *Nova et Vetera*, 1940, p. 389.

[48] See P. de Menasce, "Apostolat civilizateur et colonisation chrétienne, Considérations rétrospectives sur les réductions du Paraguay," *Annuaire missionnaire de la Suisse*, 1942, p. 68.

[49] See *Nova et Vetera*, 1934, p. 80.

[50] See "*Déchirures de l'Eglise*," *Nova et Vetera*, 1946.

[51] "There are many kinds of atheism. There are pseudo-atheists, who think that they do not believe in God but who unconsciously do so, since the God whose existence they deny is not God at all but something else. There are also practical atheists, who think they believe in God, while in reality they deny His existence by each of their actions; these make an idol of the living God. Then there are the absolute atheists, who really deny the existence of that God whom believers actually believe in; these atheists are obliged to change their entire scale of values and to destroy in themselves every vestige of His name." Jacques Maritain, "Une nouvelle approche de Dieu," *Nova et Vetera*, 1946, p. 125. See also his "La dialectique immanente du premier acte de liberté," *Nova et Vetera*, 1945, p. 231.

[52] We are following here the interpretation of Father Allo which we have summarized in *Nova et Vetera*, 1935, p. 209.

[53] She will shine then not merely as a glorious Church but as a resur-

rected one; like Christ, she will have passed the gates of death to enter into glory. See Charles Journet, *Exigences chrétiennes en politique* (Paris: 1945), p. 505.

⁵⁴ Is there not as much positive theology as there is speculative theology in the *Symbolism* of J.-A. Moehler?

⁵⁵ "In a mystical sense we call them two cities. . . ." *The City of God*, Book XV, Chapter 1, Number 1 (*P.L.*, XLI, col. 437).

⁵⁶ *Ibid.*, Book XIV, Chapter 28 (col. 436).

⁵⁷ Paul Claudel, *Positions et propositions* (Paris: 1929–1934), I, p. 170.

⁵⁸ There is even too much of this now outmoded cosmic imagery in the questions in which at the beginning of his career Saint Thomas treated the next life in his commentary on the *Sentences*. No doubt, he would have abandoned this imagery had he lived long enough to finish the *Summa*.

Paul Claudel had good reasons for pointing out the danger there is of making Dante primarily a theologian: "Many are tempted to think that theology is responsible for the beautiful imagery of this sublime poet and that it can offer us no other representation of the future life than his vivid pictures" (*op. cit.*, p. 175). As for the danger which exists for theologians themselves should they wish to transform Beatrice into an abstraction in order to make Dante one of their own profession, this has been emphasized, in opposition to Father Mandonnet's *Dante le théologien*, by Etienne Gilson with an insistence that almost amounts to cruelty in his *Dante et la philosophie* (Paris: 1939), pp. 1 and 283.

⁵⁹ These lines of an English writer are cited by Claudel, *op. cit.*, p. 172.

⁶⁰ *La pensée et le mouvant* (Paris: 1934), p. 141.

⁶¹ One of these points of view, for example, is the distinction in historical matters between roles and masks or characters. Some Christian characters can play anti-Christian roles, while some anti-Christian characters can play Christian roles which are unfortunately deformed. See on this Jacques Maritain, *Religion and Culture* (New York: 1931), p. 58.

⁶² "Everything which it is possible to divine or to believe, in other words, universal history—which was read by Bossuet to no purpose—is a mysterious and prophetic prefiguration of the *Drama of God*. This prefiguring is analogous to the ensemble of prefiguring images which constitute Biblical revelation and which remained unintelligible until the High Mass of Calvary. Nevertheless there is this difference that Jewish prophecy was concerned with the Redemption, while the universal prophecy of history is concerned with the accomplishment of the Redemption by the triumphal coming of the Holy Spirit." (Preface of *Constantinople et Byzance* as cited in *Léon Bloy, choix de textes* edited by Albert Beguin, p. 92.)

CHAPTER 8

¹ See Vladimir Lossky, *op. cit.*, pp. 35 and 40.

² See, for example, Saint Justin, *Second Apology*, Chapter 8 (*P.G.*, VI, col. 457).

³ In Book I, Chapter 3, of his *Exposition of the Orthodox Faith* (*P.G.*, XCIV, col. 793), the existence of God is proved by reason from the contingence of creatures.

4 See Denziger, *op. cit.*, Number 1173.

5 See Charles Journet, *Dark Knowledge*, p. 50.

6 Pierre Dahmen, S.J., *Un jésuite brahme, Robert de Nobili, 1577–1656* (Brussels: 1925), p. 36.

7 See Saint Thomas, *Summa Contra Gentiles*, II, 4.

8 Sacred doctrine "does not receive its principles from other sciences but immediately from God through revelation. Consequently it does not receive anything from these sciences as though they were superior to it, but uses them as its inferiors and servants." (Saint Thomas, *Summa Theologica*, I, 1, 5, *ad* 2.) To understand this is to understand why Christianity can not identify itself with the cultures which it encounters.

9 Apologetics, which, because it is the defensive part of theology, establishes its arguments by the use of reason, comes under the direction of faith because of the requirements of its essence, for it belongs to the kingdom of God. But philosophy does not come under the direction of faith except by reason of its existence in a human subject, for it belongs to cultural activities. On this see Jacques Maritain, *De la philosophie chrétienne*, p. 96.

10 Cajetan distinguishes the simple motion (*motus simplex*), which results in the natural effect of an instrument, from the artful motion (*motus virtuosus*), which raises the instrument to the level of art (*In Summam Theologicam*, III, 62, 4, Number 4).

11 See *Summa Theologica*, I, 1, 1 with Cajetan's commentary.

12 See especially *Summa Contra Gentiles*, I, 4; also read *Summa Theologica* II–II, 2, 4; I, 2, 2, *ad* 2; II–II, 1, 5, *ad* 3.

13 *Summa Contra Gentiles*, II, 4.

14 See Saint Thomas, *Summa Theologica*, I–II, 100, 1.

15 This metaphysical notion is independent of the question whether the world was created from eternity or whether there was a first moment of time. See Saint Thomas, *Summa Theologica*, I, 46, 2.

16 Etienne Gilson, *The Spirit of Medieval Philosophy* (New York: 1940), pp. 68–69.

17 See Denziger, *op. cit.*, Number 2145.

18 *Ibid.*, Number 1650.

19 "Although these natural disciplines are based on their own naturally known principles, Catholics who study such disciplines should always have before their eyes divine revelation as the guiding star by which they can avoid the shipwreck of error." *Ibid.*, Number 1681.

20 See Saint Thomas, *Summa Theologica*, I–II, 109, 1 and 2.

21 *Ibid.*, I–II, 109, 2 ad 3.

22 *Summa Contra Gentiles*, IV, 52.

23 See, for example, the commentaries of Medina, Billuart, Del Prado, and so forth.

24 The encyclical was published by Leo XIII, August 4, 1879, *Acta Sanctae Sedis*, XII, pp. 97 ff. The French translation uses the phrase "Christian philosophy" instead of "scholastic philosophy." Actually the phrase "Christian philosophy" is equivalently found in the letter of Pope Leo XIII, December 30, 1892, in which the Pope approved the constitutions of the Society of Jesus, which recommend the teaching of the doctrine of Saint Thomas. In the letter the Pope says that the Angelic Doctor has

made the philosophy of Aristotle Christian by purifying it of error: *Hanc . . . christianam fecit.*

[25] Cited in Denziger, *op. cit.*, Number 1799.

[26] In the encyclical *Aeterni Patris* the word *philosophy* is not always understood in its strict sense of a discipline differentiated from theology. At times it means the entire work of human reason, even when it is engaged in the work of defensive (apologetical) or expository theology.

This is also the meaning of the word used by Etienne Gilson in his *Spirit of Medieval Philosophy*. To realize this, it is necessary to read what he has told us of this work in his *Christianisme et philosophie* (Paris: 1936), p. 129: "I wrote from what is now the third chapter of *The Spirit of Medieval Philosophy* to the end of the first volume of that book without thinking of the notion of Christian philosophy: it was only then that I encountered this term and, since it seemed to me that it gave unity to the philosophy which I was describing, I wrote the first two chapters on the subject of this notion. I was well satisfied with my discovery, and while studying thereafter some of the documents concerning this matter, I encountered the encyclical *Aeterni Patris*, which I had completely forgotten. I saw at once that what I was trying to prove in two volumes, twenty chapters, and countless notes was exactly what this encyclical was able to teach me. It even contained the very interpretation of medieval philosophy that I was proposing. . . ."

[27] To the question whether man without grace but with only the powers of nature can love God above all things, Saint Thomas answers that it is not possible in our present state (*Summa Theologica*, I–II, 109, 3). In the following article the Saint explains that in the state of wounded nature man would not be able to accomplish all the precepts of the natural law if grace did not come to heal him.

[28] See Jacques Maritain, "*La dialectique immanente du premier acte de liberté*," *Nova et Vetera*, 1945, p. 218.

[29] See the citation from Cardinal Gonzalez as quoted by J. M. Ramirez, *De Hominis Beatitudine* (Salamanca: 1942), p. 46, note.

[30] "Though in the world of speculation to ignore a truth does not falsify one's knowledge—theodicy for instance is in no way falsified by its ignorance of the Trinity—yet in the field of practice, where direction must be given to conduct, and where reason proceeds *modo compositivo*, the ignorance or omission of an element necessary to conduct falsifies conduct itself" (Jacques Maritain, *Science and Wisdom*, p. 164).

[31] *Summa Contra Gentiles*, II, 4.

[32] See, for example, *Exigences chrétiennes en politique*, p. 509.

[33] Jacques Maritain, *De la philosophie chrétienne*, p. 147.

[34] Jacques Maritain, *The Degrees of Knowledge*, p. 355, footnote 1.

[35] To attempt to explain the superiority of Christianity over the atheistic and collectivistic movements of today by means of an Hegelean dialectic which presupposes that there exists in human nature a "power of transcendence" and a "necessity for the Incarnation," is to construct an *ad hominem* apologetics; but as long as one does not break with this Hegelean dialectic, it also entails putting oneself into a position where, in the final analysis, it is impossible to distinguish the supernatural from the natural; consequently, one can not give the true reasons for the supranationalism of

the Church nor explain why she meets the opposition that she does. See G. Fessard, *France, prends garde de perdre ta liberté* (Paris: 1946), p. 110. The Church does not just exist; it exists in a definite way, namely, as a kingdom which by its essence is not of this world.

³⁶ See Charles Journet, *Exigences chrétiennes en politique*, p. 311.

³⁷ It is equally clear that we would not be able to consider the case of human values when they are ravished by sin.

³⁸ Jacques Maritain, *Science and Wisdom*, pp. 185–186.

³⁹ We do not intend to oppose the words civilization and culture. For the definition of culture, see Jacques Maritain, *Religion and Culture*, pp. 3 ff. Except for a few additions, the lines which follow are reprinted from an article in *Vie Intellectuelle*, 1928, p. 453.

⁴⁰ "So that he might lead bestial and solitary men to civilization (*civilitatem*)." (*In libros de Anima Expositio*, Book I, Lesson 12, at the end.)

⁴¹ *In libros Ethicorum ad Nicomachum Expositio*, Book I, Lesson 1.

⁴² If these natural communities were fictitious and not real persons, it would mean the downfall of this Aristotelian, Thomistic (and even Scriptural—see Eph. 5, 21 to 6, 9: Col. 3, 18–25) division of moral philosophy.

⁴³ "Money and all wealth are a kind of instrument for economic philosophy." (Saint Thomas, *In libros Politicorum Expositio*, Book I, Lesson 6.)

⁴⁴ Social questions actually involve two kinds of questions, political and economic. The use of the word *social* as a synonym for economic is an abuse; at the same time it is an indication that the class warfare which has now become international is the great social danger of our era.

⁴⁵ "For a good . . . life two things are required. The main thing is to act according to virtue. . . . The other one, which is secondary and instrumental, is a sufficiency of material goods, the use of which is necessary for acts of virtue." (Saint Thomas, *De Regimine Principum*, Book I, Chapter 15.)

⁴⁶ See the first book of Aristotle's *Politics* together with Saint Thomas' commentary, Lessons 6 to 9. "It is necessary for the activity of the political or the economic man that those things should be acquired which are of value for the necessities and utility of the society, whether it be the family or the State; for neither the family nor the State can be governed if the necessities for life are absent."

In his *Leçons de philosophie sociale*, Father Schwalm tries to re-express these positions. He takes pains to show that the art of acquiring material things must be subordinated to the family. "In order to take care of the accidental insufficiency of the family in regard to certain things which are necessary for its own purpose, the family needs certain groups which are controlled by specialists who can help the family. These are helps to the family. Even today these groups are called by the old scholastic term of private societies. . . . It is these that constitute what is called the economic order. Etymologically, economy is the governing of the home, of the family; hence these groups which are helps to the family are rightly called private societies" (*op. cit.*, I, p. 148). At a time characterized by the breakdown of the family and the adoration of riches, it seems difficult to give the word economy the full meaning of its original sense. As a matter of fact, how-

The Wisdom of Faith

ever, the entire social effort of Christianity tends to give back to the family its true place at the center of the economic order.

It goes without saying that we would be entirely ready to use the term political economy to designate the art of acquiring wealth which can be utilized for the human values of the State.

47 Similarly the word *culture* can mean either an act or a state.

48 It is in this sense that Saint Thomas can say in *Summa Contra Gentiles*, III, 37, that the contemplative life is the end of civil government. He does not mean that the State can cause such a life as though it were the State's proportioned end, but that the State can prepare for it, since it is higher and preferable to political ends; in the same sense, to prepare the earth is to prepare the flower.

See the remarks of Jacques Maritain, *Les droits de l'homme* (New York: 1942), pp. 30 and 97. "The community can demand that a mathematician serve the community by teaching mathematics . . . but it will never have the right to tell a mathematician to hold a certain mathematical system as true."

49 See Saint Thomas, *Summa Theologica*, I–II, 109, 2, ad 3.

CHAPTER 9

1 Since it is difficult for mystical knowledge and discursive knowledge to coexist in the same person, this causes to a certain extent the problem of the diversity and the inequality of various ways and vocations to truth. This problem has been posited even outside of Christianity. See *"Texte d'Al-Ghazali traduit et annoté"* by Louis Gardet, *Revue Thomiste*, 1938, pp. 569–578. The following lines are taken from this article: "The soufis had a preference for the sciences received by way of inspiration and excluded those which were acquired by study. Moreover, they had no desire to study a science nor to learn what men had written about a science nor to investigate their teaching and their proofs.

"On the other hand, those who practiced speculation and discursive activity, did not deny the possibility of this way of the soufis nor its existence; nor did they deny that on rare occasions it could achieve its purpose; they could hardly do this, since that is the state most frequently found among prophets and saints. They did, however, regard it as a difficult way that was slow to achieve results and which demanded a number of conditions difficult to fulfill. . . . To apply oneself to the way of study was a surer and closer way to the end in view."

From a Christian point of view, we must deny this dichotomy. We would say that these ways, whatever their diversity and inequality, make use of each other. The reason for this is the unity of the Mystical Body, of which each Christian is a member.

2 See Fr. Bruno, O.D.C., *St. John of the Cross* (New York: 1932), pp. 53, 137, 226.

3 Aldous Huxley, *Grey Eminence* (New York: 1941), p. 33.

Because Jean Baruzi wishes to understand Saint John of the Cross without understanding the dogmatic beliefs of the Saint, he attributes to Saint John a mystical ecstasy which is not Christian. According to Baruzi, a philosopher is able to discover and experience in himself the same ecstasy that Saint John experienced. And in Baruzi's eyes Saint Teresa is engaged "in a tragic and irresolvable conflict between the absolute contemplation, the existence of which she senses, and the limited states from which she was never fully freed." (*Saint Jean de la Croix et le problème de l'expérience mystique*, 2nd ed. (Paris: 1931), pp. ii, iii, vii, and 87).

⁴ From a letter dictated by the Saint a few days before her death (quoted in Noële et Robert Boulet, *op. cit.*, p. 696).

⁵ Vladimir Lossky, *op. cit.*, p. 40.

⁶ See *Summa Theologica*, III, 7, 5.

⁷ *Ibid.*, III, 11, 3.

⁸ *Ibid.*, III, 12.

A NOTE ON THE TYPE

IN WHICH THIS BOOK WAS SET

This book has been set in Electra, a type face created in 1935 by W. A. Dwiggins, the well-known Boston artist. This type falls within the "modern" family of type styles, but was drawn to avoid the extreme contrast between "thick and thin" elements that marks most "modern" type faces. The design is not based upon any traditional model, and is not an attempt to revive or to reconstruct any historic type. Since its birth, Electra has met with success because of its easy-to-read quality. This book was composed and printed by the York Composition Company of York, Pa., and bound by Moore and Company of Baltimore, Md. The design and typography of this book are by Howard N. King.